THE SUPERNATURAL IN SOCIETY,

CULTURE, AND HISTORY

Edited by Dennis Waskul
and Marc Eaton

THE SUPERNATURAL IN SOCIETY, CULTURE, AND HISTORY

TEMPLE UNIVERSITY PRESS
Philadelphia • Rome • Tokyo

TEMPLE UNIVERSITY PRESS
Philadelphia, Pennsylvania 19122
www.temple.edu/tempress

Copyright © 2018 by Temple University—Of The Commonwealth System
  of Higher Education
All rights reserved
Published 2018

Library of Congress Cataloging-in-Publication Data

Names: Waskul, Dennis D., 1969– editor. | Eaton, Marc A., 1980– editor.
Title: The supernatural in society, culture, and history / edited by
  Dennis Waskul and Marc Eaton.
Description: Philadelphia : Temple University Press, 2018. | Includes
  bibliographical references and index.
Identifiers: LCCN 2017056012 (print) | LCCN 2018006621 (ebook) |
  ISBN 9781439915264 (E-Book) | ISBN 9781439915240 (cloth : alk. paper) |
  ISBN 9781439915257 (pbk. : alk. paper)
Subjects: LCSH: Supernatural.
Classification: LCC BL100 (ebook) | LCC BL100 .S87 2018 (print) |
  DDC 130—dc23
LC record available at https://lccn.loc.gov/2017056012

∞ The paper used in this publication meets the requirements of the
American National Standard for Information Sciences—Permanence
of Paper for Printed Library Materials, ANSI Z39.48-1992

Printed in the United States of America

9 8 7 6 5 4 3 2 1

CONTENTS

Introduction: The Supernatural in Society, Culture, and History • *Dennis Waskul and Marc Eaton* — 1

1 Toward a Cryptoscience • *William Ryan Force* — 18

2 On Researching the Supernatural: Cultural Competence and Cape Breton Stories • *Jeannie Banks Thomas* — 35

3 Ghosts and Hauntings: Genres, Forms, and Types • *Dennis Waskul* — 54

4 Paranormal Investigation: The Scientist and the Sensitive • *Marc Eaton* — 76

5 The Allure of Dark Tourism: Legend Tripping and Ghost Seeking in Dark Places • *Rachael Ironside* — 95

6 "The Spirits Tell Me That You're Seeking Help": Fortune-Telling in Late Capitalism • *Stephen L. Muzzatti and Emma M. Smith* — 116

7 Reading Tarot: Telling Fortunes, Telling Friends, and Retelling Everyday Life • *Janet Baldwin* — 136

8 Twentieth-Century Voodoo: Black Culture, Cultural Geographies, and the Meaning of Place • *I'Nasah Crockett* — 152

9	Vampirism: Modern Vampires and Embattled Identity Claims • *Joseph P. Laycock*	*171*
10	Cryptozoology: The Hunt for Hidden Animals and Monsters • *Tea Krulos*	*190*
11	Alien Abduction Narratives: A Proposed Model and Brief Case Study • *Scott R. Scribner*	*210*
	Contributors	*233*
	Index	*237*

THE SUPERNATURAL IN SOCIETY,

CULTURE, AND HISTORY

INTRODUCTION

The Supernatural in Society, Culture, and History

Dennis Waskul

Marc Eaton

In 1966, anthropologist Anthony Wallace confidently predicted that "belief in supernatural beings and in supernatural forces that affect nature without obeying nature's laws will erode and become only an interesting historical memory" (264). Over half a century later, it appears Wallace could not be further from the truth. In all fairness, though, Wallace simply articulated a long-standing academic position regarding the supernatural, a subject that many scholars regard as, in the words of historian Keith Thomas, "rightly disdained by intelligent persons" (1971: ix). Since the Enlightenment era, philosophers and other scholars have assumed that irrational supernatural beliefs will give way to the rational endeavors of scientific experimentation and empirical observation. Despite such confident predictions, supernatural beliefs and reported experiences persist and even flourish in the current era. Perhaps these scholars have failed to recognize that it is "far harder to kill a phantom than a reality" (J. Thomas 2007: 81).

In the twenty-first century, as in centuries past, stories of ghosts, vampires, and monsters of all kinds both thrill and terrify us, inviting us to imagine that our familiar surroundings may be more enchanted than we thought. Despite—or perhaps because of—advanced scientific understanding of the natural world, people continue to report beliefs in and firsthand experiences with supernatural phenomena. The supernatural remains a part of everyday life, and the time has come to acknowledge that such beliefs and experiences are not doomed to extinction. We are past due for a concerted effort to understand supernatural beliefs and experiences—and that is precisely the main objective of this volume.

A recent Chapman University survey (2015) indicated that approximately half of all American adults hold at least one supernatural belief, by which we mean a belief in abilities or beings whose manifestation transcends accepted scientific understandings of the natural world and conventional religious doctrine. Of these believers, 41.4 percent believe places can be haunted by the spirits of deceased humans, 26.5 percent believe the living can communicate with the dead, 18.1 percent believe aliens have visited earth in modern times, 13.9 percent believe fortune-tellers and psychics can foretell the future, and 11.4 percent believe Bigfoot is a real creature. Other surveys report even higher percentages, between 68 percent (Bader, Mencken, and Baker 2010) and 73 percent (Moore 2005), of Americans believe in at least one supernatural phenomenon. Regardless of the precise percentage, the conclusion is obvious: it is *normative* for contemporary Americans to report beliefs in the supernatural. In fact, more contemporary Americans believe in the supernatural than scientific evidence that global warming is caused by human activity (Leiserowitz et al. 2012) or that humans evolved through natural processes (Pew Research Center 2015). Furthermore, most of these supernatural beliefs have increased over the last quarter century. According to the Pew Forum on Religion and Public Life (2009), belief in contact with the dead and witnessing the presence of a ghost doubled between 1996 and 2009. Newport and Strausberg (2001) found less dramatic but nonetheless consistent increases since 1990 in reported beliefs in hauntings, alien visitation, clairvoyance, and channeling.

Americans are not alone. A recent U.K. poll, for example, found that 52 percent of Britons believe people have experienced ghosts and that 38 percent believe people have witnessed alien spacecraft visiting Earth (YouGov 2013). Likewise, Lyons (2005) reports that the populations of the United States, Canada, and Great Britain generally hold similar levels of belief in astrology, extraterrestrial visitation to Earth, and the ability to communicate mentally with someone who has died. Christopher Bader, Joseph Baker, and Andrea Molle (2012) indicate that rates of belief in astrology, communication with the dead, and telepathy among the Italian population are higher than those reported by David Moore (2005) in a Gallup poll of adult Americans. On the other hand, American teens and college students are less likely than U.S. adults to believe in extrasensory perception, telepathy, alien visitation, communication with the dead, astrology, and several other supernatural abilities (Farha and Steward 2006). Another poll (Pollack 2016) showed a less consistent generational decline in supernatural beliefs: American teens are less likely to believe in UFOs (29 vs. 35 percent) but more likely to believe in ghosts (44 vs. 41 percent) relative to their adult counterparts. Despite minor cultural and generational differences, survey data consistently show that large proportions of people living in scientifically and technologically advanced nations continue to believe in phenomena that cannot be explained by established science.

These beliefs may be both fed and reflected by the plethora of supernatural books, television shows, and movies that crowd our shelves and screens. Sales for the Harry Potter books top 400 million copies (Scholastic, n.d.), while the Twilight saga has sold over 155 million copies (McClurg 2015). In addition, the film adaptations of these book series have grossed a respective $7.7 billion (Nash Information Services, n.d.a) and $3.3 billion (Nash Information Services, n.d.b) in global sales. Aside from these fantasy fiction novels, our televisions are full of dramatized and reality-style supernatural story lines. Dramatic shows like the aptly named *Supernatural* draw nearly two million viewers each week (Porter 2016), and reality-style paranormal investigation shows like *Ghost Hunters* and *Ghost Adventures* each average approximately one million weekly viewers (Hibberd 2014; D. Holloway 2014). The supernatural is also hot at the box office, where "found footage" horror films such as the *Paranormal Activity* series capitalize on our fear that those bumps in the night may be a demonic presence (Box Office Mojo, n.d.). More recently, zombies have taken over the silver screen (Rutherford 2013). In fact, Mikel Koven found that "more zombie movies were produced in the dozen years after 9/11 than the sixty-two years before" (2015: 93). This post-9/11 zombie fascination has spilled over to television, where AMC's *The Walking Dead* consistently ranks as one of the highest-rated television shows in recent history (Kissell 2016). These patterns of media consumption reveal a voracious contemporary appetite for supernatural stories of all sorts.

These supernatural manifestations in popular culture are worthy of scholarly attention because of their symbolic significance alone: they represent our worst fears in an age of terrorism, global warming, and other large-scale changes that threaten to destabilize or destroy life as we know it. However, in an era when interactive media and reality television blur the line between fantasy and real life, these media representations have also fueled the growth of organizations and identities that are rooted in fictional—or at least dramatized—portrayals of supernatural phenomena. Some simply seek to live out fantasies, like the nearly two hundred teams in the United States that play quidditch, a fictional game depicted in the Harry Potter books and movies (US Quidditch, n.d.). Others fashion themselves as researchers seeking empirical evidence for ghosts, lake monsters, UFOs, and other such phenomena (Krulos 2015). In fact, 20 to 25 percent of Americans have actually investigated ghosts, haunted houses, astrology, UFOs, or any one of the cryptids within the field of cryptozoology (Bader, Mencken, and Baker 2010). A third group, known as Otherkin, do not engage with the supernatural in a playful or scientifically intended manner but actually believe themselves to be supernatural, in that their identities as "real" vampires, elves, and other such beings place them outside the bounds of humanity and scientifically recognized biological categories (Laycock 2009, 2012). Although such groups may seem odd at first glance, research shows that participants are usually motivated by common human interests like spiritual enlightenment, the hope of scientific discovery, or the desire to feel special in some way (Bader, Mencken, and Baker 2010; Denzler 2001; Northcote 2007). In other words, people who personally engage with the supernatural are no kookier than the rest of us.

This nonjudgmental stance relative to supernatural beliefs and participation contrasts with earlier sociological work, which theorized that disadvantaged and marginal social groups—such as racial/ethnic minorities, women, and the less educated—would report higher levels of supernatural beliefs because they had less to lose in terms of social standing by adhering to such beliefs (Bainbridge 1978; Wuthnow 1976). It also runs counter to the majority of psychological research, which argues that supernatural beliefs result from cognitive defects or psychoses. For example, Emilio Lobato and colleagues report positive correlations between "epistemically unwarranted" beliefs and "ontological confusion," which they characterize as an inability to distinguish between psychological, physical, and biological domains of reality (2014: 618, 620). Likewise, Ken Drinkwater, Neil Dagnall, and Andrew Parker (2012) found that supernatural believers exhibited lower than normal levels of critical thinking, while Matthew Sharps, Justin Matthews, and Janet Asten (2006) concluded that tendencies toward dissociation (feeling disconnected from the everyday world) predisposed study participants to make perceptual errors that increased their beliefs in ghosts, aliens, and cryptozoological creatures. Other psychological studies (French and Stone 2014; Irwin 2009) show consistent relationships between fantasy proneness, schizotypal behaviors, and supernatural beliefs.

In contrast, folkloric researchers have highlighted the cultural value of such beliefs and practices. Bullard (1989) and Dewan (2006) show, for example, how people who believe they have encountered UFOs and aliens rely on established folkloric narrative structures to make sense of this potentially traumatizing experience. Similarly, Diane Goldstein, Sylvia Grider, and Jeannie B. Thomas (2007), and a more recent volume edited by Jeannie Thomas (2015), explore how contemporary ghost lore serves moral functions by warning the living of the evils of things like violence, slavery, and persecution. Through a practice Linda Dégh and Andrew Vázsonyi (1983) refer to as "ostention," individuals sometimes reenact ghostly or other macabre legends in hopes of experiencing contact with the supernatural. While ostention can arguably be connected to murderous acts (Ellis 1989; Radford 2014), it more often takes the form of "legend tripping," as in the pilgrimage many residents of San Antonio, Texas, make to the site of an accident involving a train and a bus full of schoolchildren. As Carl Lindahl (2005) recounts, legend trippers park on the train tracks and wait for the ghosts of the children to push them to safety. Much like participants on ghost tours (Gentry 2007; J. Holloway 2010; also see Chapter 5), these pilgrims experience the excitement of possibly encountering the spirits of the deceased even as they are exposed to tragic tales that remind them to appreciate and live a moral life.

Sociologists have also begun to acknowledge the social and cultural value of the supernatural. As self-reported religious beliefs and church attendance decline in the United States and Europe (Bruce 2002; Pew Forum on Religion and Public Life 2009), supernatural beliefs can serve as a functional alternative (Emmons and Sobal 1981; Hergovich, Schott, and Arendasy 2005) or supplement (McKinnon 2003) to mainstream religious beliefs. A recent series of studies indicates that supernatural beliefs are highest among people who do not regularly attend church but nonetheless do not identify as atheists (Bader, Baker, and Molle 2012; Baker and Draper 2010; Glendinning 2006; Mencken, Bader, and Kim 2009; Mencken, Bader, and Stark 2008). It seems that the supernatural's marginality to religion provides believers with the freedom to develop their own metaphysical worldviews without the baggage of doctrinal authority, proscriptive rituals, or paying of literal and figurative dues. This flexibility allows believers to mix and match aspects of supernatural and conventional religious belief systems, as when paranormal investigators draw on their religious or spiritual beliefs for protection and interpretation of events during a ghost hunt (Eaton 2015; Fitch 2013). Moving the focus from belief to experiences of supernatural phenomena, Dennis Waskul's (2016) study of ghosts and hauntings illustrates the social-psychological processes by which strange happenings are made into ghosts. Most often, the people who conclude that they have experienced a haunting are "rational believers" (Goldstein 2007: 66) and also have settled on this interpretation reluctantly after eliminating other sensible explanations through systematic, deductive processes. Collectively, a small but growing body of literatures in the social sciences and humanities are starting to illuminate the many valuable social and cultural functions performed by supernatural beliefs and practices.

It may be fair to claim that the supernatural is experiencing a renaissance. Not only are media representations nearly ubiquitous, but increases in reported beliefs and personal experiences suggest that the supernatural has also colonized everyday life. At the very least, the popularity of the supernatural in our era rivals the enormous popularity of séances and the Spiritualist movement in the United States and Europe in the latter half of the nineteenth century (Leonard 2005; Weisberg 2005). Although scholarly research has lagged behind this cultural trend, an emerging body of literature by academics and journalists treats the supernatural as worthy of serious study. However, these investigations of supernatural phenomena are often separated by disciplinary boundaries within academia as well as divisions between what are considered scholarly and popular treatments of the supernatural. We believe that these barriers hinder understanding of the supernatural as a social and cultural product that has real significance for believers in such phenomena. Our aim in this book is to compile research from experts trained in the social sciences and humanities into one reasonably comprehensive volume that illustrates, as our title suggests, the social, cultural, and historical significance of the supernatural.

SUPERNATURAL DEFINITIONS AND PARAMETERS

Though the word "supernatural" is common in casual conversation, it is rarely if ever defined in its everyday usage. "Supernatural" is a word frequently used to refer to religious phenomena in addition to being a catch-all category for fantastic nonreligious phenomena: ghosts, vampires, Sasquatch, aliens, UFOs, fairies, witchcraft, and so on. Moreover, "supernatural" is frequently used interchangeably with "paranormal," whose meaning includes extrasensory perception, clairvoyance, telekinesis, and other alleged psychic abilities. We believe that both tendencies are a mistake, and we call for distinctions that are more precise.

According to common cultural assumptions, there is a fundamental difference between two college students conversing with a spirit via a Ouija board and an evangelical Christian who has been taken by the spirit of the Holy Ghost. Likewise, having a conversation with the ghost of a former resident of your home is considered odd, but communicating with a deity via prayer is perfectly normal. But what is the difference? The main difference is that institutionalized religious beliefs have what David Hufford (1995: 18) calls "cultural authority." These beliefs are transmitted through social institutions that, through historical power struggles and intergenerational transmission of values, are vested with the authority to declare certain worldviews more valid than others. By virtue of being embedded in these legitimated and legitimating institutions, evangelical Christians possess the power to conventionalize their beliefs as valid *religious* phenomena while discrediting nondoctrinal beliefs and rituals as invalid *supernatural* phenomena. Hence, it is not the essential qualities of a phenomenon that make it religious or supernatural but rather the dynamics of cultural authority that determine which of these seemingly equivalent phenomena achieves legitimacy. Thus, while nonhuman entities such as demons certainly fit the objective criteria of supernatural creatures, they are nonetheless religious beings according to our definition to the extent that their existence is asserted and legitimated within the context of conventional Christian teachings. Conversely, despite the subcultural growth of Wicca and goddess religions (Griffin 1995; Jensen and Thompson 2008), witchcraft itself has not been integrated into dominant religious discourse. Therefore, witches remain supernatural beings even though some people embrace some forms of witchcraft as a new religion.

By disentangling the supernatural from religion, we are better able to understand the supernatural as a modern concept, even though we see similar representations of the supernatural throughout history and across cultures. As Émile Durkheim points out, the "supernatural" refers to "all sorts of things which surpass the limits of our knowledge; the supernatural is the world of the mysterious, of the unknowable, of the un-understandable" (1915: 39). Or at the very least, the supernatural refers to everything that we cannot *make* understandable using socially legitimated means of knowledge production—especially, in our era, the application of science, technology, and reason. Hence, as Durkheim insightfully argues, the supernatural is necessarily a modern idea simply because there can be no "supernatural" without "the sentiment that a *natural order of things* exists, that is to say, that the phenomena of the universe is bound together by necessary relations, called laws" (41; emphasis in original). Durkheim further elaborates:

> When this principle has once been admitted, all that is contrary to these laws must necessarily appear to be outside of nature and, consequently, of reason; for what is natural in this sense of the word, is also rational, these necessary relations only expressing the manner in which things are logically related. But this idea of universal determinism is of recent origin. . . . [I]t is a conquest of the positive sciences. . . . In order to arrive at the idea of the supernatural, it is not enough, therefore, to be witness to unexpected events; *it is also necessary that these be conceived as impossible,* that is to say, irreconcilable with an order which, rightly or wrongly, appears to us to be implied in the nature of things. Now this idea of a necessary order has been constructed little by little by the positive sciences, and consequently the contrary notion could not have existed before them. (1915: 41–43; emphasis added)

Thus, it is correct to claim that throughout recorded history people have allegedly encountered things we might now interpret as supernatural phenomena. However, it is incorrect to label these events in historical accounts as supernatural if the experiences were interpreted and acted on in the context of a religious worldview that framed the events as evidence of religious teachings (as, for example, a sign from God). Likewise, it is historically inaccurate to refer to these encounters as supernatural if they occurred before the development of a modern paradigm in which the universe is understood as operating according to immutable laws of nature. For these reasons, we must apply the supernatural label carefully when comparing cross-cultural or transhistorical accounts of such phenomena.

We reserve the term "paranormal" for alleged psychic abilities that defy accepted scientific understanding of human mental capabilities.[1] There are several important differences between supernatural and paranormal phenomena. One difference concerns testability. A person who claims to be clairvoyant—that is, able to gain information about remote places, people, or events using no known sensory medium or physical interaction—can be subjected to laboratory tests designed to determine if such abilities are present. Such methods are scientific in that they rely on falsifiable hypotheses that are tested using controlled conditions that may be replicated by other researchers. In contrast, alleged supernatural phenomena such as ghost encounters or alien abductions are fundamentally untestable. These phenomena do not occur in a replicable fashion, the conditions in which they occur cannot be controlled, and the evidence presented is generally anecdotal. While some investigators of the supernatural, such as paranormal investigators and Bigfoot hunters, collect an enormous amount of empirical evidence, even the clearest audio or video recording cannot prove the source of what we are hearing or seeing. Although believers assert that evidence of even one exceptional case—one "white crow," according to William James (1896: 884)—is enough to disprove established science, the presence of one or two cases that appear to deviate from expectations is insufficient to overturn centuries of accumulated knowledge about the natural world. Absence of evidence is not necessarily evidence of absence, but this inability to establish scientific meth-

---

1. This distinction parallels that made by parapsychologists between psi phenomena that they attempt to test in laboratory settings, such as telekinesis or remote viewing, and other phenomena generally labeled paranormal, such as ghosts and cryptids. While such a distinction is important for parapsychological research, we use "supernatural" and "paranormal" here because these terms are more widely known to a general audience. In addition, we distinguish "supernatural" from "paranormal" to emphasize that supernatural phenomena are presumed to go against natural laws, whereas paranormal phenomena are assumed to violate social standards of what is considered normal. We make one exception for ghost hunters, who prefer to be called "paranormal investigators." While this terminology does not adhere to our definition for people who seek to accumulate evidence for the existence (or nonexistence) of ghosts—what we call "supernatural" phenomena—we respect the descriptor they choose for themselves.

ods of investigation distinguishes supernatural phenomena from paranormal abilities.

A second difference is that paranormal powers are presumed to originate in the mental capabilities of otherwise ordinary human beings rather than from nonhuman sources or manipulation of one's environment by means of magic. If someone believes he or she possesses the ability of psychokinesis—moving objects purely with the power of the mind—then, for our purposes, that is a paranormal phenomenon. However, if this person claims to move objects by use of a spell or some other form of magic then, for our purposes, that is a supernatural phenomenon. Equally, the power of telepathy—the alleged ability to send and receive messages simply through mental transference between two or more living humans—is paranormal, but the claimed ability to communicate with the dead or with otherworldly beings is supernatural. Like distinctions between religious and supernatural phenomena, the difference between paranormal and supernatural phenomena lies not in the ways these alleged abilities manifest themselves. Both psychokinesis and magic could move objects in similarly astounding ways, for example. Rather, the distinction between paranormal and supernatural phenomena rests on how those who claim such abilities *account* for the origin of these powers. In the former, such powers are presumed to be rare (but not superhuman) mental capabilities that need no additional outside influence to be effective. The latter, on the other hand, requires some external source of power or information to manifest what, on the surface, looks like the same phenomenon as that produced through paranormal means.

A final difference concerns the inclusivity of the two terms. Using our above definition, "paranormal" applies only to abilities, while "supernatural" encompasses abilities as well as entities. Because our goal in this volume is to highlight the social and cultural functions of beliefs and practices associated with both supernatural abilities (such as fortune-telling or communicating with the dead) and entities (such as ghosts or Bigfoot), use of the more inclusive term "supernatural" is more appropriate. This focus on personal *experiences* with or the historical *effects* of both supernatural abilities and entities distinguishes this work from others that frequently emphasize popular culture *representations* of the supernatural. The contributing authors in this volume place an array of supernatural phenomena in their appropriate historical, social, and cultural contexts. In doing so, they challenge the reader to not dismiss the supernatural as an unfortunate remnant of some imagined irrational past. Such a dismissive attitude simply obscures the important roles that supernatural beliefs and practices have played in Western history.

SUPERNATURAL OVERVIEW

The contributing authors of this book are diverse in many important and valued respects. They come from disciplinary perspectives within the social sciences and humanities and use different research methods to arrive at their conclusions. Some base their arguments on firsthand ethnographic experiences, while others rely more on secondary sources and historical records. The authors also vary in terms of their engagement with elements of what could broadly be called supernatural subcultures. Some authors in this volume relate to the supernatural as an object of disinterested inquiry that can be understood through archival research or similar unobtrusive methods of data collection. Those who used ethnographic methods necessarily participated in supernatural subcultures in an effort to see the world from the perspective of those they studied. Regardless of the research methods they used or their personal beliefs about the ontological status of the supernatural—that is, whether these abilities and entities are real in some objective sense—the authors have not set out to prove or disprove supernatural phenomena. Instead, the focus of this volume is on what these beliefs and alleged experiences do *to* and *for* people—in other words, their personal, social, and cultural functions in a given historical moment.

Supernatural beliefs and practices persist because they serve important social functions. They provide explanations for frightening or unexplained events, help people cope with trauma, imbue the mundane with mystery, establish social bonds between like-minded people, and even provide a platform for developing self-identities. Furthermore, as several chapters of this book illustrate, supernatural beliefs and experiences are deeply entangled within power relationships: they can be invoked as a means of exploiting disadvantaged populations or may be used as a source of self-empowerment in the face of personal troubles or social problems. As other chapters illustrate, the supernatural can also be a powerful source of meaning, community, and identity. Setting aside ontological arguments about the objective reality of the supernatural allows us to acknowledge that the things people believe—and most especially how they act on those beliefs—are undeniably real in the beliefs' personal and social consequences.

In this volume, supernatural beliefs, practices, and identities are treated as collective processes of sense making that must be understood within their sociocultural and sociohistorical contexts. Therefore, it is our position that the supernatural *is* real because belief in the supernatural has fundamentally shaped human history and continues to inform people's interpretations, actions, and identities daily. The supernatural is an indelible part of our social world that deserves sincere scholarly attention. This volume is our contribution to that effort: the following chapters approach the supernatural from many disciplinary and professional perspectives, allowing the reader to examine the supernatural in historical, social, and cultural contexts.

In Chapter 1, William Ryan Force argues for a multidisciplinary "cryptoscience" that considers mythic tales, folk stories, beliefs, and experiences with the uncanny as valuable aspects of the human experience deserving of serious scholarly inquiry. Force describes a flexible framework for *conceptualizing* the supernatural as a "social fact," a culturally embedded reality that structures perceptions of reality and helps people make sense of their everyday lives. Force further articulates several general principles of this cryptoscience that not only are highly useful for those who seek to better understand the supernatural but also are dynamics that we see reappearing frequently in subsequent chapters of the book.

Whereas William Ryan Force seeks to establish a means of conceptualizing the supernatural, in Chapter 2 Jeannie Banks Thomas lays out a *methodology* for approaching both research and general inquiry on the supernatural. Thomas emphasizes the importance of cultural competence in the kinds of questions and research that we conduct on the supernatural and provides a useful checklist for students and aspiring scholars. To illustrate her method, Thomas narrates engaging and evocative examples from the ethnographic fieldwork she conducted on Cape Breton Island.

The Introduction and first two chapters provide readers with three fundamentals: a general scholarly argument for the significance of the supernatural, a general way of thinking about the supernatural, and a general way for conducting inquiry on the supernatural. From Chapter 3 on, each chapter focuses on a specific supernatural phenomenon. Chapters 3, 4, and 5 concern different aspects of ghosts, which—as we established earlier in this chapter—are the supernatural entities people are most likely to report believing in and witnessing.

In Chapter 3, Dennis Waskul ethnographically illustrates the key elements that distinguish four genres of ghostly experiences: what he calls "everyday ghosts," "professionalized ghosts," "commercial ghosts," and "institutional ghosts." Drawing from his previous and ongoing research, Waskul further defines and illustrates four types of hauntings (intelligent, residual, anniversary, and historical) as well as six forms of ghosts that appear within those hauntings (apparitions, phantasms, wraiths, poltergeists, specters, and phantoms). Waskul seeks to provide a useful framework for sifting and sorting the enormous variety of experiences that people claim and associate with a ghostly presence.

In Chapter 4, Marc Eaton focuses on the tension between two methods of paranormal investigation: the scientific and sensitive approaches. On the basis of several years of participant observation and interviews with paranormal investigators (ghost hunters), Eaton's chapter contextualizes these two approaches within a U.S. culture that is characterized by both individualized spirituality *and* an abiding faith in science. Eaton first describes the differences between scientific and sensitive investigators in terms of their ontological assumptions, epistemologies, and reasons for investigating. Next, Eaton reveals how sensitive methods are subordinated to scientific approaches within the paranormal investigation subculture and details the strategies sensitives use to increase the perceived validity of their claims. Eaton unpacks the power dynamics that determine what qualifies as a legitimate way to investigate the existence of ghosts.

Legend tripping and dark tourism are the central topics of Rachael Ironside's Chapter 5. Legend tripping, an activity that appears in several places in this book, refers to visiting a location that is associated with the supernatural. For example, visiting a graveyard with a reputation for being haunted is a form of legend tripping, and as Ironside illustrates, people legend trip for several reasons. Some forms of legend tripping benefit businesses and communities; these forms make up what is known as dark tourism. For example, dark tourism is critical to the local economy of Salem, Massachusetts, which has commodified its legendary witch trials. Ironside grounds her discussion of dark tourism in what is surely its most common form—ghost tourism, which includes relatively low-cost adventures like a guided ghost walk or ghost hunt as well as more expensive thrills such as staying in a haunted hotel. On the basis of her ethnographic research on ghost tourism, Ironside illustrates the key elements necessary for a successful experience with dark tourism.

Turning to fortune-telling, in Chapter 6 Stephen Muzzatti and Emma Smith highlight how fortune-tellers function as life advisors for people searching for guidance in the face of economic uncertainty in late modern capitalism. Muzzatti and Smith also emphasize the persecution of fortune-tellers throughout Western history and illustrate the sharp contrast between popular culture caricatures of the fortune-teller and the actual practice of soothsaying. Muzzatti and Smith illustrate how modern and contemporary fortune-telling machines and smartphone apps both popularize and trivialize fortune-telling.

While some who seek answers about the future or the mysteries of life turn to fortune-tellers, others use tarot cards, which are the subject of Janet Baldwin's Chapter 7. Baldwin details the somewhat mysterious history of the tarot, as well as major influences on this tool of divination as the cards became more or less codified by the early 1900s. Yet tarot can serve more functions than simply being a means for gleaning clues about the future or insights about one's everyday life. As Baldwin illustrates from her ongoing ethnographic research, the use of tarot can bind people together and serve ritualized social functions that are at least as magical as the alleged powers of tarot itself.

In Chapter 8, I'Nasah Crockett focuses specifically on voodoo, especially in the city of New Orleans. As Crockett illustrates, the actual practice of voodoo sharply contrasts with how it has been characterized in the limited available literature on the topic—much of which is tainted with blatant racism. Moreover, voodoo is both an eclectic religion and a tourist commodity in New Orleans. Thus, the history and nature of voodoo—especially in New Orleans—is heavily influenced by not only the black culture of the region but also shifting geographic realities, the civil rights movement, and the marketing of voodoo as a tourist commodity.

In Chapter 9, Joseph Laycock goes beyond beliefs to trace the evolution of the vampire from a demonic to a sympathetic figure, a misunderstood outsider who appeals to many teens and young adults searching for an identity in which to ground their self-perceptions. While many may identify with the vampire as a social construct signifying outsider status, some people's commitment goes beyond mere affinity for the symbol. These people believe they are real vampires—that they were born with a condition that makes them fundamentally unlike other human beings. Laycock details the common misunderstandings about the real-vampire community, the similarities between members' claims of identity and the history of the LGBTQ community, and ultimately the challenge these identity claims make to not only what it means to be a vampire but what it means to be *human*.

In Chapter 10, Tea Krulos provides overviews of the field of cryptozoology as well as the cryptids that cryptozoologists study and hunt. From Lazarus species and living fossils to well-known (e.g., Bigfoot and the Loch Ness monster) and lesser-known (e.g., Mothman) cryptids, Krulos illustrates the struggles cryptozoologists face in their quest for legitimacy. Faced with skeptics on one side and hoaxers on the other, cryptozoologists fight an uphill battle against both scientific orthodoxy and public opinion. Yet, inspired by a few success stories, cryptozoologists remain compelled by the thrill of potential discovery and the hope that one day they will be seen as pioneering scientists. Regardless of the outcome of their efforts, Krulos argues, their efforts have value as a form of enchantment in what often feels like a disenchanted world.

In Chapter 11, Scott Scribner proposes an eight-part Teller-Narrator model for understanding alien abduction narratives. He shows how these narratives form within—and are informed by—a complex matrix of competing accounts of abduction experiences. Scribner's model embeds the alien abduction narrative within a temporal sequence in which past stories may act as interpretive resources for a given abduction account, which may in turn influence future narratives of similar experiences. At the same time, multiple people—from eyewitnesses to professionals—attempt to shape the narrative to fit their needs. To illustrate this process, Scribner draws on perhaps the best known of such narratives, the story of Travis Walton's abduction in November 1975.

We sought to bring together scholars from different disciplines and backgrounds to create one comprehensive text on the supernatural—an objective that we knew from the start could never be fully achieved. Missing from this book is any sustained attention to other topics that could just as easily have been included—worthy subjects such as witchcraft, mediumship, astrology, and nonreligious understandings of demonology. Perhaps the supernatural is simply too vast a subject for any one text to fully cover. As the content of this book clearly illustrates, the supernatural is extraordinarily rich with complex, important, and innately interesting social, cultural, and historical dynamics. Consequently, we hope this book contributes to a future in which scholars are less likely to ignore or trivialize these topics.

REFERENCES

Bader, Christopher D., Joseph O. Baker, and Andrea Molle. 2012. "Countervailing Forces: Religiosity and Paranormal Belief in Italy." *Journal for the Scientific Study of Religion* 51 (4): 705–720.

Bader, Christopher D., F. Carson Mencken, and Joseph Baker. 2010. *Paranormal America: Ghost Encounters, UFO Sightings, Bigfoot Hunts, and Other Curiosities in Religion and Culture*. New York: New York University Press.

Bainbridge, William S. 1978. "Chariots of the Gullible." *Skeptical Inquirer* 3 (2): 33–48.

Baker, Joseph, and Scott Draper. 2010. "Diverse Supernatural Portfolios: Certitude, Exclusivity, and the Curvilinear Relationship between Religiosity and Paranormal Beliefs." *Journal for the Scientific Study of Religion* 49 (3): 413–424.

Box Office Mojo. n.d. "Paranormal Activity: Total Grosses." Available at http://www.boxofficemojo.com/franchises/chart/?id=paranormalactivity.htm (accessed January 15, 2018).

Bruce, Steve. 2002. *God Is Dead: Secularization in the West*. Oxford, UK: Blackwell.

Bullard, Thomas E. 1989. "UFO Abduction Reports: The Supernatural Kidnap Narrative Returns in Technological Guise." *Journal of American Folklore* 102 (404): 147–170.

Dégh, Linda, and Andrew Vázsonyi. 1983. "Does the Word 'Dog' Bite? Ostensive Action: A Means of Legend-Telling." *Journal of Folklore Research* 20 (1): 5–34.

Denzler, Brenda. 2001. *The Lure of the Edge: Scientific Passions, Religious Beliefs, and the Pursuit of UFOs*. Berkeley: University of California Press.

Dewan, William J. 2006. "'A Saucerful of Secrets': An Interdisciplinary Analysis of UFO Experiences." *Journal of American Folklore* 119 (472): 184–202.

Drinkwater, Ken, Neil Dagnall, and Andrew Parker. 2012. "Reality Testing, Conspiracy Theories, and Paranormal Beliefs." *Journal of Parapsychology* 76 (1): 57–77.

Durkheim, Émile. 1915. *The Elementary Forms of Religious Life*. New York: Free Press.
Eaton, Marc. 2015. "'Give Us a Sign of Your Presence': Paranormal Investigation as a Spiritual Practice." *Sociology of Religion* 76 (4): 389–412.
Ellis, Bill. 1989. "Death by Folklore: Ostention, Contemporary Legend, and Murder." *Western Folklore* 48 (3): 201–220.
Emmons, Charles, and Jeff Sobal. 1981. "Paranormal Beliefs: Testing the Marginality Hypothesis." *Sociological Focus* 14 (1): 49–56.
Farha, Bryan, and Gary Steward. 2006. "Paranormal Beliefs: An Analysis of College Students." *Skeptical Inquirer* 30 (1): 37–40.
Fitch, Marc E. 2013. *Paranormal Nation: Why America Needs Ghosts, UFOs, and Bigfoot*. Santa Barbara, CA: Praeger.
French, Christopher C., and Anna Stone. 2014. *Anomalistic Psychology: Exploring Paranormal Belief and Experience*. Hampshire, UK: Palgrave Macmillan.
Gentry, Glenn W. 2007. "Walking with the Dead: The Place of Ghost Walk Tourism in Savannah, Georgia." *Southeastern Geographer* 47 (2): 222–238.
Glendinning, Tony. 2006. "Religious Involvement, Conventional Christian, and Unconventional Nonmaterialist Belief." *Journal for the Scientific Study of Religion* 45 (4): 585–595.
Goldstein, Diane. 2007. "Scientific Rationalism and Supernatural Experience Narratives." In *Haunting Experiences: Ghosts in Contemporary Folklore*, edited by D. E. Goldstein, S. A. Grider, and J. B. Thomas, 60–78. Logan: Utah State University Press.
Goldstein, Diane E., Sylvia A. Grider, and Jeannie B. Thomas. 2007. *Haunting Experiences: Ghosts in Contemporary Folklore*. Logan: Utah State University Press.
Griffin, Wendy. 1995. "The Embodied Goddess: Feminist Witchcraft and Female Divinity." *Sociology of Religion* 56 (1): 35–48.
Hergovich, Andreas, Reinhard Schott, and Martin Arendasy. 2005. "Paranormal Belief and Religiosity." *Journal of Parapsychology* 69 (2): 293–303.
Hibberd, James. 2014. "SyFy Will Never Stop Airing 'Ghost Hunters.'" *Entertainment Weekly*, October 29. Available at http://www.ew.com/article/2014/10/29/ghost-hunters.
Holloway, Daniel. 2014. "Travel Channel Tells Ghost Stories to Young, Female Audience." *Broadcasting and Cable*, August 29. Available at http://www.broadcastingcable.com/blog/bc-beat/travel-channel-tells-ghost-stories-young-female-audience/133557.
Holloway, Julian. 2010. "Legend-Tripping in Spooky Places: Ghost Tourism and Infrastructures of Enchantment." *Environment and Planning D: Society and Space* 28 (4): 618–637.
Hufford, David. 1995. "Beings without Bodies: An Experience-Centered Theory of the Beliefs in Spirits." In *Out of the Ordinary: Folklore and the Supernatural*, edited by B. Walker, 11–45. Logan: Utah State University Press.
Irwin, Harvey J. 2009. *The Psychology of Paranormal Belief: A Researcher's Handbook*. Hertfordshire, UK: University of Hertfordshire Press.
James, William. 1896. "Address of the President before the Society for Psychical Research." *Science* 3 (77): 881–888.
Jensen, Gary F., and Ashley Thompson. 2008. "'Out of the Broom Closet': The Social Ecology of American Wicca." *Journal for the Scientific Study of Religion* 47 (4): 753–766.

Kissell, Rick. 2016. "Ratings: 'The Walking Dead' Down, Still Huge in Return; Small Tune-In for HBO's 'Vinyl.'" *Variety*, February 17. Available at http://variety.com/2016/tv/news/ratings-the-walking-dead-vinyl-premiere-1201707036.

Krulos, Tea. 2015. *Monster Hunters: On the Trail with Ghost Hunters, Bigfooters, Ufologists, and Other Paranormal Investigators*. Chicago: Chicago Review Press.

Laycock, Joseph P. 2009. *Vampires Today: The Truth about Modern Vampirism*. Westport, CT: Praeger.

———. 2012. "'We Are Spirits of Another Sort': Ontological Rebellion and Religious Dimensions of the Otherkin Community." *Nova Religio* 15 (3): 65–90.

Leiserowitz, Anthony, Edward Maibach, Connie Roser-Renouf, Geoff Feinberg, and Peter Howe. 2012. "Climate Change in the American Mind: Americans' Global Warming Beliefs and Attitudes in September 2012." Available at http://environment.yale.edu/climate/files/Climate-Beliefs-September-2012.pdf.

Leonard, Todd J. 2005. *Talking to the Other Side: A History of Modern Spiritualism and Mediumship*. New York: iUniverse.

Lindahl, Carl. 2005. "Ostensive Healing: Pilgrimage to the San Antonio Ghost Tracks." *Journal of American Folklore* 118 (468): 164–185.

Lobato, Emilio, Jorge Mendoza, Valerie Sims, and Matthew Chin. 2014. "Examining the Relationship between Conspiracy Theories, Paranormal Beliefs, and Pseudoscience Acceptance among a University Population." *Applied Cognitive Psychology* 28 (5): 617–625.

Lyons, Linda. 2005. "Paranormal Beliefs Come (Super)Naturally to Some." *Gallup*, November 1. Available at http://www.gallup.com/poll/19558/Paranormal-Beliefs-Come-SuperNaturally-Some.aspx.

McClurg, Jocelyn. 2015. "Meyer, Riordan Back on Best-Seller List." *USA Today*, October 14. Available at http://www.usatoday.com/story/life/books/2015/10/14/stephenie-meyer-twilight-rick-riordan-magnus-chase-usa-today-best-selling-books-list/73877256.

McKinnon, Andrew M. 2003. "The Religious, the Paranormal, and Church Attendance: A Response to Orenstein." *Journal for the Scientific Study of Religion* 42 (2): 299–303.

Mencken, F. Carson, Christopher D. Bader, and Ye Jung Kim. 2009. "Round Trip to Hell in a Flying Saucer: The Relationship between Conventional Christian and Paranormal Beliefs in the United States." *Sociology of Religion* 70 (1): 65–85.

Mencken, F. Carson, Christopher D. Bader, and Rodney Stark. 2008. "Conventional Christian Beliefs and Experimentation with the Paranormal." *Review of Religious Research* 50 (2): 194–205.

Moore, David W. 2005. "Three in Four Americans Believe in Paranormal." *Gallup*, June 16. Available at http://www.gallup.com/poll/16915/three-four-americans-believe-paranormal.aspx.

Nash Information Services. n.d.a. "Box Office History for Harry Potter Movies." Available at http://www.the-numbers.com/movies/franchise/Harry-Potter#tab=summary.

———. n.d.b. "Box Office History for Twilight Movies." Available at http://www.the-numbers.com/movies/franchise/Twilight#tab=summary.

Newport, Frank, and Maura Strausberg. 2001. "Americans' Belief in Psychic and Paranormal Phenomena Is Up over Last Decade." *Gallup*, June 8. Available at http://www.gallup.com/poll/4483/americans-belief-psychic-paranormal-phenomena-over-last-decade.aspx.

Northcote, Jeremy. 2007. *The Paranormal and the Politics of Truth: A Sociological Account.* Charlottesville, VA: Imprint-Academic.

Pew Forum on Religion and Public Life. 2009. "Many Americans Mix Multiple Faiths." Washington, DC: Pew Research Center.

Pew Research Center. 2015. "U.S. Public Becoming Less Religious." Available at http://www.pewforum.org/2015/11/03/u-s-public-becoming-less-religious.

Pollack, Hannah. 2016. "American Teens No Longer More Likely than Adults to Believe In God, Miracles, Heaven, Jesus, Angels, or the Devil." *PR Newswire*, November 1. Available at https://www.prnewswire.com/news-releases/american-teens-no-longer-more-likely-than-adults-to-believe-in-god-miracles-heaven-jesus-angels-or-the-devil-300355416.html.

Porter, Rick. 2016. "Wednesday Final Ratings: 'SVU' Finale Adjusts Up, 'Supernatural' Finale Adjusts Down." *TV by the Numbers*, May 26. Available at http://tvbythenumbers.zap2it.com/2016/05/26/wednesday-final-ratings-may-25-2016.

Radford, Benjamin. 2014. "The Slenderman Stabbing: Are Urban Legends Really to Blame?" *Live Science*, June 5. Available at http://www.livescience.com/46129-slenderman-stabbing-and-urban-legends.html.

Rutherford, Jennifer. 2013. *Zombies.* New York: Routledge.

Scholastic. n.d. "Harry Potter: About the Series." Available at http://harrypotter.scholastic.com/series_information (accessed January 15, 2018).

Sharps, Matthew J., Justin Matthews, and Janet Asten. 2006. "Cognition and Belief in Paranormal Phenomena: Gestalt/Feature-Intensive Processing Theory and Tendencies Toward ADHD, Depression, and Dissociation." *Journal of Psychology* 140 (6): 579–590.

Thomas, Jeannie B. 2007. "Gender and Ghosts." In *Haunting Experiences: Ghosts in Contemporary Folklore*, edited by D. E. Goldstein, S. A. Grider, and J. B. Thomas, 81–110. Logan: Utah State University Press.

———, ed. 2015. *Putting the Supernatural in Its Place: Folklore, the Hypermodern, and the Ethereal.* Salt Lake City: University of Utah Press.

Thomas, Keith. 1971. *Religion and the Decline of Magic.* New York: Scribner's.

US Quidditch. n.d. "About US Quidditch." Available at https://www.usquidditch.org/about/mission (accessed January 15, 2018).

Wallace, Anthony. 1966. *Religion: An Anthropological View.* New York: Random Books.

Waskul, Dennis, with Michele Waskul. 2016. *Ghostly Encounters: The Hauntings of Everyday Life.* Philadelphia: Temple University Press.

Weisberg, Barbara. 2005. *Talking to the Dead: Kate and Maggie Fox and the Rise of Spiritualism.* New York: HarperCollins.

YouGov. 2013. "Ghosts and UFOs." Available at http://www.assap.ac.uk/newsite/Docs/Ghost%20UFO%20Survey%202013.pdf.

1

TOWARD A CRYPTOSCIENCE

WILLIAM RYAN FORCE

This chapter articulates an argument for the academic exploration of the supernatural. By "supernatural" I mean assorted phenomena: ghosts and hauntings; psychics, mediums, and myriad "seers"; tarot and astrology; vampires, lycanthropes, and other semihuman creatures; UFOs and extraterrestrial beings (including encounters therewith); spooky spaces like the Bermuda Triangle; bizarre happenings like unexplained weather patterns; and witchcraft and magic(k). Abstracted from these examples, I propose we define "supernatural" to mean any phenomenon encountered by human beings that is currently unexplained or unexplainable.[1] These topics, however, are typically considered outside the domain of serious, scholarly inquiry or academic attention. It is therefore worth considering that many—maybe even all—of the above-listed examples *could be* subject to appropriate intellectual scrutiny. Indeed, much of what is now supernatural *could* eventually be folded into our notions of the natural because what is accepted as a legitimate subject for research is less dependent on the actual scope of science than its socially prescribed boundaries (Gieryn 1983).

David Hufford argues that experiences can find explanation, or exegesis, in myriad narratives, but which narrative is considered legitimate is a mat-

---

1. Note that in the Introduction, Dennis Waskul and Marc Eaton further refine the distinction between supernatural (phenomena that lie outside the realm of what is understood to be natural reality) and paranormal (phenomena that "violate social standards" of the collectively defined normative understanding of how natural reality works). While this is a useful *epistemological* distinction, here I conflate the two for the purposes of revealing their *ontological* overlap as potentially hidden or obscure aspects of the so-called natural universe.

ter of "cultural authority" (1995: 18). Similarly, Peter Berger observes that a "sane" or "normal" person is one who "lives within assigned coordinates" (1963: 67)—and that our sense of what is plausible or implausible is derived from our socialization. Dennis Waskul and Marc Eaton echo this view in their definition of the supernatural in the Introduction, noting that whether an experience is appropriately described as plausible or implausible depends more on the alignment of individual experiences with culturally supported, (inter)subjective interpretation than any argument about the objective facts of the matter. In other words, whether a monster or a ghost is a *realistic* possibility in a given person's worldview depends on the prevailing versions of reality that are institutionalized in, say, organized religion or natural science.

Likewise, someone claiming to hear voices when alone can be deemed credible in that assertion through the diagnosis of certain psychological conditions. Similarly, when accounts of sanity are used as a mitigating circumstance in a legal case, the criminal justice system becomes another site for the power-laden process of defining what is real. In these ways, institutional forms, including science and the state in this case, clearly have a vested interest in arbitrating between competing definitions of reality and have the power to make their definitions hegemonic. Whether dealing with a legal standard for evidence, an appeal to theological doctrine, or the hallowed facts of empirical science, one is drawn into a self-contained logical worldview that Berger called a *plausibility structure* (1967: 45). Although each perspective (be it religious, scientific, or legal) claims a monopoly on what counts as true, individuals within a complex society such as ours are assailed by multiple and equally assured frameworks for "the real."

Putting it plainly, I suggest that "supernatural" is a word we tend to use when unusual, uncanny, or otherwise spooky stuff does not fit into a dominant religion's system of orthodoxy or with some other culturally sanctioned version of reality (including that of science). The supernatural is what gets marginalized in the dominant paradigm's version of reality (Gieryn 1983) or the culturally authoritative narrative (Hufford 1995). However, the very fact that a substantial number of people say they have had supernatural experiences—or believe in that possibility—tells us that *some* narrative and cultural spaces of "reality" are carved out for these things. These are the spaces in which we are left to sort between dissonant definitions of the world as it is.

As the editors of this volume explain in the Introduction, "Approximately half of all American adults hold at least one supernatural belief, by which we mean a belief in abilities or beings whose manifestation transcends accepted scientific understandings of the natural world" and can include ghosts, sentient beings from other places in the galaxy, or creatures like the Loch Ness monster. It is therefore evident that mythic tales, folk stories and beliefs, legends (both historical and contemporary), and other weird or uncanny aspects of our cultural worldviews require serious examination. If a thing has consequences and effects for the lives of everyday people, it is real(ity) for those who experience it (Thomas and Thomas 1928), and hence, for all intents and purposes, the supernatural is therefore very real.

When I was a graduate student I worried that my decision to research white masculinity in bars was a potentially career-killing idea. Wayne Brekhus was my advisor, and he remarked that, not long ago, graduate students in the social sciences who studied culture would be expected to write about "higher" forms instead of popular ones—Herman Melville instead of Michael Jackson. As Brekhus saw it, this was myopia: the average person is likely to have spent more time with "Billie Jean" than *Billy Budd*. Of course, he is right. Likewise, if so many of us feel that our lives have been in some way touched by the supernatural, it is elitist posturing to refuse to take it under consideration. One can be incredulous while still remaining flexible—we are not obligated to agree with the people we try to understand or even like the things we research. That does not mean we are excused from a sober(ing) look, and my primary objective in this chapter is to articulate a starting point for conceiving the supernatural as a series of subjects that is worthy of close scholarly attention.

KNOWING THE UNKNOWN

> As our circle of knowledge expands, so does the circumference of darkness surrounding it.
> —Attributed to ALBERT EINSTEIN

This chapter is not about the study of the supernatural's representation but about the *social fact* of supernatural reality. Émile Durkheim ([1895] 1982) defined a social fact as anything felt to be external to a person that asserts coercive force over perceptions, self-concept, or behavior. These social facts are often simultaneously both intangible and powerful. For example, most people cannot articulate the dynamics of class exploitation or corporate power but still know it when they feel exploited by their bosses or let down by the failed promises of pointless consumer products. Similarly, the supernatural is composed of social facts. I previously suggested that the supernatural comprises any phenomenon that is currently unexplained or unexplainable. Yet if folks tell us that they have seen a Sasquatch or been visited by a spirt, they are conveying to us their experiences regardless of whether they can explain that reality through theory or empiricism. This pushes us to make an attempt at analyzing those assertions, even if we find them to be incredible.

Aside from not attempting to scientifically explain such things, another fundamental issue with making sense of the supernatural is that some phenomena may elude our understanding, not because of a lack of the needed analytic equipment but because we misapply it. That is, something may be unknown as of yet but not unknowable. A basic misapplication of any discipline's methodology and theory lies in using it exclusively and without connection to other bodies of knowledge. To avoid that error, I outline here a general conceptual framework for considering the sociocultural and historical dimensions of supernatural phenomena—what I label a *cryptoscience*—and at its core this model requires a ruthless transgression of disciplinary boundaries to be effective.

The prefix "crypto-" is apt because it means to be hidden or secret rather than being impossible to know. It is helpful to consistently remind ourselves that much of our now mundane wisdom was once hidden from us in the past. Before Hippocrates, what people of his time might now call medical science was a hodgepodge of quasiscientific practices and superstition. Two thousand years later, the earliest surgical procedures in Europe and the United States were still viewed with suspicion by medical science and relegated to barbershops rather than hospitals. Meanwhile, relatively advanced surgical and medical practices had already been widely embraced and practiced in northern Africa. Many things likely went unknown or were puzzled over for too long because the thinkers of various cultures worked in isolation to answer big questions, unable or unwilling to acknowledge the work of others.

A broad cryptoscientific perspective—literally, *a science of the hidden or unknown*—ideally bridges aspects of disciplines more conventionally described as social science (sociology, psychology, religious studies, anthropology) or the humanities (literary theory, folklore studies) to emphasize the strength of their mutual application in exploring the unexplained. Necessarily, the so-called natural sciences are also of massive importance in this regard. It ought to go without saying that physics and biology are likely filled with untapped applications to the research program described here. Linkages across all disciplines—from particle physics to poststructural anthropology—are the likeliest way toward anything resembling a satisfying answer to questions about the supernatural.

A perhaps surprising example of this work comes from renowned astronomer and public scientist Carl Sagan. In *The Demon-Haunted World*, Sagan (1995) speculates about the scientific bases for phenomena, including ghosts and so-called alien encounters, in which individuals witness or interact with extraterrestrial beings (often in the form of being forcibly abducted by those beings). Sagan was infamous for his militant agnosticism about the supernatural. He refers repeatedly to the notion that absence of evidence is not evidence of absence—never dismissing any explanatory possibilities without grounds to do so while subjecting all explanations to thorough scrutiny. Sagan (1995) reminds us of what most scientists already know, if only implicitly: that science does not now (nor is likely to *ever*) offer a complete or infallible model of natural reality.

This is a separate matter, however, from nonscientists being typically unaware of the full breadth of explanations available to account for the seemingly inexplicable. Consequently, "spurious accounts that snare the gullible are readily available. . . . Sparse and poor popularizations of sciences abandon ecological niches that pseudoscience promptly fills" (Sagan 1995: 5–6). Sagan then goes on to provide, for example, potential explanations for the conditions that may give rise to reports of an unidentified flying object:

> unconventional aircraft, conventional aircraft with unusual lighting patterns, high-altitude balloons, luminescent insects, planets seen under unusual atmospheric conditions, optical mirages and looming, lenticular clouds, ball lightning, sundogs, meteors including green fireballs, and satellites, nosecones, and rocket boosters spectacularly reentering the atmosphere. (1995: 70–71)

In the absence of these explanations, and compounded by folk stories or preexisting supernatural beliefs, an alien aircraft can be proffered as a potential explanation for contact with a UFO.

Encounters with extraterrestrial life (or their technology) may also be accounted for by hallucinations. Contrary to commonplace assumptions, hallucinations are not uncommon or the exclusive province of the mentally ill. Many factors can trigger auditory and visual hallucinations: lucid recollections, emotional stress, seizures, fever, and the prolonged deprivation of sleep, food, light, sound, or human contact (Sagan 1995). Hallucinogens can also of course be unwittingly ingested—whether by humans foraging for food (who may consume particular kinds of cacti or mushrooms) or eating prepared food on which molds have developed, like ergot (which grows on rye and can induce both hallucinations and prolonged unconsciousness). Regardless of their origin or cause, hallucinations essentially involve sensory input being misprocessed by the human brain. A preconscious stream of data, constantly processed by the human brain, is among the explanations for where our dreams derive from. Similarly, Sagan (1995: 106) describes how the conscious mind can sometimes become temporarily aware of the data stream and mix its content with waking perceptions to produce hallucinatory effects. Ghosts, monsters, and many other phenomena likewise could be the result of hallucinatory episodes.

As Sagan's arguments illustrate, the natural sciences are excellent for explaining the potential physical bases for many things attributed to the supernatural. However, the domain of any science is limited and necessarily provincial. And, as this book repeatedly illustrates, Sagan and others like him are focused on explaining the supernatural phenomenon itself—not its existence as a social fact, which is grounded in social and cultural realities that are relatively impervious to radical empiricism. In short, these scientistic perspectives tend to explain away the supernatural rather than regard it as a partial and tentative account. While suited for an explanation of the workings of the human body and brain, the natural environment, and the basic laws governing the existence of matter and energy, these disciplines must be combined with the insights of social sciences and the humanities to produce something closer to a complete analysis of these experiences, events, and objects. As Berger (1963, 1967) and countless others have explained, human beings occupy a twofold world: a physical, objective reality and a symbolic world *through which* the first is encountered. Albert Einstein himself acknowledged that "physical concepts are free creations of the human mind, and are not, however it may seem, uniquely determined by the external world" (1938: 31).

Hostility between the natural and social sciences abounds on both sides of the divide but is misguided and counterproductive (Pigliucci 2013). It is through the lenses provided by the social sciences and humanities that we can understand the processes by which the raw facts of experience (as described by natural scientists) are made into social reality. In the social sciences and humanities, research and writing has already developed to make sense of the supernatural. Perhaps the most logical first stop for answers is psychology, which typically focuses on the human mind and the internal mechanisms that drive human behavior. Here, too, mainstream psychology has historically been antagonistic toward supernatural beliefs, characterizing them as the product of delusions or psychoses. However, exceptions can be found. Even Carl Jung (1979) acknowledged that the prominence of UFO abduction reports leads to questions about what psychological functions they may provide. Recent work also entertains claims of alien encounters, even while remaining critical of empirically unverifiable assertions. In many cases, alien abduction narratives are understood as earnest, albeit distorted, memories of childhood sexual molestation or related to the phenomenon of sleep paralysis (McNally and Clancy 2005).

In a different vein, psychologists have begun looking into the scientific bases for supernatural experiences like certain ghostly encounters (Nees and Phillips 2015). The human brain is, in part, a pattern-recognition machine that searches for meaningful recurrences in the raw data of experience. This allows for the development of language acquisition among other things, but it can misfire. Pareidolia is a naturally occurring form of hallucination in which the human brain perceives patterns within random data—like the face of Jesus in a potato chip or voices within the din of rain or wind. Michael Nees and Charlotte Phillips (2015) explain that this can be readily used to explain the discovery of ghostly voices or sounds in audio recordings of haunted spaces. By extension, this phenomenon may help explain the appearance of faces or other images during firsthand experiences or in visual data like photographs.

Folklore studies are another obvious source for tools to help unpack the supernatural experience. Perhaps most widely regarded is Hufford (1982) for his work on sleep paralysis and the Old Hag mythos that shows up in consistent ways across cultures. A plethora of phenomena fit the model of sleep paralysis symptoms: shuffling footsteps, an uncanny presence, the inability to move, a sensation of being held down or choked, and even nightmarish visions. Variations on the Hag explanation abound across human cultures—taking the form of ghosts, succubae and incubi, or in our contemporary world, space aliens. Sleep paralysis is also raised by Sagan (1995), in a way that is very much consistent with Hufford, to explain alien encounters. Folklorist Thomas Bullard (1989) also supports this analysis of the extraterrestrial abduction as a modern riff on supernatural abduction motifs. The pliability of sleep paralysis makes it the basis for many narrative constructions and speaks to the interpretive authority of folk stories or cultural myths (including religion and science) in shaping our understanding of experience. The work of Jeannie Banks Thomas (2015; Goldstein, Grider, and Thomas 2007) employs a similar sensitivity to the subjectivity of human experience in exploring how folktales about ghosts function as moral narrative devices that communicate core values (and fears) within a society.

Further work that crosses disciplinary lines also proves promising for adding to the bricolage of methods and theories needed for the cryptoscientific project to succeed. Mainstream anthropological studies of peoples' experiences with witchcraft, ghosts, and aliens provide another entry point. In Jack Hunter's online journal and edited volume, the idea of "paranthropology" is advanced as an interdisciplinary project for exploring the "paranormal, supernatural or anomalous" experiences recounted by people (2015: 11).[2] Paranthropology in many ways straddles anthropology, religious studies, sociology, and folklore studies (among other fields), taking a multifaceted look at the meaningful relationship between human beings and the supernatural belief

---

2. See also the website of the *Paranthropology* journal, at http://paranthropologyjournal.weebly.com.

systems they develop. It is clear that social scientific work on human experience has already begun to examine seriously and rigorously the supernatural as a fateful dimension of everyday life. To advance and extend this analysis, I suggest that the microsociologies of everyday life are a crucial addition.

EXPANDING OUR UNDERSTANDING OF THE EVERY DAY

> Reality is a consensus.
> —Chuck Palahniuk, *Rant*

Borrowing heavily from the tradition of symbolic interactionist and constructionist sociology with the insights of cultural cognitive sociology to explore the supernatural as a sociomental experience, my primary goal for the remainder of this chapter is to identify central assumptions of my proposed cryptoscience. To begin with, *cryptoscience approaches the ontological reality of the supernatural as less important than the meanings these phenomena have for people who experience them.*

Social reality is a product—a consequence of the natural world being perceived and experienced through the symbolic forms available to people. Primary among these symbolic constructions are what Durkheim ([1915] 1995) called collective representations: core values, fundamental ideas, and dominant beliefs crystalized in the shape of widely shared stories and images. Our shared notions about the world result from interpretations that draw from this common stock of knowledge (Berger and Luckmann 1966). Erving Goffman (1974) uses the term "frames" to describe these prevailing models for making sense of social life. The frame analogy is apt because these dominant collective representations do indeed focus our attention and limit our gaze to only certain versions of reality. Similarly, Judith Butler argues that it is "recognition" by other members of a culture that grants a thing its status as real; a phenomenon must be made comprehendible or "legible" to others before it can become part of our stock of collective representations (2004: 32).

Taken together, these sociological insights are especially useful for understanding the supernatural as a category of phenomena that are out of frame—or illegible—to most of us because we perceive reality as exclusively defined by the collective representations we have inherited. At the same time, we must account for many people continuing to assert that they have experienced the supernatural despite such phenomena not being granted legitimacy by the dominant belief systems of our era, science and religion. To understand the persistence of the supernatural at the level of individual perception it is helpful to suspend cantankerous ontological questions about what is real and to focus instead on how a person's *belief* that a supernatural phenomenon—

a ghost or Sasquatch, for example—is real results in certain consequences. From this perspective, "reality" is defined less by collective representations than by experiential knowledge and the consequent actions taken on the basis of this experience.

Perhaps the simplest way to understand this interplay between experiential and collective definitions of reality is by considering a real-world example. The question of whether one is really a man, for example, can be settled by several standards: a legal document (such as a birth certificate) that verifies a person's status as a male, medical tests for the presence of a Y chromosome, or behaving in ways that others understand as appropriately manly (spitting in public, expressing sexual interest in women, memorizing useless sports trivia, etc.). The former two standards define masculinity as a matter of biological sex, while the latter defines it as a certain type of gendered performance or self-identification. Moreover, manhood is likely to be defined by observers on the basis of surface-level information and collective representations of what a man *should* look like. Think, for example, of how often we presume the gender of people without ever knowing for certain their biological sex or self-identification. Struggles may ensue over which ways of defining masculinity are more accurate, but all these definitions are real in the sense that they have consequences for the individuals so defined—in the same way that those who were defined as witches in various times in history suffered the consequences of this definition regardless of its validity.

To continue with this illustrative example, a person's self-definition as a man is the product of gender socialization, a process in which he was taught what a man looks like and how he talks or behaves. Once he internalizes these gender norms, this person will "do gender" (West and Zimmerman 1987: 126) in ways that conform to social expectations and will judge his own manhood by how well he exhibits certain characteristics that are culturally coded as masculine. His manhood will also be judged by others, who may implement "technologies of person production" (Cahill 1998: 141) to correct or punish behaviors that they perceive as insufficiently masculine. This person may have male genitalia and a thick beard, listen to heavy metal, and have a reputation as an accomplished heterosexual; nonetheless, if he stumbles in front of a stranger and begins to weep, it is likely that the stranger's first response will be to participate in humiliation or harassment designed to teach him to realign his behavior with widely understood beliefs about what it means to be a man. In short, one's definition of manhood is policed both internally and externally on the basis of internalized preconceptions of what real masculinity looks and acts like.

These same kinds of arbitrary frames inform how people define, interpret, and act on other aspects of social life—including supernatural ones.

For example, Dennis Waskul explains that a "ghost" is another abstraction that refers to a wide variety of experiences. Notably, he reports that ghosts occur "most frequently in no visual or identifiably human acoustic form at all" (Waskul 2016: 21). Despite the word "ghost" being used in many cases (and disproportionately in popular culture) to describe humanlike apparitions with malicious intent, 68 percent of the descriptions in Waskul's sample lacked any human characteristics at all (2016: 139). Hence, despite people experiencing strange happenings that have no human characteristics, individuals commonly *presume* that those oddities are evidence of the ghost of a former living person on the basis of application of cultural stock knowledge that they have learned through the course of their life. Alternatively, a more skeptical interpreter of these claims may note that nearly all the ways that ghosts are experienced (Waskul 2016)—sounds with no detectable origin, bodily sensations that appear to have no physical stimulus, and visual apparitions in the form of what appear to be shadows or smoke—are equally explainable as forms of hallucinatory experience (Sagan 1995). Thus, the reality of ghosts is essentially the result of an interpretation that, in turn, is greatly influenced by the stock of collective representations internalized as facts.

Ultimately, the reality of a thing is an epistemological privilege secured by that phenomenon's enshrinement in the normative codes of a social system—what Eviatar Zerubavel calls "sociomental lenses" (1997: 31). Individuals in a given society learn to see, or make sense of, their experiences and observations through optical socialization (Zerubavel 1997). This means that what we perceive as natural or supernatural—our definition of reality itself, in other words—is a product of interpersonal, collaborative exchanges of meaning. Butler has claimed that "gender is a kind of imitation for which there is no original; in fact, it is a kind of imitation that produces the very notion of the original . . . a *phantasmic* ideal" (1993: 313). Put another way, gender is merely a ghost story that has ascended to the level of cultural taken-for-grantedness. Given that gender is no less a constructed category than the supernatural, there is reason to believe that societal attitudes about the reality of supernatural phenomena also have the capacity to change.

THE SOCIOMENTAL PRODUCTION OF REALITY

> The face of the beast always becomes known, and the time of the beast always passes.
> —STEPHEN KING, *Silver Bullet*

The chapters in this book provide an impressive and varied series of considerations from a range of disciplines on myriad supernatural phenomena: ghosts and hauntings (Chapter 3, Chapter 4, and Chapter 5), fortune-tellers (Chapter 6), tarot (Chapter 7), voodoo (Chapter 8), vampires (Chapter 9), Bigfoot and other cryptozoological creatures (Chapter 10), and aliens (Chapter 11). The goal of this chapter is to outline a new analytic strategy—a cryptoscience—with which to fully elucidate the supernatural in a multidirectional, transdisciplinary manner. It ought to go without saying that there is no single way this approach would (or should) work. Nonetheless, I conclude by providing a preliminary illustration of how to engage this new conceptual framework.

Consider again that our shared cultural definition of the supernatural is filtered through particular forms of knowledge (typically science or religion) that exert interpretive authority over our perceptions. Supernatural phenomena are those that are excluded from these dominant paradigms' versions of reality. Nevertheless, the ubiquity of the supernatural in our culture tells us that some corners of reality act as refuge for these ideas. Folk stories and cultural myths act as plausibility structures, shaping our understanding of the world around us (Bullard 1989; Hufford 1982; Sagan 1995). Zerubavel's (1991, 1997, 2015; see also Brekhus 2015) description of human cognition as sociomental—a process wherein raw experience is filtered through available social scripts, particularized to individual cultural worlds—moves this idea further forward. A fruitful analytic implication of this argument is that the pattern-seeking human mind is subject to something I call *sociomental pareidolia*. By this I mean that when one experiences a stimulus or sensory input that cannot be sorted into a mundane cultural category, the mind may place it into a category that is the closest fit. As in the case of auditory pareidolia, in which meaningful sounds (like voices) are heard among a din of noise, the human mind is likely to seek out a meaning for any stimulus that impresses itself on its consciousness.

Zerubavel (1997, 2015) writes that we routinely ignore vast amounts of stimuli or experiential information in the act of perceiving what we are *taught is relevant* by our social groups. The raw facts of experience are processed into reality, guided by the interpretive sovereignty of whatever cultural authority prevails (Berger 1967; Bullard 1989; Gieryn 1983; Hufford 1995). Paradigms like religion and science exclude explanations—or even preclude one's recognition of experiences—that fall outside their boundaries. These plausibility structures delegitimize transgressive claims and attempt to domesticate seemingly supernatural phenomena by reframing them in ways that conform to a religious or scientific mode of understanding. Apparently supernatural experiences—say, hearing voices or visitation by a strange being—may be interpretively transformed into the assuring presence of one's God or the work of malevolent demons.[3] Alternatively, modern Western psychology would say these same reports are symptoms of mental illness.

Because religion and science coexist as culturally endorsed ways to understand such experiences, both are available as interpretive resources for people who are trying to make sense of uncanny experiences. Many people who have such an experience initially attempt to find space for this experience *within* reason. Both the contemporary rise in stories of alien abduction related in therapy settings (Sagan 1995) and the use of technology in attempting to prove the existence of ghosts (Eaton 2015) illuminate how people attempt to make sense of the supernatural by interpreting it through a scientific frame. Similarly, Waskul (2016) finds that ghosts are the end product of social psychological work. Individuals who claim to have observed ghosts typically test the data of their experience against folk theories, examine the evidence at their disposal, and whittle down potential explanations until they arrive rationally at a ghost story (Waskul 2016: 52). Waskul's research supports Diane Goldstein's (2007) conclusion that ghosts are the rational interpretive result of systematic, analytic deduction. On the other hand, Marc Eaton (2015) also found that paranormal investigators used preexisting religious beliefs to make sense of what they believe to be ghostly experiences.

Steve Bruce (1996) describes this coexistence of religion and science as the incomplete or uneven secularization of the social world. The unevenness of this secularization means that some parts of society—the academic community, for example—are almost exclusively dominated by a secular worldview, while others—such as fundamentalist faith communities—are dominated by a religious worldview. Logically, this also means that some parts of the social world are not dominated by either worldview. These places—including, I argue, the broad community of supernatural believers—afford people the freedom to develop understandings of their experiences that lie outside the widely accepted parameters of reality.

To return to Zerubavel's (1997) important insight, some stimuli are never interpreted (or even noticed) by most people because they are perceived as incongruent with religious and scientific versions of reality. From this sociomental perspective, when we attend to a stimulus that nobody else noticed, one that exists outside the boundaries of what we think of as reality, we lack a mundane category with which to label that stimulus. Because we are not taught to believe that supernatural phenomena are part of our reality, those

---

3. Indeed, similar tropes appear in accounts of visits from angels, demons, ghosts, and aliens: beings appear from the sky or simply materialize, emit an otherworldly glow or move through physical objects, and telepathically communicate messages to those they visit.

who think they have experienced such things are left struggling to explain the discord between what is collectively defined as real and what they just experienced.[4] They are likely to engage in the kind of cognitive work described by Waskul (2016) in the social psychological production of a ghostly encounter. At the end of this logical process of elimination, some may find that the cultural category of supernatural—that space between the scientific and religious paradigms made possible by uneven secularization—may best fit with their experience. This leads us to another core principle of cryptoscience: *if some alternative (albeit less legitimate or credible) explanation is available, using that interpretation becomes a rational, sociomentally innovative decision in the face of interpretive strain.*

Once the supernatural is accepted as a culturally legitimate explanation, coding certain experiences as supernatural no longer feels like an error in judgment or a willful delusion. As Waskul points out, once a person accepts as a possibility the existence of the supernatural, "everyday happenings can (and do) take on new meanings" (2016: 134). If the concept of a ghost, wraith, or specter is available for use in the interpretation of reality, then belief that one has encountered a spiritual being is no longer dismissed as a symptom of irrationality or mental illness. Instead, the existence of the supernatural as a viable discourse by which we can make our experiences "legible" (Butler 2004) to others provides a third means—along with scientific and religious discourses—by which we can make sense of the world around us.

An analytic approach that accepts supernatural explanations as legitimate neither accepts without scrutiny supernatural accounts of individuals' everyday lives *nor* engages in caustic dismissals of the possibility that a person has experienced some aspect of the world for which a "pure" scientific version of reality lacks an explanation. *A concept like sociomental pareidolia allows us to honor the lived reality of human beings (including their more fantastic contours) while maintaining a degree of incredulity necessary to critical inquiry.* We cannot deny that many people believe they have experienced the supernatural; nor can we deny that these beliefs alter their perceptions of reality and how they live their lives. To paraphrase William Thomas and Dorothy S. Thomas (1928), these phenomena are real because they are real in their consequences. Moreover, categories of supernatural entities and abilities—such as aliens, ghosts, monsters, and fortune-telling—are pervasive in our social

---

4. It appears that there are interesting attentional differences between neurotypical and autistic people, as well as between men and women (Zerubavel 2015). This is worth considering alongside findings that women are more likely to (believe in and) observe ghosts than are men (Bader, Mencken, and Baker 2010; Waskul 2016). Another, more Foucauldian, possibility is that what we now call autism might mirror the behavioral and cognitive functions that qualified one as a shaman in the days before the scientification of reality (see Foucault 1977).

world. Their ubiquity makes them flexible instruments of perception that lend themselves to processes of sociomental pareidolia—the placing of one's experience into an available category that makes sense of the experience as a certain *type* of phenomenon (scientific, religious, or supernatural).

History certainly shows that when people do not have a preconceived framework with which to interpret the world they invent new explanations to make sense of these confusing experiences. Hufford (1982) discusses how sea creatures (like walruses) were interpreted as mermaids and mermen by sailors who had never before encountered these animals. The historian Nell Irvin Painter (2010) notes that early attempts at scientific human classification (including those of Carl Linnaeus in his *Systema Naturae*) frequently included monsters and other semihuman creatures as fact. Cyclopes and animal-human hybrids (like a person with the head of a dog) were considered credible as were grotesque, offensive portrayals of people from Africa and Asia. Human beings who were more hirsute or with facial features uncommon to the region of the explorer could, through a combination of ethnocentric contempt and shock, be transformed into monsters. The imprecise artistic re-creations of explorers' observations, when filtered through racial and cultural prejudices, turned these distorted caricatures into monstrous creatures that Europeans believed to be scientifically proved.

Consider one final example of mythic creatures: giants. Recently, genetic research published in the journal *Human Mutation* indicates that a particular gene that contributes to gigantism is ten times more common in Ulster (a province in the northern part of Ireland) than elsewhere in the United Kingdom and can result in people who grow to nearly eight feet tall (Fowler 2016). Not coincidentally, the folklore of Ulster is densely populated with giants and their accomplishments. Perhaps most well known is the Irish folktale of Finn McCool, who created the Isle of Man when he threw a chunk of the earth into the sea. It is not difficult to surmise how, across the passage of time in a preliterate culture dependent on the oral transmission of fact, stories about people who towered over their fellows were quite literally blown out of proportion. This research illuminates the underlying genetic truth behind folktales about giants in this region. In conjunction with the other examples referred to above, it also illustrates a recurring pattern in human history: when faced with the unfamiliar, humans will create monsters when they can find no other way to categorize this reality.

CONCLUSIONS

In this chapter I outline what I call a *cryptoscience*: a transdisciplinary program of research for exploring the supernatural as an aspect of everyday reality. Throughout, I refer to cryptoscience as a "perspective," "model," "framework," "project," "strategy," and an "analytic approach." I carefully avoid more deterministic or loaded terms like "theory" because I feel that a science of the hidden or unknown is best treated through the use of sensitizing concepts and grounded, nimble research unfettered by disciplines or the confines of a single theory. I try to illustrate some of the promising contributions already developed in the natural sciences, social sciences, and humanities. The myriad explanations and conclusions borne from these disparate fields provide a starting point for a set of tentative conclusions about the nature of the supernatural. The diversity of these arguments, I suggest, increases the strength of their mutual application in exploring the unexplained.

The cryptoscientific lens is a contribution toward a very daunting project: learning to understand the supernatural as a legitimate third paradigm—alongside science and religion—that offers explanations of reality that are grounded in widely shared collective representations of the social and natural worlds. My hope is to contribute to the academic conversation about the supernatural by providing some preliminary ideas about the way forward. Unusual, uncanny, or otherwise spooky stuff is experienced as such because it does not tend to fit with any system of orthodoxy (like religion or science). Scholars of many disciplines understand the difficulty of articulating the unmentioned, of speaking about what usually goes unspoken. It is not always easy, and sometimes it sounds to other people like crazy talk. This means we have to work a bit harder to explain it.

REFERENCES

Bader, Christopher, F. Carson Mencken, and Joseph Baker. 2010. *Paranormal America: Ghost Encounters, UFO Sightings, Bigfoot Hunts, and Other Curiosities in Religion and Culture.* New York: New York University Press.
Berger, Peter. 1963. *Invitation to Sociology.* New York: Anchor Books.
———. 1967. *The Sacred Canopy.* New York: Anchor Books.
Berger, Peter, and Thomas Luckmann. 1966. *The Social Construction of Reality.* New York: Anchor Books.
Brekhus, Wayne. 2015. *Culture and Cognition: Patterns in the Social Construction of Reality.* Cambridge, UK: Polity Press.
Bruce, Steve. 1996. *Religion in the Modern World: From Cathedrals to Cults.* Oxford: Oxford University Press.
Bullard, Thomas. 1989. "UFO Abduction Reports: The Supernatural Kidnap Narrative Returns in Technological Guise." *Journal of American Folklore* 102 (404): 147–170.
Butler, Judith. 1993. "Imitation and Gender Insubordination." In *The Lesbian and Gay Studies Reader,* edited by H. Abelove, M. A. Barale, and D. M. Halperin, 307–320. New York: Routledge.
———. 2004. *Undoing Gender.* New York: Routledge.

Cahill, Spencer. 1998. "Toward a Sociology of the Person." *Sociological Theory* 16 (2): 131–148.
Durkheim, Émile. (1895) 1982. *The Rules of Sociological Method*. New York: Simon and Schuster.
———. (1915) 1995. *The Elementary Forms of Religious Life*. New York: Free Press.
Eaton, Marc. 2015. "'Give Us a Sign of Your Presence': Paranormal Investigation as a Spiritual Practice." *Sociology of Religion* 76 (4): 389–412.
Einstein, Albert, and Leopold Infeld. 1938. *The Evolution of Physics*. New York: Simon and Schuster.
Foucault, Michel. 1977. *Discipline and Punish*. New York: Vintage.
Fowler, Julian. 2016. "Mid Ulster Identified as 'Giant Hotspot' by Scientists." *BBC News*, October 12. Available at http://www.bbc.com/news/uk-northern-ireland-37622249.
Gieryn, Thomas. 1983. "Boundary-Work and the Demarcation of Science from Nonscience: Strains and Interests in Professional Ideologies of Scientists." *American Sociological Review* 48 (6): 781–795.
Goffman, Erving. 1974. *Frame Analysis*. New York: Harper and Row.
Goldstein, Diane. 2007. "Scientific Rationalism and Supernatural Experience Narratives." In *Haunting Experiences: Ghosts in Contemporary Folklore*, edited by D. Goldstein, S. Grider, and J. B. Thomas, 60–78. Logan: Utah State University Press.
Goldstein, D., S. Grider, and J. B. Thomas, eds. 2007. *Haunting Experiences: Ghosts in Contemporary Folklore*. Logan: Utah State University Press.
Hufford, David. 1982. *The Terror That Comes in the Night: An Experience-Centered Study of Supernatural Assault Traditions*. Philadelphia: University of Pennsylvania Press.
———. 1995. "Beings without Bodies: An Experience-Centered Theory of the Beliefs in Spirits." In *Out of the Ordinary: Folklore and the Supernatural*, edited by B. Walker, 11–45. Logan: Utah State University Press.
Hunter, Jack, ed. 2015. *Strange Dimensions: A Paranthropology Anthology*. Llanrhaeadr-ym-Mochnant, UK: Psychoid Books.
Jung, Carl. 1979. *Flying Saucers: A Modern Myth of Things Seen in the Skies*. Princeton, NJ: Princeton University Press.
McNally, Richard J., and Susan A. Clancy. 2005. "Sleep Paralysis, Sexual Abuse, and Space Alien Abduction." *Transcultural Psychiatry* 42 (1): 113–122.
Nees, Michael A., and Charlotte Phillips. 2015. "Auditory Pareidolia: Effects of Contextual Priming on Perceptions of Purportedly Paranormal and Ambiguous Auditory Stimuli." *Applied Cognitive Psychology* 29 (1): 129–134.
Painter, Nell Irvin. 2010. *The History of White People*. New York: W. W. Norton.
Pigliucci, Massimo. 2013. "Physicists against Philosophers." *Skeptical Inquirer* 37 (1): 21–22.
Sagan, Carl. 1995. *The Demon-Haunted World: Science as a Candle in the Dark*. New York: Ballantine Books.
Thomas, Jeannie Banks. 2015. *Putting the Supernatural in Its Place: Folklore, the Hypermodern, and the Ethereal*. Salt Lake City: University of Utah Press.
Thomas, William, and Dorothy S. Thomas. 1928. *The Child in America: Behavior Problems and Programs*. New York: Knopf.
Waskul, Dennis, with Michele Waskul. 2016. *Ghostly Encounters: The Hauntings of Everyday Life*. Philadelphia: Temple University Press.
West, Candace, and Don Zimmerman. 1987. "Doing Gender." *Gender and Society* 1 (2): 125–151.

Zerubavel, Eviatar. 1991. *The Fine Line: Making Distinctions in Everyday Life.* New York: Free Press.

———. 1997. *Social Mindscapes: An Invitation to Cognitive Sociology.* Cambridge, MA: Harvard University Press.

———. 2015. *Hidden in Plain Sight: The Social Structure of Irrelevance.* Oxford: Oxford University Press.

2

ON RESEARCHING THE SUPERNATURAL

Cultural Competence and Cape Breton Stories

Jeannie Banks Thomas

It is a cool June evening in 2016 on Cape Breton Island, which is a part of the province of Nova Scotia, Canada. I am talking about supernatural legends with Peter, and he cuts right to the chase. He leans in toward the table that sits between us in his family's dining room and asks me, "What do you *do* with the ghost stories you collect? Do you debunk them?" His question is a good one; it shows his recognition that both of us exist in a culture that values "scientific" explanations of ambiguous events instead of those that tilt toward the supernatural. It is also a fair question: he has entrusted some of his own legends to me and wants to know what I will do with them.

I say to him, "No, I'm not much interested in debunking, and I'm more intrigued by what a story can teach me about the culture from which it comes." Peter and his family tell me several more narratives over the course of the evening. At one point, with the enthusiastic optimism typical of legend trippers,[1] Peter's family, folklorist Burt Feintuch, and I cram ourselves into Peter's Volkswagen and drive off to visit local legend sites. We end the evening near a fairy hill and a house where a man was murdered by his former neighbor. We sit quietly in the car and watch the sun as it expeditiously abandons itself to the gray blackness of the Northumberland Strait and the night.[2]

---

1. A legend tripper is a person who goes to the site associated with a legend (see Ellis 1996; also see Chapter 5).

2. The fairy hill is described as such in local folklore. See "Murder Charge" 2011 for more on the murder.

Figure 2.1 *Fairy hill. Photograph by the author.*

CULTURAL COMPETENCE AND THE SUPERNATURAL

I have thought a lot about Peter's question, and I have encountered similar versions of it from legend tellers and students over the years; other scholars of the supernatural have also confronted related questions (Waskul 2016: 129). In fact, drawing on years of fieldwork experience—both mine and other folklorists (Glassie 2016; Ives 1995; Jackson and Ives 1996; Mills 1991; Shutika 2011)—I have developed a simple protocol, a checklist, that I find useful in working with supernatural legends and in doing any kind of thinking about culture or fieldwork. This set of procedures is the answer to two of my questions over the years: What conduct can I encourage students to employ to best understand folk cultures as we discuss them in the classroom and as students experience them in field? And what conduct can I undertake before, during, and after fieldwork to document the culture responsibly?

My intent in this chapter is not to introduce new ideas about fieldwork. A rich body of literature about fieldwork and reflexivity already exists (see Clifford and Marcus 1986; Clifford 1988; Emerson, Fretz, and Shaw 2011; Jackson and Ives 1996). My contribution lies in distillation and utility; I communicate basic aspects of a culturally competent approach in a way that makes them easy to recall and employ in the classroom, in the field, and in scholarly analysis. Stated simply, the checklist gets to the point in a manner that is easy to remember. My approach to supernatural narratives is also informed by the scholarship on intercultural communication, which is defined as "what transpires when people engage in communication with others whose experiences, assumptions, sense making, and behaviors are different" (Condon 2015: 451).[3] However, I do not adopt the phrase "intercultural competence." Instead, I say "cultural competence" to suggest that we do not just need basic competencies when working with *other* cultures. We need them while working with any culture, our *own* included. I use the term "cultural competence" to emphasize that that we never gain perfect knowledge of culture, which is fluid and varies because of individual perception. However, we can hope to do a capable, responsible, and less ethnocentric—that is, competent—job of trying to document and understand culture and the supernatural. We need mental habits that help us come to a better understanding of culture, whether we interpret it from an insider's or outsider's perspective. Of course, as with any approach, mine should be refined, expanded, modified, and complicated according to the situation and the needs of the student of the supernatural or the fieldworker.[4] The bottom line is whether you are doing fieldwork related to the supernatural or are simply trying understand it both processes involve some basic cultural competencies.

To return to the question Peter posed at the beginning of this chapter, my checklist is a more detailed response to his query about what I do with the material I collect and study. This approach helps me document what I am seeing and generate an interpretation that is both responsible to the culture and analytically defensible. This checklist is, if anything, an even more apropos starting point for examining supernatural accounts because they are still too frequently trivialized in ethnocentric ways that cause their meaning to be overlooked or misunderstood (Goldstein 2007). Put another way, the supernatural is a part of the human experience, and as such it deserves the same treatment and study accorded to other aspects of culture.

I divide the seven-point checklist, which I call the Cultural Competence Checklist, into three parts—prepare, approach, and analyze—that give some brief basics on how to undertake the study of the supernatural and culture.

---

3. I like the concern with understanding a culture (and the people who comprise it) that I see in the various intercultural competence models (see Howard-Hamilton, Richardson, and Shuford 1998; Bennett and Bennett 2004; Spitzberg and Changnon 2009; Deardorf 2009; Cuyjet, Howard-Hamilton, and Cooper 2012; Leeds-Hurwitz 2012; Lustig and Koester 2012). However, as communication scholars have rightly noted, the approach is often "identified with a bewildering set of terms" (Hammer 2015: 483). Its complicated conceptual models with multiple components do not necessarily translate well into the contexts in which I work. I am interested in emphasizing a few basic steps that someone can recall when working in the field or when trying to understand supernatural accounts.

4. For approaches to fieldwork that go into more detail, see Fetterman 2010, along with Winick and Bartis 2016; for one that focuses on writing ethnography, see Chiseri-Strater and Sunstein 1997.

For any academic endeavor, the prepare and analyze parts of the checklist are so ingrained that they almost go without saying. However, for those learning how to study culture and the supernatural, it is important to call attention to them because they are fundamental: no good study can proceed without them. Here is the full checklist, separated into its three parts:

Prepare
1. *Do background research:* Do your homework about the group, culture, or event from whence the thing that you are studying originates; be sure to review the scholarly literature. Try to find both primary sources (such as direct observation, oral interviews, statistics, and historical documents from the time period under study) and secondary sources (such as newspaper articles, scholarly articles, and scholarly books) in your research.

Approach
2. *Be humble:* Enter into studying culture or fieldwork with a humble attitude. Think about how your worldview, customs, and behaviors are different or weird to others. Before, during, and after your research or fieldwork, ask yourself, "Have I set aside my ego enough?"
3. *Get consent and listen:* If you are in the field, listen more than you talk, and do not interrupt. When you have the chance to write field notes, focus on accurate and detailed notes; emphasize observing and describing. Before, during, and after the fieldwork, ask yourself, "Am I listening enough? Am I talking or interrupting too much? Do I need to return and listen some more?" Follow proper research protocols for your field, such as getting informed consent.
4. *Do not judge:* Be aware of your tendencies to judge what you are seeing; try to turn that off while researching or in the field. If something strikes you as strange or weird, recognize that you are judging and try to unpack that response. What might a nonjudgmental approach be? What might an empathetic approach be? Remember that romanticizing a culture is a form of judgment, so periodically ask yourself if you are romanticizing (or conversely, demonizing) what you are seeing. Before, during, and after the fieldwork and analysis, ask yourself, "Did I jump to a judgment too quickly? Am I romanticizing or being too critical about what I observed?"

Analyze
5. *Engage in analysis:* Identifying what appear to be patterns is often a good place to begin. Before analysis, review the prior research

(point 1 above) related to what you are studying. Then ask yourself, "Does what I am seeing relate to the existing research or not? Does it fit any of the patterns described in existing research? Is it different from them? Why? What would members of the group identify as significant?" This last question often calls for follow-up with and input from the people in the group that you are describing.

6. *Cite evidence:* Support your analysis and any conclusions you draw with specific evidence. While preparing analysis, ask yourself, "Have I supported each assertion with enough evidence?"

7. *Draw conclusions:* Ask yourself why anyone else should care about your research. Be sure to identify a relevant question or questions that your analysis and evidence address. What conclusions can you defensibly assert about your cultural artifact, event, or supernatural story? Are you certain your analysis and the evidence you cite are sufficient to support your claims?

In the classroom, when I am teaching students not to judge, I acknowledge that some judging is a part of our culture and that it is normal to make judgments, including snap judgments. Indeed, judging a situation is probably an evolutionarily advantageous activity that helps us rapidly perceive and deal with potential dangers. However, such judgments can lead to incorrect perceptions and misunderstandings, too. Understanding the supernatural and culture requires enough flexibility to rethink initial judgments. It also asks you to go through some sort of cultural competence process and engage in analysis while recognizing that analysis is itself a kind of judging. Good analysis should be self-aware, well informed, well reasoned, questioned, and open to revision—as opposed to an unexamined, knee-jerk reaction. Analytic assertions that are supported by vetted research and sound evidence are *earned conclusions*, which are different from quick judgments.

For example, if my class is looking at ghost stories on the Internet and trying to understand their possible cultural meanings, and a student says (as they sometimes do), "These are dumb!" My response is, "Sure, you're entitled to respond to them however you want. You certainly do not have to like them; everyone has likes and dislikes. However, for the sake of understanding Internet culture, let's look at the stories through the lens of the Cultural Competence Checklist. What would a humble, nonjudgmental approach sound like? What kind of research can you do to better inform yourself about their popularity? If you studied many of these stories, do you think you might begin to see some patterns? Do you have any idea what they might be?" And so on. I have found this method very productive in class. It respects student opinions and responses; it does not require students to love every cultural object and behavior they see. It simply asks them to be respectful, responsible, and analytic in their understanding of the cultural artifact, which is a competent way to approach the supernatural. Also, if someone already likes a topic, taking this tack asks them to be thoughtful, be analytic, and to question any romantic views that they might hold.

With this basic checklist in mind, along with Peter's query to me about how I approach ghost stories, let us return to Cape Breton Island and attend to some stories told by Peter and his friends.[5] Throughout my work with these supernatural stories, I used the checklist points. As I listened to the stories in the field, I engaged the approach part of the checklist. That is, I tried to actively *listen* and not interrupt; when I talked, it was to try to encourage interviewees to tell their stories (points 2 and 3 in the checklist). When the three friends started narrating, I asked if we could videotape them. I was not expecting to do fieldwork, so I did not have release forms for obtaining their informed consent with me at the time. I had to go back to each of the narrators to request consent to publish the stories in this article (point 3 in the checklist). What follows in the next sections are some of their narratives and my discussion of how I attempted to maintain a *humble attitude* (point 2), and question my *judgments* about the narratives (point 4). Of course, I cite other scholars' *research* throughout the rest of this paper (point 1), and I *analyze* the stories with an eye toward the patterns that emerge (point 5), citing *evidence* (point 6) to support the *conclusions* that I draw from the narratives (point 7). Thus, all seven points of the Cultural Competence Checklist inform my understanding of these supernatural stories.

A HOUSE CÈILIDH IN CAPE BRETON

Before our legend trip in June of 2016, several years earlier on an August night in 2009, Peter and two friends told me several legends in the living room of his family's home in Cape Breton. The storytelling took place during a raucous house party, or *cèilidh*, complete with live music in the garage provided by talented local musicians. The word *cèilidh* comes from the Gaelic "to visit" and refers to a "social gathering with information, entertainment (music, song, dance, storytelling), and conversation with refreshments being served" (Doherty 2015: 80). Peter's family often refers to this event as their "garage party," and it happens on a larger scale than the typical house *cèilidh*. In the excerpt that follows, Peter is joined by his friends Lesley and Jarrod; all of three of them were home from college for the summer and were relax-

---

5. I extend deep gratitude to Peter, Lesley, Jarrod, and Margie for their assistance and commentary on drafts of this chapter. Also, thanks go to Alain for help with a citation.

Figure 2.2 *West Mabou Square Dance sign. Photograph by the author.*

ing over beers, which they had retrieved from a dory in the backyard that was filled with ice and beer. Traditional Cape Breton fiddle and piano music coming from the garage can be heard in the background throughout the narrating session, as can the sounds of partygoers talking.

The three take turns telling stories. Jarrod begins with a local legend.[6] Then with Keith's beer in her hand and an animated expression, Lesley recalls an earlier evening when the three were together telling ghost stories. She mentions the Cape Breton tradition of hosting community dances with live fiddle and piano music, which has brought some fame to the island (Feintuch

---

6. I have lightly edited these excerpts to make them easier to read. As Feintuch says, "Raw interview transcripts are the stuff of research, but because they attempt to reproduce verbatim everything said—and because in conversation people don't follow the rules of formal or written English—they can be awkward or uninviting for readers. Consequently, I have edited those transcripts for public presentation. . . . That means in some cases I've removed digressions and false starts . . . and—very rarely—inserted a word or two for continuity" (2015: 15). I follow this model when presenting the narratives in this chapter.

2010). Lesley also talks about what it is like to live with a *buidseach*, which is Gaelic for "curse." Peter then refers to a common Cape Breton legend motif: the forerunner, which is a sign that foretells the future. The narrating ends when Peter goes to the garage to sing and play. As the session winds down, Jarrod tells a family story about his grandfather, but he begins with a legend from nearby Port Hood Island.

> JARROD: People used to live on Port Hood Island. This family lived over there, and there was a good-looking girl and a younger sister who was not good-looking at all. All the men liked the older one. She had longer hair; she was beautiful. The other girl was jealous. And one day, the younger sister said, "Let me braid your hair; I want to braid your hair. Come down by the beach, and I'll braid it." She braided it for about an hour, and the young girl braided it to a ring on a rock, and it tied her to the rock. And the tide came in, and the older sister drowned. . . . Lesley, you tell your story now.
>
> LESLEY: We had gone down to go to the West Mabou dance, the square dance, and the power went out, so we were all sitting here. I felt like we were in the 1940s; we had homemade biscuits, homemade jam, homemade cheese, sitting in the dark, telling ghost stories.
>
> PETER: We had candles.
>
> LESLEY: Yeah, candles, so we started in on the ghost stories, eh? Anyways, my grandmother bought a house, and everyone was like, "Mary! Why would you buy that house? It's got a *buidseach* on it." A *buidseach* is a curse. "The woman who lived there before you *buidseached* it," and it was right across the street from a church. And my grandmother is like, "Oh, my God, you guys are crazy believing in that stuff." Anyways, they moved in, and they had four children. I've never been upstairs in the house, and it's my grandparents' house. You know when you go in the house and get that feeling? Does anyone get it?
>
> PETER AND JARROD: Yeah, the heebie jeebies.
>
> LESLEY: I've never been anywhere but the kitchen. My mother told me that when she was little, she would have this recurring dream. She was probably thirteen or something; she would walk to the top of the stairs. As soon as you pass the kitchen, it's like the heebie jeebies, a queer feeling. The stairs are so high; it's the weirdest feeling. This is her dream: She'd leave her bed, go to the top of

the stairs—and my mom cried when she told me this. My mom is like a tin man; she had a hard life, and she is tough as nails.

"Lesley, I was standing at the top of the stairs, and three stairs down it was the devil. I can't describe it as anything else."

And my mom's not one ounce full of shit. Not at all.

"Three stairs down was this man. I can't describe him; he was the weirdest-looking man." They would stand there, and they would stare at each other, and he would, like, kind of jolt, and she would run to her bed. She said everything was a dream up until her running. And she says she can remember being awake, jumping in the bed, and pulling the covers over her head. She says to this day, she doesn't know if it was a dream or not. And there was a *buidseach* was put on the house.

After my grandmother got feeble, she moved into the senior citizens' [housing] and she gave the house to my Uncle Ronnie and his wife. Ronnie's wife is so holy. She'll be coming up for visits, and she'll sit for tea and say, "Everyone thinks I'm so crazy when I tell this, but I'll be doing the dishes, and I'll feel someone grab me on the shoulder!"

I can't even describe how weird the house is. She was alone one night, and she was sitting on the couch. From the couch you can see the flight of stairs, which is the creepiest part of the whole house. They're so high, creaky and wooden. She could hear someone walk down the stairs. She heard them go down five stairs. She heard them go down the stairs and up the stairs and then leave. She said, "I know it was a ghost. I know it."

She's not one ounce crazy; she's the most spiritual woman.

The lady who lived there before, she put a *buidseach* on it. My grandmother bought that house; they were so poor. They bought the house for some crazy price. It was the cheapest house, and it's a pretty big house. She bought it for so cheap; she got a huge deal on it.

PETER: There's nothing they can do to remove the curse?
LESLEY: Actually, they did two exorcisms on the house, and it didn't do anything. *Two exorcisms!*

Despite all my years of studying culture, as I began to analyze Jarrod and Lesley's stories, I made a hasty *judgment*; I initially forgot point 4. That is, I initially omitted Jarrod's story about the younger sister who drowns her older sister. I knew from prior research (point 1) that this story exists in fuller form elsewhere (Chisholm 2000: 44–46), and Jarrod's version is so abbreviated that I did not think he was very invested in it as a narrator. I wondered if he might politely have brought it up solely because he knew I was interested in supernatural stories. He later told me that he learned the story in elementary school. After a school fieldtrip to Port Hood Island, a guest speaker from the island told the children the legend. In the longer versions of the story, the jealous younger sister kills her older sibling so she can marry the older sister's fiancé. Before the elder sister dies, she says to her murderous sister, "You will regret it because you will see seaweed and the mark of the fish." The surviving sister then marries the fiancé and becomes pregnant with their first child. She gives birth to a fishlike child; he has fins for arms and is wrapped in seaweed. Thus she receives supernatural retribution for her crime. As I continued to think about Jarrod's stories, I reviewed the points in the competence checklist. I asked myself if I had been too quick in my initial omission of Jarrod's story. When I wondered if including the story might add to my understanding of the entire storytelling session, I realized the answer was yes.

As I began thinking about the story in the context of the entire evening, I saw that Jarrod set in motion an important thematic frame that continued throughout the stories: the importance and impact of family. Reviewing the Cultural Competence Checklist (point 4) was crucial in helping me overcome one of my scholarly biases: an overemphasis on form and structure, which initially caused me to overlook thematic connections. Just as in Jarrod's story, in Lesley's narrative, family is also a significant theme. Her story details a recurring and unusual sleep experience described by her mother and also her aunt's otherworldly experiences in the family home. Lesley is a particularly engaging narrator; she is expressive and often uses colorful phrases to underline her points, such as "My mom's not one ounce full of shit." Her story describes anomalous events on or near the stairs, an "odd" part of the house. This is a liminal, or betwixt and between, part of the home, and it is a supernatural commonplace for otherworldly events to happen in such spaces (Turner 1970). The story also provides character insight into Lesley's mother. We learn that she has had a hard life, and she is a survivor. The story details her confronting the devil, which operates as a powerful metaphor for a strong woman who has had to face difficult circumstances. The event described is dramatic, and it was appealing to me to understand this story by linking it to the research (point 1) about sleep experiences.

Any folklorist who studies supernatural legends is aware of David Hufford's (1989) groundbreaking work on the "Hag," or the experience of sleep paralysis. Hufford describes this experience as the loss of voluntary movement during the period just before sleep or right after (1989). It was tempting to locate Lesley's story somewhere in relation to sleep research. I could argue that the narrative's source lies in some form of lucid dreaming, nightmare, sleepwalking, sleep paralysis, hypnopompic or hypnagogic visions, or night terrors. However, I would need textual details (narrative evidence, point 6) to make such a link, and I did not see enough evidence to feel confident that I could make a strong argument (point 5). Just because I cannot place the components of the narrative in relation to existing research does not mean that the story has nothing to say. In fact, it is rich with meaning. I can mount arguments supported by textual evidence that identify the key thematic ideas communicated by the narratives. That is, I can make assertions about *meaning* (as opposed to *source*), much as one does in literary scholarship (Thomas 2007).

Most obviously, the story could be about religious worldviews ("it was the devil") or, at the very least, the presence of dark and frightening experiences in everyday life. Other stories about encounters with the devil are part of Cape Breton's oral tradition (see Caplan 2002: 9–11, 41–46, 63–70, 75–77; point 1). Lesley's story fits within the parameters of this practice. Also, the account is not just about the supernatural figure her mother sees. Lesley clearly uses the story to characterize family members in a positive fashion. Narrative evidence (point 7) for this can be found when she says her mother is strong ("tough as nails") and her aunt is spiritual ("so holy"). The story not only depicts family members but also goes beyond the confines of the family and refers to local Scottish culture as well. Lesley uses a Gaelic word, *buidseach*, or "curse." This word carries traces of the settlement history of Cape Breton Island. As Feintuch writes:

> By the early nineteenth century, much of what we might call the cultural patterning of Cape Breton was established. It was French. It was Scottish. It was Mi'kmaq. Irish people, many by way of Newfoundland, and Loyalists from New England rounded out the population. . . . The Scots who came followed a pattern known as *serial* or *chain migration*. People from one community of origin tended to follow kin and neighbors and settle together. . . . Today the preponderance of particular family names in certain places is evidence of families migrating together or at least following one another. (2010: 10)

In the nineteenth century, Gaelic was the island's dominant language; however, it declined dramatically in the twentieth century (Morgan 2008). At the end of the twentieth century, a revival had begun, following the lead of the successful language revivals among First Nations Mi'kmaq communities, such as Wycocomagh, and French communities, such as Cheticamp (Feintuch 2010). Road signs are often in both Gaelic and English, but Gaelic is not a dominant language today. Therefore, I was a little surprised to hear Lesley use a Gaelic word in this everyday context. It suggests that parts of Gaelic culture, in this case a word, still exist in her family and are used in ordinary contexts, perhaps like Yiddish phrases exist in some Jewish-American communities. Here, the Gaelic word also functions to give this family's supernatural story a Cape Breton Scottish regional flavor.

Lesley then relates a ghostly experience that her aunt had in the house: a hand grabs her while she is doing dishes, and she also hears anomalous footsteps, both common supernatural motifs. In discussing these incidents, Lesley sketches her aunt's character: "She's not one ounce crazy; she's the most spiritual woman." She talks about the house being appealing to her grandmother because it was so inexpensive, and she characterizes her grandmother's family as "so poor." These details speak to not only the family but also the region (point 7). Cape Breton has a long history of being one of the most impoverished regions in Canada. In 2015, Cape Breton had the highest rate of child poverty in Atlantic Canada, with one of every three children living in poverty ("Cape Breton" 2015; point 6). Lesley's story about her family's cursed house takes a place among other Cape Breton ghost stories that detail the economic harshness faced by those among the living (Thomas 2007).

Lesley concludes her narrative by saying that two exorcisms failed to rid the house of its supernatural occupants. That the house is across the street from a Catholic church adds irony. This part of the story again points to a quality of Cape Breton: it has many predominantly Catholic communities (points 1 and 6). The majority of early Gaelic-speaking, Scottish settlers to Cape Breton were Catholic (Feintuch 2004). Like the Scottish culture and the Gaelic language, Catholicism is an underlying cultural factor that contributes to Lesley's story (point 7). The religion persisted in Cape Breton to a greater degree than did the language.

As noted earlier, I am not interested in debunking the story. If I were to look solely at these narratives in terms of a "Is this bunk?" framework, I would miss all the narrative work that the story actually does—and it does a lot. It describes anomalous experiences, contains traditional motifs, and it is also a family story that depicts some of the defining character traits of Lesley's mother and aunt. Lesley is an excellent narrator; she is animated and clever. Not only does her story portray traits of family members, but her *performance* also reveals some of her personality. The story is effective in terms of remembering the personal and familial; it communicates details about both Lesley and her family. It also speaks to the local: it tells us something about everyday Scottish culture for some Cape Bretoners (point 5). It shows the continued, if partial, existence of the Gaelic language on the island. It points to important aspects of Cape Breton culture and history, including the Gaelic language, Scottish culture, Catholicism, and economic difficulty (point 5). It gives me as a listener more of an insider sense of the place (Thomas 2015).

In that engrossing narrative session in Peter's living room on that summer night in 2009, after Lesley tells her story, Peter refers to forerunner legends and says, "Even our house here—my dad told me that my grandmother used to say that you'd always see lights up here. It was a forerunner to this party." The three then tell some legends that take place off the island, and Jarrod ends the session with the following story.

> JARROD: [*Smiles.*] My grandfather turned ninety-seven yesterday. He's probably the smartest man alive, too. I don't know how he does it. He takes care of my grandmother, and my grandmother is eighty-six, and she's got really bad Alzheimer's.
> LESLEY: Wait! How old is he?
> JARROD: Ninety-seven.
> LESLEY: He robbed the cradle, bigtime! [*All laugh.*] He did! That's a big age difference!
> JARROD: Yeah, I guess so, but he learned how to make biscuits and rolls just recently, two years ago. And he cooks all the meals. He drives every single day. He's only got good vision in one of his eyes.
> LESLEY: [*Laughs.*] Really?! He drives?! He's ninety-seven?!
> JARROD: He is so smart. He is an electrician and a plumber. He wired a house forty years ago, and they had a problem recently. They called him, and over the phone, he could remember where he did something in the basement.

The stories ended at this point when the three friends headed to the garage for music. Peter's mention of the forerunner mirrors the real-life house party context in which the stories were being told on that August evening in 2009. As I thought about it, I realized that being at the house party was an unknowing ostension, or the enacting of a legend (Ellis 1996); that is, I felt as if we were inadvertently acting out one of the parties that the forerunners predicted. Forerunner legends were more commonly told in the nineteenth and early twentieth centuries in other parts of North America, but they remain in circulation in Cape Breton. A forerunner, as the word suggests, is a sign that reveals something that will happen in the future. Often it is some sort of anomalous light (Thomas 2007) or a noise such as a rapping sound, and earlier, it was quite common for the sign to foretell an impending death. For example, a rapping noise could be the forerunner of the sound of a coffin being nailed together (see Caplan 2002: 28–29, 58, 59, 114–115). However, in Peter's story, his dad says the forerunner predicts happy future events: parties at the site that will eventually become their family home. The forerunner was accurate: his family hosted many notable house parties over the years. They also ran the weekly square dances in West Mabou, so they have done much to fuel the kind of mix of community, sociability, and live traditional music that is Cape Breton (Feintuch 2010; MacKinnon 2009; McDavid 2008; Sparling 2014).

Scholars have noted the social genius that is easily found in many parts of the island; Feintuch writes, "I am convinced that there is something about Cape Breton that encourages people to value good talk. . . . Consider good talk as one of the ways to maintain good connections with family, friends, and neighbors" (2010: 5, 16). This house party was a venue in which "good talk" was shared, and connections were made and maintained. As Peter finishes talking about forerunners, he is asked to go out to the garage and play music, so the session begins to wind down. To my surprise, it did not stop right at that time. It ended with Jarrod telling a family story—not a supernatural one. Given the pressure to end the narrative-telling session, which Jarrod did not capitulate to until he told this story, it is apparent that he wanted to share it and that it was important to him.

Initially, when I was preparing to write this chapter, I thought I would exclude Jarrod's narrative about his grandfather. Even though it was a charming portrait of his grandfather's devotion to his wife—and funny in its incongruities—it is a family story, not a supernatural one. However, as I worked through the Cultural Competence Checklist and queried my analytic choices, I realized that my judgment was, again, perhaps too hasty (point 4). I thought about being humble: shouldn't I listen (points 2 and 3) to what he was trying to tell me? Shouldn't I pay attention to something that Jarrod thought was significant enough that it caused him to ignore the pressure to end the session in order to tell this narrative about his grandfather? This evidence of the story's importance made me rethink my earlier decision. When I began reviewing the narratives that were told that evening, I realized that Jarrod begins and ends the storytelling session; he frames it. He starts with a story that is supernatural, but it is fundamentally about family, specifically family dysfunction and disequilibrium. He ends with a narrative about his family, but it is about a functional family. Equilibrium is restored at the end of the session. All three of the narrators take up these same themes over the course of the evening's stories. The stories are often fundamentally hopeful in that they either demonstrate that means exist to resolve disequilibrium or that tough times and frightening events can simply be lived with and through.

Jarrod ends the storytelling with a narrative that details family hardship: his then ninety-seven-year-old grandfather, who has vision primarily in one eye, has had to learn to take care of his wife, who has Alzheimer's disease. The story is about meeting difficulties with intelligence, resilience, and grit, which is a theme that appears in the other stories as well, such as the one about Lesley's mother (point 7). Lesley's comments show that she sees the humor and incongruity in Jarrod's story, and she enjoys it. Culture and memories are important in the construction of identity and in making sense of everyday life. Jarrod's account reminds me that family stories carry these memories and values, just as do supernatural narratives.

Jarrod's narrative specifically mentions that his grandfather learned how to make biscuits. This detail also recalls the beginning of the storytelling, when Lesley remembers eating homemade biscuits and jam at an even earlier legend-telling session. Lesley describes the biscuits and storytelling as objects and a process that link her to the past: "I felt like we were in the 1940s." The three are connected to the past: the island's traditions, culture, and history flow vibrantly through them when they tell their stories.

Answering the question of whether the supernatural is real is not especially germane to these stories. They are about bigger, more important, and sometimes more mysterious things: How do you survive difficult experiences that you cannot even fully explain? How do you endure hardships, such as your spouse having Alzheimer's? The evening provides a good example of a supernatural storytelling session that is not limited to one genre. The supernatural stories prompt other narratives, such as family stories, that share a thematic connection. To understand which themes were repeated and emphasized, it is instructive to not only think about the supernatural narratives but also look at the other stories performed that night. Jarrod, Lesley, and Peter's narratives—regardless of their genre—depict family, tough times, and resilience. They exemplify good talk and nod to the local music, house *cèilidh* traditions, Catholicism, and the Gaelic language (point 5). They show that out of challenge and hardship can come endurance—both of a culture and of individual people. This theme is perhaps best embodied by Jarrod's grandfather, who was still alive in 2016, well past the hundred-year mark.

I am intrigued by the connection between the supernatural and family stories told at the house party. It is probably not unusual for a family-themed, supernatural narrative to lead to a family story that is not focused on the supernatural, as is the case with Jarrod's story about his grandfather. Then again, it is not uncommon for a supernatural story to also be a family story, as is the case with Lesley's story about her grandmother's house. In fact, merging the familial with the supernatural in narrative form can serve multiple functions. Such accounts can be an effective and gripping narrative form for containing musings on life and family, especially the ambiguities thereof.

Figure 2.3 *Cape Breton Piper. Photograph by the author.*

Simultaneously, such stories can also share and maintain culture, identity, and values.

The process of analyzing the supernatural and family stories from that Cape Breton summer night underlined the importance of using the fundamentals of the Cultural Competence Checklist to guide me in my research. Using these basic principles as touchstones helped me do a responsible job of interpretation by familiarizing myself with previous research (point 1); trying to humbly listen to the narrators (points 2 and 3); questioning my initial judgments (point 4); looking for patterns (point 5); citing evidence (point 6); and, therefore, drawing reasoned conclusions (point 7) about supernatural narratives. Whether one has studied the supernatural for years, as I have, or is new to the process, using such a cultural competence approach works as a guide to researching and understanding. In my case, it led to a better understanding of the cultural work that the stories were doing in terms of how they helped the narrators and me understand the construction of self, family, and place. They also reflected local realities, including economic conditions, cultural traditions, including Gaelic phrases, and the influence of religion.

On that August evening in 2009, Burt and I went to Peter's home to attend a party and enjoy some local music. We were not expecting it, but we left rich with stories. Later, on a June night in 2016, when we again visited Peter's family, they were in the midst of work. Peter was mowing their substantial lawn. Hoping not to impose, we planned only a brief stop. But the visit was longer and better than intended because it was again full of stories and included some legend tripping. Then Peter's family graciously sent us home with oat cakes (a Cape Breton staple), freshly made rolls, homemade jam, and butter. As we drove to Port Hood, toward our appropriately named bed-and-breakfast, the Fiddle and the Sea, I reflected on how people can connect with others and make their best selves material and warm with small but good things: rolls, homemade jam, and stories.[7]

REFERENCES

Bennett, Janet M., and Milton J. Bennett. 2004. "Developing Intercultural Sensitivity: An Integrative Approach to Global and Domestic Diversity." In *Handbook of Intercultural Training*, edited by D. Landis, J. M. Bennett, and M. J. Bennett, 147–164. Thousand Oaks, CA: SAGE.

"Cape Breton Child Poverty Rates Highest in Atlantic Canada." 2015. *CBC News*, November 25. Available at http://www.cbc.ca/news/canada/nova-scotia/poverty-report-children-cape-breton-1.3335561.

Caplan, Ronald. 2002. *Cape Breton Book of the Night: 75 Stories of Tenderness and Terror Told by 68 Storytellers*. Wreck Cove, NS: Breton Books.

Chiseri-Strater, Elizabeth, and Bonnie Stone Sunstein. 1997. *FieldWorking: Reading and Research Writing*. Upper Saddle River, NJ: Prentice Hall.

Chisholm, Archie Neil. 2000. "Jim St. Clair 49." In *"As True As I'm Sittin' Here": 200 Cape Breton Stories from Archie Neil's Cape Breton*, edited by B. Sutcliffe and R. Caplan, 44–46. Sydney, NS: Breton Books.

Clifford, James. 1988. *The Predicament of Culture: Twentieth-Century Ethnography, Literature, and Art*. Cambridge, MA: Harvard University Press.

Clifford, James, and George E. Marcus. 1986. *Writing Culture: The Poetics and Politics of Ethnography*. Berkeley: University of California Press.

Condon, John. 2015. "Intercultural Communication." In *The SAGE Encyclopedia of Intercultural Competence*, edited by J. M. Bennett, 450–453. Los Angeles: SAGE Reference.

Cuyjet, Michael J., Mary F. Howard-Hamilton, and Diane L. Cooper. 2012. "Understanding Multiculturalism and Multicultural Competence among College Students." In *Multiculturalism on Campus: Theory, Models, and Practices for Understanding Diversity and Creating Inclusion*, edited by M. Cuyjet, M. Howard-Hamilton, and D. Cooper, 11–18. Sterling, VA: Stylus.

---

7. I am aware that this could be interpreted as a romantic statement, and I have asked myself whether my view here is too romantic. In response, I note that something being positive does not automatically equate it with romanticism. So it simply seems accurate in this circumstance to acknowledge the positivity that I saw in that moment. I also do not think I am overstating—which would be romanticizing—that positivity.

Deardorf, Darla, ed. 2009. *The SAGE Handbook of Intercultural Competence*. Thousand Oaks, CA: SAGE.
Doherty, Liz. 2015. *The Cape Breton Fiddle Companion*. Sydney, NS: Cape Breton University Press.
Ellis, Bill. 1996. "Legend Trip." In *American Folklore: An Encyclopedia*, edited by J. Brunvand, 439–440. New York: Garland.
Emerson, Robert M., Rachel I. Fretz, and Linda L. Shaw. 1995. *Writing Ethnographic Fieldnotes*. Chicago: University of Chicago Press.
Feintuch, Burt. 2004. "The Conditions for Cape Breton Fiddle Music: The Social and Economic Setting of a Regional Music." *Ethnomusicology* 48 (1): 73–104.
———. 2010. *In the Blood: Cape Breton Conversations on Culture*. Logan: Utah State University Press.
———. 2015. *Talking New Orleans Music: Crescent City Musicians Talk about Their Lives, Their Music, Their City*. Jackson: University Press of Mississippi.
Fetterman, David M. 2010. *Ethnography, Step-by-Step*. Los Angeles, CA: SAGE
Glassie, Henry. 2016. *The Stars of Ballymenone*. Bloomington: Indiana University Press.
Goldstein, Diane E. 2007. "The Commodification of Belief." In *Haunting Experiences: Ghosts in Contemporary Folklore*, edited by D. E. Goldstein, S. A. Grider, and J. B. Thomas, 171–205. Logan: Utah State University Press.
Hammer, Mitchell R. 2015. "Intercultural Competence Development." In *The SAGE Encyclopedia of Intercultural Competence*, edited by J. M. Bennett, 483–485. Thousand Oaks, CA: SAGE Reference.
Howard-Hamilton, Mary F., Brenda J. Richardson, and Bettina Shuford. 1998. "Promoting Multicultural Education: A Holistic Approach." *College Student Affairs Journal* 18 (1): 5–17.
Hufford, David. 1989. *The Terror That Comes in the Night: An Experience-Centered Study of Supernatural Assault Traditions*. Philadelphia: University of Pennsylvania Press.
Ives, Edward D. 1995. *The Tape-Recorded Interview: A Manual for Field Workers in Folklore and Oral History*. Knoxville: University of Tennessee Press.
Jackson, Bruce, and Edward D. Ives. 1996. *The World Observed: Reflections on the Fieldwork Process*. Urbana: University of Illinois Press.
Leeds-Hurwitz, Wendy. 2012. "Writing the Intellectual History of Intercultural Communication." In *The Handbook of Critical Intercultural Communication*, edited by T. Nakaymama and R. Halualani, 21–33. Chichester, UK: Blackwell.
Lustig, Myron W., and Jolene Koester. 2012. *Intercultural Competence: Interpersonal Communication across Cultures*. London: Pearson.
MacKinnon, Richard. 2009. *Discovering Cape Breton Folklore*. Sydney, NS: Cape Breton University Press.
McDavid, Jodi. 2008. "The Fiddle Burning Priest of Mabou." *Ethnologies* 30 (2): 115–136.
Mills, Margaret. 1991. *Rhetorics and Politics in Afghan Traditional Storytelling*. Philadelphia: University of Pennsylvania Press.
Morgan, Robert J. 2008. *Rise Again! The Story of Cape Breton Island, Book One*. Wreck Cove, NS: Cape Breton Books.
"Murder Charge in C.B. Senior's Death." 2011. *CBC News*, April 8. Available at http://www.cbc.ca/news/canada/nova-scotia/murder-charge-in-c-b-senior-s-death-1.1022022.

Sherman, Sharon R. 1998. *Documenting Ourselves: Film, Video, and Culture.* Lexington: University Press of Kentucky.

Shutika, Debra Lattanzi. 2011. *Beyond the Borderlands: Migration and Belonging in the United States and Mexico.* Berkeley: University of California Press.

Sparling, Heather. 2014. *Reeling Roosters and Dancing Ducks: Celtic Mouth Music.* Sydney, NS: Cape Breton University Press.

Spitzberg, Brian, and Gabrielle Changnon. 2009. "Conceptualizing Intercultural Competence." In *The SAGE Handbook of Intercultural Competence*, edited by D. Deardorff, 1–52. Thousand Oaks, CA: SAGE.

Thomas, Jeannie Banks. 2007. "The Usefulness of Ghost Stories." In *Haunting Experiences: Ghosts in Contemporary Folklore*, edited by D. E. Goldstein, S. A. Grider, and J. B. Thomas, 25–59. Logan: Utah State University Press.

———. 2015. "Which Witch Is *Witch*? Salem, Massachusetts." In *Putting the Supernatural in Its Place: Folklore, the Hypermodern, and the Ethereal*, edited by J. Thomas, 49–89. Salt Lake City: University of Utah Press.

Turner, Victor. 1970. *The Forest of Symbols: Aspects of Ndembu Ritual.* Ithaca, NY: Cornell University Press.

Waskul, Dennis, with Michele Waskul. 2016. *Ghostly Encounters: The Hauntings of Everyday Life.* Philadelphia: Temple University Press.

Winick, Stephen, and Peter Bartis. 2016. *Folklife and Fieldwork: An Introduction to Cultural Documentation.* Washington, DC: Library of Congress. Available at http://www.loc.gov/folklife/fieldwork.

3

GHOSTS AND HAUNTINGS

Genres, Forms, and Types

Dennis Waskul

In surveys and polls, ghosts are consistently identified as the most common of all supernatural beliefs. In a random sample survey of 1,637 people, Christopher Bader, F. Carson Mencken, and Joseph Baker found that "nearly half of Americans believe in ghosts" (2010: 44). Almost identical findings have been reported in other polls (see Ramsey, Venette, and Rabalais 2011; Speigel 2013; Taylor 2003) and in the United Kingdom (YouGov 2013). Furthermore, there is evidence that a large portion of this sizable believing population also report *experiences* that they attribute to a ghostly presence. In their study of 241 students at a southern American university, Matthew Ramsey, Steven Venette, and Nicole Rabalais (2011) found that 28.5 percent report experiencing a ghostly presence at least once in their life. Likewise, a survey from the Pew Research Center (Lipka 2015) reports that 18 percent of Americans claim to have seen a ghost, and 29 percent sensed the presence of someone who is dead (also see Alfano 2005). Indeed, far from outlandish or even eccentric, beliefs about and experiences with what people attribute to a ghost are quite common, maybe even normative.

Since 2013 I have been studying people's reported experiences with ghosts and conducting ethnographic research at locations thought to be haunted (see Waskul 2016). My research is built from a simple premise: one does not have to believe that ghosts are real to acknowledge the reality of belief in ghosts; likewise, one does not have to accept the notion that people can experience a ghostly presence to acknowledge that some people claim to have such experiences.[1] These beliefs and experiences are undeniably real in that they have real consequences and can be studied independent of one's position regarding the "truth" or "reality" of ghosts. Thus, my research is mainly focused on how people report experiencing a ghostly presence, the processes by which people arrive at the conclusion that they have experienced a ghostly encounter, what those ghosts do to and for people, and the consequences thereof.

On the basis of the reports that I have collected, I have also created a general typology of ghosts and hauntings. This typology is useful for sifting and sorting the diverse array of experiences that people attribute to a ghostly presence, and that is the main focus of this chapter. Because reported encounters with a ghostly presence are enormously diverse, it is helpful to have a framework that allows us to compare and contrast ghostly experiences that share common characteristics. In this chapter, I illustrate four ghostly genres, four forms of hauntings, and six types of ghosts by drawing on my previously published research (Waskul 2016) and more recent data.[2]

GHOSTLY GENRES

I identify four analytically distinct genres of ghostly experiences: "everyday ghosts," "professionalized ghosts," "commercial ghosts," and "institutional ghosts." Although these genres share some important characteristics, they differ in the ways they affect how people define, interpret, and ultimately experience ghostly encounters.

Everyday Ghosts

The term *everyday ghosts* refers to uncanny experiences that are not conventionalized by religious or spiritual beliefs. While religious beliefs and experiences share much with the supernatural, it is a mistake to conflate the two (see the Introduction). The key difference is that religious beliefs and experiences are vested with what David Hufford aptly coined "cultural authority" (1995: 18). That is, religious beliefs and experiences are institutionalized, bestowed with power, and made normative and thus provide "core beliefs"

---

1. And for the record, I began this research agnostic on the subject and remain so. Like most people, I have experienced things I cannot explain—especially during the course of this research. Still, I cannot say if those experiences are, or are not, attributable to a ghost, and I do not feel a compelling need to have an answer for that question.

2. The main source of data for this chapter draws from interviews of seventy-one people who described a total of 91 hauntings involving 144 distinct ghosts. Portions of this chapter are adapted from *Ghostly Encounters: The Hauntings of Everyday Life* (Waskul 2016, chap. 3).

(Hufford 1995: 29) that, to the faithful, can conventionalize encounters with things like "spirits." Everyday ghosts fall outside that cultural authority and legitimizing institutional structures.

Traditional Hmong religious beliefs provide an excellent contrasting example. For those who adhere to traditional Hmong beliefs, the spirit realm is highly influential on the physical world, all things possess a spirit, and deceased ancestors directly influence one's health and well-being. Thus, traditional Hmong people commonly encounter what we non-Hmong people of the Western world would call ghosts, but such encounters are interpreted and ritualized through the cultural authority of their belief system. In contrast, a person who encounters a ghostly presence but does not adhere to a religious or spiritual belief system that conventionalizes this experience is left to his or her own means to make sense of what occurred. This individualized meaning making in the absence of social and cultural resources that normalize such experiences is what I mean by an "everyday ghost." Since the majority of Western religions do not supply conventionalizing beliefs or practices for experiences with ghosts, it is fair to presume that the majority of ghostly encounters are experiences with everyday ghosts.

Professionalized Ghosts

In the fall of 2016 I arranged to meet with forty-three-year-old Jackson. Jackson contacted me to share the odd experiences he has had in his 1920s former farmhouse. Like many others I have spoken to, Jackson is eager to tell his story. But there is something unique about Jackson; something new has happened that compels him to even greater urgency. Since living in the home, Jackson has experienced a number of relatively minor oddities; most commonly, lights in his home randomly turn on and off by themselves. These and many other odd occurrences piqued Jackson's curiosity but never summoned a great deal of his attention; as Jackson states, "I didn't think anything of those things." Not anymore.

Jackson recently installed a security system in his home that includes motion-activated cameras. When the security system is armed, the cameras send photos to Jackson's cell phone if movement is detected. Not long ago, Jackson had armed his security system and exited his house when his phone gave him a notification. "I sat down. I thought it was a text message, but it wasn't. It was this image [shown in Figure 3.1]."[3] Despite the low image resolution, there is no mistaking what the photo appears to have captured: a

---

3. I am grateful for Jackson's permission to reproduce this image.

Figure 3.1 *Image from Jackson's home security system.*

child in the middle of Jackson's kitchen at a time during which "no one was home," Jackson assures me. "It scared me."

In conducting my research I always seek to interview people at the locations where those ghostly experiences have happened. In this case, I and my wife (also coresearcher) were scheduled to interview Jackson at his home at 3:00 P.M. on a Sunday afternoon. At noon, however, my wife got a strange text message from Jackson pleading for us to meet him somewhere else. Although less than ideal for our purposes, we willingly agreed to meet at a bar and grill. When we got there Jackson sheepishly explained:

> I met with a medium, and just this morning she said that because of the interviews you guys have been doing [for ongoing research on ghosts]—and the nature of the subject—that she feels that there could be bad energy associated with you two. So the very first thing she said was that I need to meet you guys on neutral ground—not come into my house—and definitely not when my children are present. And when I get home [*pauses*]—and see, this is where I struggle [*laughs nervously*]: before I walk in the door, I'm supposed to ask my spirits to cleanse any negative energy that would have come off you guys to me [*laughs more loudly*]. I think that's a little crazy, but I

dunno. I just don't need anything wrong going on at my house or in my life right now, 'cause things are going really good, and I don't wanna take any chances.

Jackson's ghost has been professionalized. *Professionalized ghosts* refers to ghostly experiences that are subject to and at least partially understood within the discourses, practices, and technologies of mediums, paranormal investigators, or what can be called a "priesting" (Brady 1995) of the dead.

Jackson's experience provides an excellent example of how professionalized ghosts are different from, and perhaps not comparable to, other genres of ghostly encounters. In this case, the medium altered not only how Jackson chose to participate in our research—and what he will do when he gets back home—but also his fundamental understanding of the ghost. The image from Jackson's security camera was enough to convince him that there is a ghost in his home, but until he met with the medium he assumed that there was only one ghost in the house. The medium told him otherwise, saying that there were three but assuring him that none were harmful or anything to fear. Because of the medium's professional status, Jackson accepted her claims at face value and thus altered his understanding of these now professional*ized* ghosts. When people seek out the services of mediums, paranormal investigators, and religious authorities to assist them in understanding and contending with alleged ghostly presences, these professionals offer new information, narratives, and strategies for action that greatly alter an individual's experiences with the ghosts.

Commercial Ghosts

"You must have been to the Palmer House, haven't you?" a participant in my research says to me at the conclusion of an interview. I have been asked that question many times before and for good reason. The Palmer House[4] is arguably the most well-known purportedly haunted location in the region where I live. It is routinely identified in the media as one of the best places to visit for an encounter with the dead, and it has been featured on Biography Channel's *My Ghost Story* (episode 15) and Travel Channel's *Ghost Adventures* (season 7, episode 4). But there is another reason the Palmer House is so widely known to be haunted: the owners and management of this historic hotel actively *promote* its haunted reputation, on which they literally capitalize.

---

4. The Palmer House, in Sauk Centre, Minnesota (birthplace of Sinclair Lewis), was originally built in 1863; the building went by many names until it was rebuilt in the early 1900s by R. L. Palmer after it was destroyed in a fire. It is a beautiful work of architecture and listed on the National Register of Historic Places.

Anyone can witness how the Palmer House seeks to cash in on a haunted reputation; it is readily apparent on its website. The website supplies links to major television and news coverage of the hotel's hauntedness. The page "Paranormal Findings" on the website features the detailed results of a 2006 investigation by Midnite Walkers of the Paranormal Research Society.[5] The "Event Calendar" was especially revealing when I viewed it in October 2017: for the "Spirit Experience Weekend," guests could "explore multiple avenues of interacting with Spirits and paranormal energy"; during the "SPIRIT Search and Psychic Energy Gathering," guests "learn about energy fields, auras, ghosts and spirits, psychic skill training, investigative equipment, PLUS experience an actual spirit search and investigation of paranormal activity"; and at "Things That Go Bump in the Night," attendees got a full weekend (for sixty-five dollars, not including hotel stay) of "presentations on ghosts, spirits, investigation techniques and equipment as well as daytime and nighttime investigations of the Palmer House—voted Best Haunted Hotel in the Nation by *USA Today*." Indeed. The Palmer House is most certainly haunted with what I call *commercial ghosts*.

Commercial ghosts are found within establishments, even entire communities, that have vested economic interests in a haunted reputation. Haunted hotels and bed-and-breakfasts are among the most obvious and copious of examples, but commercial ghosts are found in any establishment for which "the business of ghosts" is closely tied to "the *business* of ghosts" (Clarke 2012: 286; emphasis in original)—and these are common enough that I strongly suspect that there is a Palmer House reasonably close to virtually all my readers. To be clear, locations allegedly populated with commercial ghosts may or may not be haunted—that is not the issue—and I am not chiding business owners and managers for seeking to capitalize on spookiness. All I am suggesting is that commercial ghosts have to be at least partially understood in the context of their literal capital, and their presence has to be at least partly foreshadowed by obvious economic incentives. And, to answer the oft-stated question from my research participants, no, I have not visited the Palmer House, at least not yet. I am not currently interested in commercial ghosts and strongly suspect that their inherent nature has as much to do with economics as with the supernatural.

Institutional Ghosts

Unless you have lived near Owatonna, Minnesota, then chances are you have never heard of the Minnesota State Public School for Dependent and

---

5. The home page is available at http://www.thepalmerhousehotel.com. "Paranormal Findings" is available at http://www.thepalmerhousehotel.com/paranormal-findings.

Neglected Children. If you live in the United States, then it is also likely that there was once an institution like this one in your state—and I suspect you are unaware of it as well. I have lived in Minnesota most of my life and had never heard of the State Public School for Dependent and Neglected Children until I started conducting research on ghosts and hauntings. Residents from the Owatonna area started telling me spooky stories about the former institution, which is undoubtedly haunted in more ways than one.

From 1886 to 1945, the Minnesota State Public School for Dependent and Neglected Children housed 10,635 children. Those institutionalized children were shipped to Owatonna by train for reasons that ranged from abusive families to neglectful living conditions to sometimes nothing more than being poor. Although the reform efforts that led to the construction of institutions like this were well intentioned, most frequently the results were not. Life at the school was not easy: it involved strict and frequently abusive discipline, moral training, a stringent regimen, and emotional neglect. And all too often children would be indentured to farm families for what essentially amounted to state-sanctioned slave labor.

A few happy stories came from this school, but far too few. Instead, the school is the epitome of a dark and sad history that only the most coldhearted could not feel if they were to visit the museum that now resides in the administrative building of the former institution. It is impossible for visitors to the museum to avoid noticing some things: bluntly displayed items that cottage matrons preferred to use for corporal punishment (radiator brushes were the favorite), a plethora of photos of children with somber and empty expressions, and an overabundance of personal accounts with a theme of longing and hopelessness. If visiting the museum does not move you, the campus graveyard surely will: it holds 198 markers for the children who died here, the average age at interment a mere and tender four years old (see Figure 3.2).[6]

Ghosts may or may not lurk in institutions such as these, but these locations are surely haunted—at least metaphorically—with many institutional ghosts. *Institutional ghosts* haunt hospitals, churches, schools, and so on, but appear especially prevalent in places where people have been institutionalized (asylums, prisons, orphanages, etc.). Among the unique features of institutional ghosts is how they so often appear as an ephemeral embodiment of profound human drama—pain, suffering, neglect, hopelessness, inhumane

---

6. As an illustration of the extent of institutionalization that occurred, the vast majority of the 198 children who died at the school were buried without a headstone. Instead, a small cement slab merely indicated each child's case number, not name. In 1993 crosses were constructed with names and added to bestow greater dignity and humanity to the young people who are buried here. Because of poorly kept records, in several instances the identity of the deceased child is unknown; several crosses have only a descriptor, such as "Baby Girl."

Figure 3.2 *Graveyard of the Minnesota State Public School for Dependent and Neglected Children. Photograph by the author.*

treatment, illness, death—and they are often profoundly historical. Institutional ghosts frequently haunt the remains of bygone days that are either forgotten or remembered with a guilty collective conscience; a place that once served as a tragic dumping ground for the living human waste of society. In those circumstances, institutional ghosts can (and do) hauntingly reveal a dark history of a painful past in which ghosts epitomize "that which has been forgotten, whether through deliberate political strategies or because the horrors of the recent past are too painful to confront" (Edensor 2005: 835).

TYPES OF HAUNTINGS

"Haunting" refers to the general charactcristics of a ghostly encounter—the conditions, circumstances, and overall demeanor of the ghosts that people experience. In my research I found four types of hauntings, although there may be others. The first two types of hauntings, intelligent and residual, are mutually exclusive, and all hauntings appear to be one or the other. The other two types, anniversary and historical, appear to be much less common but merit consideration.[7]

---

7. Because my research has focused on everyday ghosts, the few numbers of anniversary and historical hauntings I found may be the result of a selection bias. Other genres of ghostly

Intelligent Hauntings

The basic distinction between intelligent and residual hauntings is common knowledge among paranormal investigators and ghost enthusiasts. An intelligent haunting is defined as a ghostly presence that interacts with the environment, living people, or both. Those interactions are taken to signify that the ghost is aware of the living world, even self-aware, and hence intelligent. In my research, the majority of reported hauntings are intelligent (76 percent). Interaction, the crucial sign of an intelligent haunting, is broadly defined but can at least be separated into direct interactions with living people and indirect interactions with objects in the environment.

In intelligent hauntings in which a ghost is reported to interact *directly* with a living person, those ghosts typically either vocalize or leave some unheard but otherwise sensed somatic impression. Of the two, vocalizations—and especially speech—are the least common; only rarely do ghosts speak. When ghosts speak, they seldom utter more than a simple word, name, or phrase. Twenty-five-year-old Paige gives a good account for what people typically report of speaking ghosts:

> My boyfriend slept over one night. He got up in the middle of the night to go to the bathroom, and as he was crossing the stairs at two or three in the morning, he heard a whispered, "Hey!" coming from the bottom of the stairs. That really freaked me out 'cause I was, like, now we are hearing voices in my house! So maybe there really is something going on here!

More often, when ghosts are reported to vocalize, it is a nonlinguistic expression of an emotional state—such as crying, screaming, or moaning. Here are a few reported examples:

> We'd often hear the crying and then go check on the infants—and nothing [was there]. We just got used to it. We called it a ghost baby. (Amy, age nineteen)

> My cousin and I were playing upstairs. My cousin was playing next to me, and we heard what we thought was a whisper. We both stopped, and my cousin turned to me and said, "Did you hear that?" And I said, "Yeah! I thought I was hearing things!" All of a sudden a

---

encounters may contain much more frequent anniversary and historical hauntings and, especially, institutional ghosts.

middle-age-sounding woman just started screaming. It sounded like she was in the room—it didn't sound like it was outside or anything. Just ballistically screaming at us. (Vicki, age nineteen)

I often hear a woman crying in the stairway going upstairs. (Mike, age twenty-one)

When people report experiences of *nonvocal* direct interaction in an intelligent haunting, it is in the form of immediate somatic impressions—tugs, pushes, taps, distinct odors, and sometimes an electric or choking sensation—that are distinctly experienced but in the absence of any observable source or cause:

I felt the same sensation as, like, when a kid tugs at your pants to get your attention. And, obviously, I turned around and nothing was there. (Josh, age twenty-three)

I could smell the Ivory soap she always used. It was very soothing, and I was at peace. (Lana, age fifty-seven)

It was during the middle of the night when I woke up to something grabbing my ankle and pulling me down the bed. (Elise, age twenty-four)

Most frequently, intelligent hauntings entail *indirect* interactions that involve an inexplicable manipulation of objects in the environment: doors open or close, electrical devices operate erratically, items move, sounds are heard of footsteps on floors and stairs or of banging or knocking on windows and doors. Here are just a few of many examples:

My brother was just watching TV, and the remote on the coffee table started moving, maybe an inch at a time, slowly. And at one point, it just shot across the coffee table onto the floor. The batteries flew out of it. Basically, it exploded all over the floor. (Diane, age twenty)

The lights would flicker at night as the pots and pans in the kitchen would rattle. (Tiffany, age thirty-eight)

The water would turn on by itself, like in the bathtub. The water would turn on in the bathtub in the middle of the night. It was just [*pauses; sighs deeply*]—it was really nonstop. It happened all the time, and we never had explanations. (Nikki, age eighteen)

It's just all the banging and knocking! It knocks from the second-floor window—knocking from the outside, where it is physically impossible for someone to be. Sometimes we will see a dark shadow through the window or just hear the knocking. (Dylan, age thirty-five)

Yet whether the interaction is direct or indirect, intelligent hauntings entail a lot of physical activity that appears deliberate and attention seeking.

Residual Hauntings

A residual haunting entails a ghostly presence that does not interact with its environment or living occupants. In my research, residual hauntings are significantly less common (24 percent), and I find only two major forms. The first, and the most common, is a single fleeting and isolated uncanny event that is indifferent to the environment or people within it:

We could hear the front door open and close. When we went to look, there was no one out there. But it sounded like someone was coming into the house. (Lana, age fifty-seven)[8]

We saw a shadow in the basement. It was on a wall, and probably about eight feet high. The big shadow moved right across the wall. (Vicki, age nineteen)

The classic definition of a residual haunting involves seeing or hearing a ghostly presence repeatedly and in a manner with little or no deviation.[9] For example, in the house twenty-seven-year-old Luke grew up in, he said, "all the time I would hear footsteps coming down the steps, walking through the playroom that was downstairs, and then walk right alongside my bed, and

---

8. This is a helpful example of the difference between intelligent and residual hauntings; had the door actually opened and closed, this would be an intelligent haunting, since the ghost was reported to have interacted with the physical environment.

9. Because of this, paranormal investigators and ghost enthusiasts often do not consider residuals a true haunting. Rather than a ghostly presence with a will and volition of its own, residuals are frequently regarded as some kind of inexplicable supernatural recorded playback of events that previously occurred. For the purposes of my research, I do not treat residual hauntings any differently from intelligent ones.

then walk back up the steps." Luke remembers this same pattern of footsteps occurring repeatedly: "The same thing over and over. Just pacing back and forth all night."

These repeating patterns—as if something were stuck in a "*compulsion to repeat*" (Freud [1919] 2003: 145; emphasis in original)—is frequently regarded as a common characteristic of residual hauntings. In my research, however, I found only two reported instances of this kind of repetitive residual haunting. All the other residual hauntings are of apparitions, shadows, mists, and orbs with uncanny characteristics but that otherwise do not interact with people or the environment.

Anniversary and Historical Hauntings

I found two other types of hauntings in my research—anniversary and historical hauntings—but both are relatively uncommon. An anniversary haunting entails witnessing a ghostly presence on (or very close) to the date of a specific or corresponding event of significance to the ghost. For example, an anniversary ghost may appear on the date of his or her death, birthday, or an annual holiday. Twenty-three-year-old Krystal provides a good example:

> My best friend killed himself on May 7th of 2009. He did it at 4:40 A.M., just minutes after talking to me. In the summer of 2009, precisely one month after—precisely to the day—I woke up and thought I was seeing white lights, like reflections on a white wall but kind of blurry. I kept waking up and seeing them, waking up and seeing them. When I woke up the final time, I looked at my phone and saw it was June 7, 4:40 A.M., and I all of a sudden felt a warm, peaceful, comforting sensation. I know it was John.

Paranormal investigators and ghost enthusiasts often claim that anniversary ghosts are almost universally intelligent hauntings. All the anniversary ghosts reported in my research were intelligent, but the numbers are too few to allow for much comment. On the basis of the research I have conducted, it appears that anniversary ghosts are much more common in popular culture than everyday life, and people seem to expect anniversary ghosts more often than they are actually experienced.

Historical hauntings occur in places of historical significance, and people primarily report seeing apparitions whose chief characteristic, when seen in a human form, is wearing period-appropriate clothing or uniforms. Nineteen-year-old Vicki provides an example:

> I got out of the car and looked up the hill, and I saw fifteen or so colonial-dressed people standing there. I looked away and then looked back, and they were all gone. I saw men and women of all ages, but mostly middle age—not too many younger or older. . . . Later that night we went home, and one of the guys that was with [us] did some research on the area—the hanging that happened there. According to legend, the hundred or so people that watched the hanging were doomed to roam [the area]. I just chalk it up to that and feel that the fifteen or so people I saw in the hill were those spectators of the hanging.

Paranormal investigators and ghost enthusiasts typically claim that historical hauntings are almost always residual. All the historical hauntings in my research are residual, but the numbers are too few to allow for much comment.

FORMS OF GHOSTS

People commonly report experiencing ghosts in a variety of forms, and in my research I identify six: apparitions, phantasms, wraiths, poltergeists, specters, and phantoms. These forms, however, are not mutually exclusive. All reports of ghosts in my research fall into at least one of these six forms and some reported experiences have characteristics of more than one form.

Apparitions

The word "appearance"—the process of coming into sight, becoming visible—is the root for *apparition*. Thus, an apparition implies an evanescent visual presence that approximates something physical or material; a ghost that is seen. Of the reported ghosts in my research, 45 percent are apparitions.[10] Fifty-one-year-old Ralph gives a rich account:

> Three nights in a row I woke up at exactly 3 A.M. and was, like, "There's a third person in bed!" I could literally see a shape, a human figure, lying on the bed between my wife and I. My wife and I are edge sleepers—she's on one end of the bed, and I'm on the other—and there was this shape in between us. Once I became aware of it, I looked at it, although sometimes trying not to, but eventually as I was looking at it, [it] just kinda faded away. As it faded away I could see

---

10. When people think about ghosts, most often they imagine an apparition. It is worth noting that only about half of all reported ghostly encounters involve a visible presence of any kind.

my wife again. It was like a solid shape, human form; I couldn't see any detail, but it was laying above the covers. It was nerve-racking. I mean, my wife woke up and said, "Boy, you're really crowding me!" And I was like, "Well, it wasn't me!" It weirded me out.[11]

Consistent with Ralph's account, reports of apparitions most frequently involve seeing a human form—either partial or complete. In my research 68 percent of reported apparitions involve seeing a human form of some kind and often quite vividly:

I saw an adult male figure come in [my bedroom], wearing a light-green short-sleeves shirt, and he had light skin. He touched my hips in a way of sympathy, walked toward the window, and vanished. (Claire, age twenty)

We see a little girl in pajamas, too—really specifically detailed, in her pajamas. I have a little display of golf balls outside my office, and she will knock those off, tip the clubs, knock things over—almost as if to drive me absolutely crazy! Most recently, my best friend told me he saw a young girl in pajamas standing in my office doorway. (Dylan, age thirty-five)

My sister saw a lady in a red dress singing. My uncle who lives downstairs saw a really pretty lady down there, too. But when I see her, she's not a beautiful lady—just a typical-looking one. She's usually seen singing or just walking around. Once my sister heard singing downstairs through the vent, and she thought it was my uncle, but he wasn't home the whole weekend. (Ella, age twenty)

Other accounts of apparitions involve seeing something nonhuman. The majority of those reports (67 percent) entail seeing eerie shadows. Twenty-five-year-old Paige provides one of the richest examples:

I would see shadows moving in the room. I'd never seen darkness like that before. I used to feel comfort in the darkness. I was used

---

11. Although Ralph's experience is fairly typical of reports with apparitions, it is also unique in that he saw it in his bed. People who report experiencing a ghost in their bed are often extremely unsettled by the experience—and for good reason. One's bed is among the most private of all spaces; what we do in bed—and with whom—is among the most intimate and vulnerable of all human activities. Encountering an unknown entity in one's own bed is understandably disconcerting.

to the darkness. I liked being in darkness. But this darkness scared me. It was so dense that I couldn't see through it at all—that's how dark it was. Even with the moonlight, outside lights, clock lights, and everything else, I couldn't see certain areas of my room 'cause it was so dense.

Popular media is saturated with alleged experiences with ghostly orbs and mists—especially photos purported to have captured an apparition. In my research, however, people only occasionally report experiences with elusive orbs and mists:

I wasn't sure as to what I was seeing, but it wasn't walking on the ground. It was floating. It was light blue with illuminating flowing colors of white and blue. It seemed to flow in the wind, which there wasn't much of that night. (Lana, age fifty-seven)

Right at the foot of my bed there was this misty-white thing. It came at me, and it wasn't like it was going to hurt me. Still, I screamed because I didn't know what it was! It was really weird, because it wasn't like a figure—not like a person or anything—just a misty white thing. (Samantha, age forty-two)

My husband . . . would wake up to a white light circling above our bed. He would get really freaked out by that. I didn't believe him and what he was telling me. But one night he woke me up, and I saw it. It didn't last long, but it was kinda like a white circle, maybe the size of a golf ball—almost smoky, like you could see through it—and it just spun in a circle really fast above our bed, and then it was gone. (Tiffany, age thirty-eight)

Phantasms

All of the sixty-five reports of apparitions in my research appeared to people when they were fully conscious. In some instances, just 6 percent, people report seeing a ghostly presence but in a dream or some other altered state of awareness, which I refer to as *phantasms*. With apparitions, people are reasonably confident of what they see or remember seeing. In contrast, people are less certain of what they experience in a dream or some other altered state of awareness. Thus, the term "phantasm" signifies those apparitions' much more illusionary nature. Twenty-year-old Diane, for example, reported three distinct ghostly encounters. In her first experience, she is certain that she saw an apparition: "I saw a figure—and it was, like, very, *very* visible. I could *easily* see it." However, the second experience she qualifies by saying, "I didn't really see a ghost. It was actually a dream"—precisely the kind of distinction people frequently make that prompted me to treat phantasms as a distinct form of their own. Diane continues:

> The dream was this last year. It was with my dad's dad, who has passed. He came to me in my dream and told me that he needed me to pass on a message to my grandmother, who is still alive. He said, "It's very important! Don't forget!" So I was like, "Okay." And he said, "Just tell her that it's gonna be okay, don't be sad, and he is all right."

The next morning, on the recommendation of her father, Diane called her grandmother:

> I told her what my grandpa said to tell her. She was really confused, and I think, if anything, she was more ticked off at me for even bringing him up and saying something weird like that. The next week her cat—which actually my grandpa adopted from a shelter—passed away. That cat was very significant to my grandma—a huge symbol of my grandpa to her. So that was a huge loss for her. I feel like that was what my grandpa was trying to tell her—that the cat was going to pass away and that it's going to be okay.

The people I have interviewed seldom report experiences with phantasms, and that is understandable. In dreams and other altered states of awareness people routinely experience things that they understand are products of their own mind. The experience may be pleasurable, terrifying, strange, awkward, or even mundane. But, with the exception of a few psychoanalysts and psychedelic mind trippers, people seldom take the content of these altered states of mind seriously. Something else has to happen for people to report an experience with a phantasm, such as we see in Diane's account, and that is consistent with the process by which uncanny events become ghosts (see Waskul 2016). Thus, most often, explanations for experiences with phantasms emerge from coinciding life events for which people find simple coincidence hard to accept.

Wraiths

Traditionally defined, a wraith is a known person who visits the living around the time of his or her death. Reports of wraith experiences are not common in my research, a mere 3 percent of reported experiences. In the data I have collected, accounts of wraiths universally feature appearances of loved ones that portend their death and comfort the grief of the living. Here, for example, twenty-one-year-old Karen recalls her wraith experience:

> I was in the fifth grade, so I'm assuming I was around ten or eleven. She [grandma] was on a machine keeping her alive at home. The doctor came over while my family all stood around her, and he shut off the machine. It was a very traumatizing moment for us, being so young, but my mom thought that we would want to be there. We all sat around her while she slowly slipped away. Once she had, I felt something touch my shoulder, and I turned around and it was a faint image of my grandma. I thought I was just seeing things, but each one of us in the room felt and saw the same thing. My grandma probably was just trying to comfort us and let us know that she was going to be okay.

Consistent with Karen's experience, wraiths are commonly either apparitions or phantasms, since some kind of visual confirmation of the (soon to be) deceased loved one is present in almost all the accounts I collected:

> When my dad died I was in my apartment, and my daughter was, oh, maybe a week and a half old. I walked out of my bedroom, and I saw my dad just sitting at my dining room table just looking at me. He was just sitting there. (Grace, age forty-eight)

> I found myself sobbing and drenching my pillow with my tears. My mother was suddenly there, in the room with me. She placed her soft warm hand on mine, . . . on my chest. She said, "Oh honey, it's going to be okay. Stop crying now. It's going to be okay." (Lana, age fifty-seven)

Poltergeists

Geist is the German word for ghost, and *poltern* means to crash about, bang, or otherwise make noise. Hence, a literal definition of a *poltergeist* is "noisy ghost"—one that mainly makes its presence known by inexplicable sounds. I broadened this literal definition to include an alleged ghostly presence that makes itself known with baffling sounds but also moving objects, turning electrical devices on or off, opening and closing doors, and other similar mysterious manipulations of physical objects in the environment:

We hear that kind of stuff often. Like things falling to the floor, but nothing's fallen. Or when I'm down here on the main floor, I hear footsteps—people walking around. It just sounds like there's a bunch of people walking around upstairs. (Brooke, age twenty-six)

We were sitting at our dining room table, and my entire family witnessed this box move across the kitchen counter by itself. It just slowly slid across the counter. (Nikki, age eighteen)

I had a TV in my bedroom. I was sleeping, and everything was off. All of a sudden the TV turned on, and the channels started randomly flipping all on its own. The remote was on the floor next to my bed; nothing was touching it—the dog wasn't even in my room. I don't know how, but the TV just turned on and was flipping channels. (Sarah, age twenty-eight)

Poltergeists account for 32 percent of all reported ghosts in my research, and of the six ghostly forms that I have identified, they have the most consistent and stable characteristics. The poltergeists that people report in my research are almost universally place bound; they haunt a specific building, mostly homes in my research, and sometimes explicitly one room within it. Poltergeists are associated with an enormous range of strange noises and physical activity, but they almost never appear as an apparition. Other ghostly forms are mostly experienced as isolated, fleeting events, but poltergeists are far more persistent; people frequently report experiencing a poltergeist over the course of months, years, and even decades. Whereas other ghostly forms often rely on accounts that are not (or cannot be) corroborated by others, poltergeists are most often experienced by multiple people who report the same uncanny happenings over time. Finally, people often report feeling startled, even annoyed, by poltergeists—but almost never do they feel threatened by them.

Mischievousness is the most common characteristic of the poltergeist. "He feels like a jokester," says nineteen-year-old Amy, describing the character of the poltergeist she has been living with for years. "He takes stuff and hides it,"[12] she adds, and she details objects that inexplicably disappear only to be

---

12. An especially observant reader may have noticed that people commonly refer to ghosts with male pronouns. In my research only 21 percent of reported encounters with a ghost involve descriptions of something with an observable gender. Yet, regardless, when people refer to these ghosts they use male pronouns. As I argue elsewhere (Waskul 2016), this is not a coincidence but, instead, a product of an androcentric culture.

found in peculiar places. Reports of poltergeists frequently describe them as tricksters that subject the living "to a wide variety of ghostly pranks" (Jones 1959: 63). Sixty-one-year-old Martha provides a good example of the kinds of pranks that are typical of a poltergeist:

> I have toys that play musical things, but I don't have any toys that play "London Bridge Is Falling Down." One night I woke up hearing that song somewhere in the living room. And then the next night it was in my room, and as soon as I turned the light on, it stopped. The next night it kept playing after I turned the light on. I went to look for it, but I could not find it anywhere—and I knew I did not have a toy with that song. . . . My daughter and her friend were here [another time], and they rented a few movies. They placed them on that table [*points toward the dining room*], and they were in the living room the whole time. . . . [Later] we went over for the movies, and they weren't on the table. So we looked all over. We could not find them. So I took the garbage out piece by piece, and there was those two movies on the very bottom. It couldn't have slipped through. I don't understand how they can move and no one saw them moving. And, you know, we have the usual things—TVs going on and off, lights going on and off.

Specters and Phantoms

I use the word "specter" to refer to any form of a menacing ghost, one that the living feel distinctly threatened by and that they can experience in any of the other four ghostly forms. While people commonly think of ghostly encounters as a harrowing experience, available literatures suggest the opposite (see Goldstein, Grider, and Thomas 2007; Jones 1944, 1959), and my research arrives at the same conclusion. Ghosts may startle, or even annoy, but only rarely are they experienced as threatening or menacing. People often use "freaked out" to describe their reactions to ghostly encounters but, when asked, explain they usually mean the phrase to imply surprise or feeling alarm and seldom fear. Only 10 percent of reported ghosts in my study are specters.

Ghosts are sometimes reported as playful or sad, curious or indifferent, but only rarely are they angry, violent, intimidating, or aggressive. I have found only two exceptions, and neither is especially frequent. The first exception is ghosts of people who died through suicide:

> The only time I felt nauseous or, like, that I needed to get away is when my brother and his wife moved into a house, and they were giving us the whole tour. We went upstairs to these really raggedy,

short stairs—they were really narrow and wooden. And I go up to this room, and she is telling me about it. I walk in, and [*pauses*] there was this certain spot. I was fine until I crossed the doorway, and I got this feeling like I really, really, *really* need to get out! I couldn't breathe. I felt like someone was pressing on my chest. I said, "I don't know about anyone else, but I really need to get out of here quick!" So we go downstairs, and as we go down the stairs, my sister-in-law informed me that a guy hung himself on those stairs. The Realtor informed them of it. (Amy, age nineteen)

The second exception is the result of experiences with Ouija boards. In my research all six reported ghostly encounters involving Ouija boards resulted in unpleasant experiences with specters. For example, twenty-year-old Diane agreed to try a Ouija board with her brother and friends. "I wasn't buying it," Diane says, acknowledging that the planchette "was moving, but I thought the boys were just screwing around, and I was, like, this is stupid!" But in the middle of the session,

this six-four star football player of the high school team started screaming to stop. So we stopped, turned on all the lights, and he was crying and hyperventilating. He said it felt like something, or someone, went inside him and took his breath from him. He felt like he had no control over his body. He had a severe panic attack. We stopped and didn't do that anymore! But we kept the Ouija board at our house for a while after that, and while the Ouija board was in our house all kinds of really weird things happened. It didn't stop until we got rid of that Ouija board.

Consistent with my previous distinction, a specter is encountered in a conscious state of mind. If the specter appears in, say, a dream or some other altered state of awareness, I use the term "phantom." Experiences with phantoms are rare—just 4 percent of the ghosts reported in my research. Twenty-year-old Julia, for example, experiences a recurring "pattern of dreams" in which

there's something. I don't know what it is, but it's not pretty. It's like an ugly, red [*pauses*] something. Like a red, blackish shadow. It's a patterned nightmare, where it's the same thing over and over again. At first I thought it was just a really, really scary dream—and I probably just ate something too late or whatever. But then I shared this dream with one of my roommates, and she said she's had those same realistic nightmares, too—and one where she swears there is somebody standing in the corner of her room. And then our third roommate said the same thing, that she is having those nightmares, too. We don't want to put too much into it, but that's kinda freaky!

CONCLUSIONS

In this chapter, I detail a framework for categorizing ghostly experiences. This framework is useful for illuminating both the commonalities and the differences between the highly diverse genres, types, and forms of ghosts and hauntings that people experience. Further research on ghosts and hauntings may reveal additional categories, but the framework I articulate provides a starting point.

"Yes, others have come to me with very similar kinds of experiences," I reassure an informant in my ongoing research—as I must have done at least a dozen times before. And I understand; people often ask about and are comforted to know that they are not alone in the strange things they have experienced. I elaborate a bit further. "In fact, what you described to me is highly characteristic of what is called a poltergeist," and I proceed to point out the common features that people report in poltergeist experiences. "Wow! A poltergeist!" my young respondent says at the end of our conversation, immediately followed by, "*I feel a lot better knowing that!*" (emphasis added).

As fundamentally symbol-making creatures, people inevitably label things with words. Relatedly, having words allows people to conceive of things, and acquiring new words changes how (and with what) we are able to think. Thus, I am not surprised that my informant is comforted to know that the things she experiences have a label; nor am I shocked that she feels better knowing this. But in seeking to understand people's experiences with ghosts and hauntings we must be careful. In this chapter I provide a lot of labels—many of which are not my invention and are commonly used by ghost enthusiasts and paranormal investigators. Still, it is a common human error to mistake having a word for something as being the same as *understanding*, and this mistake is common enough to warrant caution.

Affixing a label to something is useful and, indeed, necessary for sorting out what is otherwise an undifferentiated mass of seemingly unrelated experiences, phenomena, or things. But those words alone do not, and cannot, bestow understanding. That is, as helpful as it may be to have labels to describe common genres, types, and forms of ghosts and hauntings, in the end none of those words bestow any deeper understanding of what exactly those people experienced. Yet, fortunately enough for the student and scholar of the human animal, as long as people continue to react to what they define as or attribute to a ghostly presence, their thoughts and consequent actions are relevant, meaningful, and worthy of our recognition and attention. In short, what the ghost is, is far less important than what it means to the people who claim to have experienced one and their reaction toward what they define as a ghost.

REFERENCES

Alfano, Sean. 2005. "Poll: Majority Believe in Ghosts." *CBS News*, October 29. Available at http://www.cbsnews.com/news/poll-majority-believe-in-ghosts.

Bader, Christopher, F. Carson Mencken, and Joseph Baker. 2010. *Paranormal America: Ghost Encounters, UFO Sightings, Bigfoot Hunts, and Other Curiosities in Religion and Culture*. New York: New York University Press.

Brady, Erika. 1995. "Bad Scares and Joyful Hauntings: 'Priesting' the Supernatural Predicament." In *Out of the Ordinary: Folklore and the Supernatural*, edited by B. Walker, 145–158. Logan: Utah State University Press.

Clarke, Roger. 2012. *Ghosts a Natural History: 500 Years of Searching for Proof.* New York: St. Martin's Press.

Edensor, Tim. 2005. "The Ghosts of Industrial Ruins: Ordering and Disordering Memory in Excessive Space." *Environment and Planning D: Society and Space* 23 (6): 829–889.

Freud, Sigmund. (1919) 2003. *The Uncanny*. New York: Penguin.

Goldstein, Diane E., Sylvia A. Grider, and Jeannie B. Thomas. 2007. *Haunting Experiences: Ghosts in Contemporary Folklore*. Logan: Utah State University Press.

Hufford, David. 1995. "Beings without Bodies: An Experience-Centered Theory of the Beliefs in Spirits." In *Out of the Ordinary: Folklore and the Supernatural*, edited by B. Walker, 11–45. Logan: Utah State University Press.

Jones, Louis. 1944. "The Ghosts of New York: An Analytical Study." *Journal of American Folklore* 57 (226): 237–254.

———. 1959. *Things That Go Bump in the Night*. New York: Syracuse University Press.

Lipka, Michael. 2015. "18% of Americans Say They've Seen a Ghost." Pew Research Center, October 30. Available at http://www.pewresearch.org/fact-tank/2015/10/30/18-of-americans-say-theyve-seen-a-ghost.

Ramsey, Matthew, Steven Venette, and Nicole Rabalais. 2011. "The Perceived Paranormal and Source Credibility: The Effects of Narrative Suggestions on Paranormal Belief." *Atlantic Journal of Communication* 19 (2): 79–96.

Speigel, Lee. 2013. "Spooky Number of Americans Believe in Ghosts." *Huffington Post*, February 2. Available at http://www.huffingtonpost.com/2013/02/02/real-ghosts-americans-poll_n_2049485.html.

Taylor, Humphrey. 2003. "The Religious and Other Beliefs of Americans 2003." *Harris Poll*, February 26. Available at http://theeffect.org/wp-content/uploads/2016/05/Religious-Beliefs-US-2003.pdf.

Waskul, Dennis, with Michele Waskul. 2016. *Ghostly Encounters: The Hauntings of Everyday Life*. Philadelphia: Temple University Press.

YouGov. 2013. "Ghosts and UFOs." Available at http://www.assap.ac.uk/newsite/Docs/Ghost%20UFO%20Survey%202013.pdf.

4

PARANORMAL INVESTIGATION

The Scientist and the Sensitive

Marc Eaton

The question of what happens after we die has haunted humanity from our earliest days. Out of this fear have emerged myriad religious and spiritual belief systems that purport to make the unknown knowable, to explain in great detail what lies beyond the veil of physical death. These belief systems differ in their descriptions of the afterlife—some declare eternal salvation or damnation, while others offer a cycle of rebirth as one moves toward enlightenment—but all offer comfort to those who have faith. However, religious faith is harder to come by these days, at least in the Western world. Religious "nones"—those who respond "none" when asked about their religious beliefs and attendance—are on the rise in the United States, with over 20 percent of the population identifying as such (Pew Research Center 2015). Similar increases in religious nonaffiliation have, at least until recently, been evident in Britain (Bruce 2002, 2011) and other European nations (Kaufmann, Goujon, and Skirbekk 2012). Accompanying this trend is a shift toward individualized spirituality. People in Western nations are increasingly engaging in deinstitutionalized forms of spiritual practice (Davie 1994; Heelas and Woodhead 2005) or even inventing their own personalized belief systems (e.g., Bellah et al. 1985).

Even as the contemporary Western world shifts away from organized religion, science and technology are both revered and feared—much like the gods of the past. We are awestruck, for example, when the phone that enables us to talk with others begins speaking back to us; the artificial intelligence behind this seems mystical and even a bit disconcerting in its powers. On the other hand, scientific evidence proves that climate change is occurring at a scale and speed that makes it seem apocalyptic in its implications. Although most of us do not fully grasp the theories and equations that make such knowledge possible, we have faith that the prevailing wisdom emanating from climate scientists is, frankly, as close to absolute truth as we can get in this secular era. The key word here is "faith": today, we *believe* in technology and science as a means to truth.

This faith is known as "scientism," which Richard N. Williams describes as "a dogmatic overconfidence in science and 'scientific' knowledge" (2016: 10). According to a scientistic worldview, science is treated as an unquestionable, unerring way to achieve understanding of the natural world. However, someone who espouses scientistic views does not adhere to the strict methodology of natural science but "borrows the apparatus of science . . . to create the *appearance* of a scientific question, the appearance of data, and the appearance of a question that will arrive at an answer" (Scruton 2016: 135). Scientism traffics in the trappings and language of science to apply a veneer of scientific legitimacy to claims that are not actually based in rigorous scientific investigation. In the context of an increasingly secularized Western world, Williams argues that "scientism has become the new orthodoxy" that raises our trust in science to the level of metaphysical commitment to things that look and sound like "science" (2016: 2). Whereas the word of God used to be the unquestioned truth, in a scientistic culture, appeals to science perform the same discursive function, undercutting the legitimacy of any claims that challenge this orthodoxy.

I argue that paranormal investigation lies at the intersection of individualized spirituality and scientism and is a product of the cultural context that is shaped by these concurrent trends.[1] This assertion is based on five years of ethnographic study of paranormal investigation teams. During my research, I have interviewed forty-four investigators, conducted participant observation on twenty investigations, and attended five paranormal conferences. At its most basic level, paranormal investigation is driven by a desire to make contact with what are commonly called ghosts or spirits—the disembodied consciousness of deceased beings (usually humans). Despite this shared goal, investigators differ in their preferred approaches: some who are more aligned with the cultural trend of scientism advocate a "scientific" approach, while others who represent the individualized, New Age spirituality of our

---

1. What I refer to as paranormal investigation is colloquially known as ghost hunting. Members of the subculture prefer the label paranormal investigation, which I use throughout this chapter out of respect for their self-identification.

era argue that their "sensitive" abilities are the best tool for making contact with spirits.[2]

Scientific paranormal investigators rely heavily on technology in an attempt to collect empirical data to prove the existence of ghosts. In doing so, they hope to prove the existence of an afterlife in which humans retain self-consciousness and agency beyond physical death. The vast majority of scientific investigators are not actually trained in science and technology but gravitate toward using such equipment because of a scientistic faith that this is the best way to gather definitive evidence. This faith is further supported by reality-based paranormal investigation television shows such as *Ghost Hunters* and *Ghost Adventures* that emphasize the use of technology as a way to communicate with and collect data about spirits.

Unlike scientistic paranormal investigators, whose primary goal is to collect definitive evidence for the existence of ghosts, sensitives are already certain of the existence of these ephemeral beings. These people—who call themselves "mediums," "psychics," "clairvoyants," "empaths," "intuitives," and other similar terms—claim to possess abilities to sense the presence of spirits and communicate with departed souls. Sensitives focus more on making contact with spirits, determining the reasons for their continued presence in the physical world, and—if they feel it is best for their clients or the spirits themselves—encouraging these spirits to "cross over" into a spiritual realm, often described as a form of paradise. Rather than placing faith in science, sensitives exhibit spiritual beliefs and practices that could be broadly categorized as New Age, such as belief in reincarnation and the manipulation of spiritual energies through the practice of Reiki. Most say that their abilities manifested at a young age, though several I interviewed reported that their abilities "turned on" after an accident or illness that led them to the brink of death.

In practice, paranormal investigation teams frequently include a combination of scientific and sensitive members; some individuals use both approaches. Teams are generally characterized by an "epistemological pluralism" (Eaton 2015: 408) that allows multiple investigative approaches and belief systems to peacefully coexist. However—to paraphrase George Orwell's *Animal Farm* (1946)—in the subculture as a whole, all investigators are equal but some are more equal than others. In general, sensitive approaches are subordinated to methods that rely on technology and scientific-sounding

---

2. To prevent the text from appearing cluttered, I refrain from using scare quotes around "scientist," "scientific," and "sensitive" in the remainder of the chapter. However, the absence of scare quotes is merely a stylistic consideration and should not be taken as an assertion of the legitimacy of claims to scientific methods or sensitive abilities.

terminology. This has important implications for the types of voices that gain legitimacy in the paranormal investigation subculture and, alternatively, which voices are silenced.

Before turning to a discussion of these power relations and how they are resolved, it is important to understand the features and scale of the paranormal investigation subculture. Below, I describe the origins, demographics, and size of the paranormal investigation subculture. Then I distinguish scientific and sensitive approaches from one another in terms of their ontology, epistemology, and reasons for investigating. Last, I present several strategies used by sensitives to increase the perceived validity of their claims before turning to a discussion of how these strategies ultimately reinforce structural inequalities based on gender and economic class.

THE PARANORMAL INVESTIGATION SUBCULTURE

Stories of ghosts and hauntings echo throughout human history (see Clarke 2012; Finucane 1996). Moreover, people have attempted to communicate with and capture evidence of ghosts for hundreds if not thousands of years. Most notable in this regard were the concurrent development of Spiritualism and psychical research during the latter half of the nineteenth century. Spiritualists claimed to be able to communicate with the dead through a coded language of knocks, automatic writing, "talking boards" (the precursor to Ouija boards), trance mediumship, and other methods (Blum 2006; Weisberg 2005). After these claims captured public attention in the mid-1800s in the United States and England, scientists and scholars from a variety of backgrounds created psychical research organizations—the Society for Psychical Research (founded 1882) in England and the American Society for Psychical Research (founded 1885) in the United States—to use the latest in scientific methods and technologies to investigate spiritualists' claims.

This tension between psychic claims and attempts to scientifically prove or disprove such claims is reflected in the bifurcation between scientists and sensitives in the current paranormal investigation subculture. This, in conjunction with the more recent trends toward individualized spirituality and scientism described above, set the sociocultural context for paranormal investigation in the twenty-first century. However, another critically important factor must be mentioned: reality-based paranormal investigation television shows. Since the early years of the twenty-first century, shows like *Ghost Hunters* and *Ghost Adventures* have drawn millions of viewers each week as they follow teams of investigators who attempt to communicate with ghosts, use technological gadgets to detect and record the presence of these spirits, and—especially in the case of *Ghost Adventures*—challenge these entities to show themselves. Almost universally, paranormal investigators with whom I spoke pointed to these shows as inspirations for joining or forming their own teams. Likewise, they stated that they at least initially modeled their investigative styles on the methods and tools used on these shows. If deinstitutionalized spirituality and scientism help explain the *why* of paranormal investigation, these television shows go a long way in explaining the *how* of investigation.

My ethnographic experience in the subculture enables me to make some claims about demographic trends within the population of paranormal investigators. Most apparent in my observations is that the paranormal investigation subculture is almost exclusively white. Despite interviewing investigators from many urban and rural or semirural locations across the country, I interviewed only one investigator who identified as anything other than non-Hispanic white. Likewise, I never observed more than about half a dozen people of color in attendance at paranormal conferences filled with several hundred people. The gender breakdown in the subculture is far more evenly split. Roughly equal numbers of men and women participate, although men are more likely to be team leaders and to be speakers at conferences. From the hundreds to even thousands of dollars most of the investigators I met spent on equipment, I infer that the subculture is generally middle class. However, as explained below, a working-class element among paranormal investigators uses less expensive equipment and places more emphasis on intuitive methods of investigation. On average, paranormal investigators reported some college experience, with a median of roughly two years of college and a range from high school graduates to several with master's degrees.

In terms of religious beliefs, the most common category among investigators was "spiritual but not religious." Some self-identified as such while others are so defined on the basis of characteristics outlined by Robert C. Fuller (2001) and Linda A. Mercadante (2014). Many expressed disillusionment with organized religion, either in general or because of specific experiences of disappointment or unbelief. At the same time, they rejected an outright atheistic worldview and held out hope that a spiritual realm exists. This position of what one may call hopeful skepticism is a consistent feature of the worldview shared by investigators of the supernatural, including those who investigated claims made by spiritualists in the late nineteenth and early twentieth centuries (Braudy 2016). In keeping with the trend toward individualized spirituality, these spiritual-but-not-religious investigators desired a direct connection to the spirit world and felt that paranormal investigation could help them achieve this goal (Eaton 2015). A smaller group of investigators still identified with an organized religious belief system; in my interview pool, all these believers except one identified as Christian. Only two investigators

I interviewed identified as atheists and even then admitted that they hoped to be proved wrong through the discovery of irrefutable evidence of spirits.

It is difficult to accurately estimate the number of paranormal investigation teams in existence at any given moment because many are short-lived enterprises, consisting of small groups of friends who watch paranormal investigation television shows and decide to try it out. These teams quickly fold after realizing that paranormal investigation is not nearly as action-packed as it seems on television and requires hours of data review in hopes of capturing a few seconds of potential audio or visual evidence. The subculture also includes more serious teams with a committed core of investigators who commonly purchase expensive equipment and conduct investigations at least once a month, depending on demand and access. According to an online directory of paranormal investigation teams, as of May 2017 there are over four thousand paranormal investigation societies in the United States.[3] After weeding out teams with defunct websites, no recent investigations listed, and those not strictly dedicated to searching for ghosts (for example, teams that also hunt for Bigfoot or UFOs), I found that approximately six hundred active paranormal investigation teams are dedicated to searching for ghosts in the United States as of 2017. This represents thousands of people who dedicate a significant part of their free time to investigating claims of hauntings in homes, businesses, and abandoned buildings all across the country.

SCIENTIFIC AND SENSITIVE APPROACHES TO PARANORMAL INVESTIGATION

The paranormal subculture is characterized by two distinct approaches to investigation: the scientific and the sensitive. To clarify the differences between these two approaches, it helps to consider how they differ in three important ways: underlying ontological assumptions, epistemological authority claims, and reasons for investigating the existence of ghosts.

Ontological Status of Ghosts: Skepticism versus Certainty

Ontology concerns one's beliefs about the nature of reality. In other words, an ontological claim asserts not only what *is* and *is not* present in the world but also what *can* or *cannot* exist in the world. Beliefs about the ontological status of ghosts are one way to distinguish scientific and sensitive approaches to paranormal investigation.

---

3. See the directory at http://www.paranormalsocieties.com.

For scientific investigators, the ontological status of ghosts is ambiguous; these investigators are not willing to assert the existence of ghosts but yet hold out hope that they may be able to discover evidence of such spiritual beings. Treading this line puts scientific investigators in a tenuous position in which they attempt to balance skepticism with hope. Articulating her experience of this balancing act, Terri, a forty-four-year-old white female investigator says, "What I call myself is a skeptical believer. I believe there's a possibility that paranormal can happen, but I'm skeptical until I have more data to back it up." Indeed, many scientific investigators proudly identify as skeptics and proclaim that their primary goal during investigations is to debunk supernatural claims. Chad, for example, is a thirty-four-year-old white male who has "always been kind of a skeptic" about supernatural claims. As a member of a team that prides itself on being very scientific, he reports, "We have a rule in the group: when in doubt, throw it out. You know, if there's any doubt that it could be something else, we're not going to present it as evidence. We have to be 100 percent sure that we have no explanation for what we just caught."

By identifying as skeptics and highlighting their ability to debunk most supernatural claims, scientific investigators assert their rationality in the face of criticism that paranormal investigation is pseudoscience (see, for example, Goode 2013; Hines 2003). Implicit in this skeptical attitude is an underlying belief that it may be possible to separate the wheat from the chaff—to discern genuine evidence of ghosts from unsubstantiated claims. This attitude is expressed by Jack, a thirty-three-year-old white male investigator:

> I'm known as Killjoy—that's my nickname—because I came into this 100 percent skeptic and debunked everything. . . . You don't say something's a ghost if you can prove otherwise. Occam's razor, you know: the simplest explanation is usually the correct one. So basically I debunked *almost* everything, but there's a few things I really couldn't debunk, and that's what kept me going.

In this regard, the ontological position of scientific investigators is one of hopeful skepticism in which disbelief in *most* claims sustains belief in the possible validity of *some* claims.

In contrast, sensitive investigators do not hesitate to state unequivocally that ghosts are real. Many times, these ontological claims are based on personal experiences in which the sensitive saw, heard, or otherwise sensed the presence of a spirit. Sensitives often claim that they were born with the ability to sense spirits. They report childhood experiences with ghosts as evidence of the legitimacy of their abilities as well as of the indisputable existence of ghosts. Raven, a twenty-four-year-old Hispanic female investigator, reports that as a child she could see shadow figures (black human-shaped forms) and once witnessed a full-bodied apparition (a ghostly human figure visible to the naked eye) forming in her mother's closet. Although most people would probably be terrified of such experiences, Raven said, "It was normal. It didn't terrify me. It was just another entity that I could feel, sense, or hear. . . . I just *knew* that there's something else." Likewise, Jeremiah, a forty-eight-year-old white male investigator, explains, "What some people consider paranormal is more normal for me, because I hear the things or see the things that they're trying to find. I've lived with it pretty much my whole life, so to me it's more *normal* than not normal." Sensitives like Raven and Jeremiah share a certainty in the ontological reality of ghosts. By framing their experiences as "normal," even mundane, they imply that communication with the dead is an unquestionable reality. From their perspective, doubting the existence of ghosts is as irrational as doubting the existence of living human beings.

Epistemological Authority Claims: Empiricism versus Intuition

Epistemology follows from ontology, in that one's beliefs about the nature of reality dictate to a large degree one's opinions about how we can best understand this reality. From epistemology one develops a methodology, which includes the tools and methods that are actually used to investigate and collect data about the nature of reality. As may be presumed by their different ontological positions relative to the existence of ghosts, scientific and sensitive paranormal investigators do not share a perspective on what forms of knowledge constitute reliable evidence of ghosts.

Those who are grounded in a scientific approach claim that only empirical data collected through direct observation, and recorded using objective instrumentation, can be considered authoritative. Investigators in this camp purchase expensive equipment that is either adapted for paranormal investigation or (more recently) explicitly designed for such uses. The most common equipment adapted for paranormal investigations includes digital audio recorders, still cameras, digital video recorders, electromagnetic frequency (EMF) detectors, geophones (which detect vibrations), motion detectors, thermometers, and barometric pressure detectors. Since the early years of the twenty-first century enthusiasts and entrepreneurs have developed equipment especially for paranormal investigation. Most popular among these devices are the Ovilus (which records changes in environmental conditions and converts this data into words that it speaks in a robotic voice) and the spirit box (also called a ghost box; an instrument that rapidly scans radio channels and produces a staccato white noise that some investigators believe can be used by ghosts to communicate from the other side).

Scientific investigators simultaneously employ multiple technological devices in an effort to gather data from multiple sources and thereby increase the validity of evidence recorded by these instruments. Phil, a forty-three-year-old white male investigator, explains the logic of using multiple devices this way:

> All of a sudden this paranormal thing happened. I got a spike on my EMF meter; at the same time . . . I had the barometric pressure in the room change. Um, when you're able to tie a lot of these different things together, I think it's at that point in time when you go, "Eh, you know what? You may have something."

Jack, the investigator who was nicknamed Killjoy, similarly stated, "One of my mantras, I guess you could say, is that I follow the law of three, which is [that] getting three pieces of evidence is a very strong case. So if you get an EMF spike, with a cold spot register[ing] on a device, with a photo, you know, that's strong evidence."

Unlike scientific investigators who want to *think* their way through an investigation, sensitives prioritize *feelings* as the best way to ascertain the truth about reported ghostly presences. These feelings, whether physical or emotional, are interpreted as evidence of direct contact with the spirit world. During one investigation of a reportedly haunted theater, I observed Paul, a white male in his early fifties, as he claimed to communicate with numerous spirits in the building, including a small boy who died in the early twentieth century. Later, while the team and I walked to another part of the theater to conduct an electronic voice phenomenon (EVP) session, I asked Paul what it felt like when he channeled spirits. He emphasized the physical sensations as well as the emotional empathy he experienced in this trance state:

> Usually what happens when they want to enter you is, literally, I feel like I want to go to sleep right away, . . . and usually I feel a tingling at the top of my head too. And that's the signal, "Hey, it's time," you know, somebody wants in. . . . You can actually feel and think what they're thinking without actually hearing words. Sometimes I hear words. Sometimes literally my eyes are closed, and I'm letting them walk me around. And literally as that's happening, I'm seeing [my surroundings] as they see things, even though it's not like that anymore.

Paul said that he had inherited his abilities from his mother's side and claimed that his sensitivity to spirits was present at an early age. Likewise, Kenneth, a thirty-six-year-old white male who describes himself as an "empath" (someone who can feel others' emotions, including those of the deceased), explains that he was "very sensitive about emotions" and had "always been that way." When I asked how he used his abilities during investigations Kenneth replies, "I sit down, and I'm quiet, and I close my eyes and feel the environment.... Just because they don't have a body doesn't mean you can't feel them emotionally, because that's what they are: disembodied emotions."

Paul and Kenneth are somewhat unusual among sensitives in that they are male. In keeping with essentialist and stereotypical notions that men are more rational and women are more intuitive, more women, I found, identified as sensitive within the paranormal investigation subculture. Moreover, female sensitives are more adamant than their male counterparts that intuition should take precedence over empirical data collection. As Allison, a thirty-four-year-old white female medium, put it, "I'd love for logic and reason to take a back seat for a bit and let the closeness we felt to our natural world return. I would like to see people return to trusting their gut and not just toss it aside as if it isn't really a part of them." Similarly, Kaye, a forty-six-year-old white female investigator, describes equipment as a distraction from her more powerful ability to simply feel the emotional energy in a reportedly haunted location:

> When I first started, I wanted to grab all my equipment and put it out, and then I realized I was looking more at my equipment instead of just sitting and paying attention to what was going on around me. And now I feel like it's so much more important to go in and just be in the building or whatever the location is, and *feel* it for a while, you know?

Sensitives believe that feelings are a more valid way of knowing the truth about ghosts because they are unmediated by technological gadgets. Rebuffing the scientists' emphasis on collection of empirical data, they argue that we must shed our technological gadgetry if we wish to truly connect with the spirit world in an intuitive way.

Reason for Investigating: Proof versus Communication

This distinction between empirical and intuitive ways of knowing is also reflected in scientific and sensitive investigators' reasons for investigating. In keeping with their emphasis on scientific discovery through systematic observation and data collection, scientific investigators are motivated primarily by a desire to collect evidence that definitively proves the existence of ghosts.

This approach is reflected in the comments of Roger, a fifty-nine-year-old white male who has been investigating ghosts and hauntings since the 1970s:

> My idea getting into this field was always to look for scientific data, scientific truths, evidence for the existence of ghosts. I could always find people who said they had seen a ghost, had felt a ghost, come in contact in one way or the other. But it was always trying to find *evidence*, corroborating evidence, that you could present, you know, either though sound or even pictures or through video.

Roger's statement about gathering evidence that one could present to others touches on two of the three motivations behind attempts to scientifically prove the existence of ghosts.

First, scientific investigators believe that debunking claims and capturing evidence on technological equipment are the best ways to demonstrate to clients whether a location is haunted. As Steven, a thirty-eight-year-old white male team leader put it, "I need that audio clip, that video clip to go to the client. I'll never go to the client and say, 'You have a ghost because I *feel* it.'" Second, scientific investigators want to find evidence that they believe will convince the mainstream scientific community of the reality of ghosts. This is especially—though not exclusively—true for investigators who work in the fields of science and technology. Matthew, a twenty-nine-year-old investigator, works in a scientific laboratory during the day and investigates the paranormal most weekends. He sees these two practices as consistent with his goal of achieving new scientific discoveries:

> In my job every day I'm trying to make a discovery that is unknown and trying to publish it; that's basically my goal in life. So I'd like to make a discovery and make some sort of conclusion based on the readings I've taken. . . . If you can figure out the comings and goings of activity in some way, shape, or form, . . . then maybe you can start to measure parameters [for the activity]. . . . By measuring these different parameters and the environment and trying to correlate them along paranormal events, we might be able to figure out what's going on.

A third reason that scientific investigators seek proof is to reassure themselves that some form of life exists beyond physical death. This motive was expressed by Barb, a sixty-three-year-old white female investigator. When I asked what she hoped to find evidence for, Barb replied, "You know, as I get older I'm starting to wonder what's coming next. I like to think that I'm not just going to be dust in a grave somewhere. So, you know, I'm trying to figure out what's out there." Another investigator, Tommy, a fifty-seven-year-old white man, similarly stated, "For me it's more of a life-after-death kind of thing but approaching it from more of a scientific viewpoint." Regardless of whether they are hoping to prove the existence of ghosts to themselves or others, scientific investigators place utmost importance on technological documentation of apparently supernatural events.

For sensitives, in contrast, there is no need to find proof of the existence of ghosts. Because sensitives believe that ghosts are simply disembodied human consciousness, they approach investigations as an opportunity for interpersonal interaction, not data collection. For example, Suzanne, a fifty-two-year-old white female investigator, describes herself as a "social worker to ghosts" and explains, "I treat them as if they're people. You know, try to understand what they're doing, why they're here, what they need, what they want. I guess I just want to be helpful and compassionate." Likewise, Raven says she is interested in understanding why the spirits remain in a location, not in proving their existence:

> A lot of people say they want to find a ghost because they want knowledge or proof that there's another side. I already know that. I know there's another side, that dying isn't where we just sort of go away. For me . . . [death is] a transition. . . . I want to know *why* they're here. What made them stay?

Consistent with their desire to develop respectful relational patterns with the spirits, sensitives are adamant that paranormal investigators should not engage in "provoking." Provoking is a technique in which investigators verbally abuse or challenge the spirits with the goal of angering the ghosts enough to cause them to vocalize, manipulate the physical environment, or even attack an investigator. Some scientific investigators endorse this technique on the grounds that the ends—empirical evidence of ghosts—justify the means. However, sensitives think the practice is rude, counterproductive, and potentially dangerous. Jeremiah explains his opposition to provoking this way:

> I'm not into the "Well, if you're here, why don't you scratch me, you bastard!" and that kind of stuff. That's not how I work. Because at one point in time or another these [spirits] were somebody's loved one. And how would you like somebody going up to your grandma and saying, "You blah blah blah!" No! That's not the way it works.

Allison reiterates Jeremiah's point about continuity of identity beyond physical death but phrases it in a slightly more ominous way, saying, "Just because you can't see them, you know, they're still people. And now they're invisible, so that just seems like a bad combin[ation]—I'm in the dark, and maybe you'll [the spirit] throw something at my head." These moral and practical objections to provoking are rooted in sensitives' belief that the main purpose of investigating is to communicate with ghosts.

STATUS TENSION IN THE PARANORMAL INVESTIGATION SUBCULTURE: THE DEVALUATION (AND REVALUATION) OF SENSITIVE IMPRESSIONS

Given their differences in ontology, epistemology, and reasons for investigating, scientific and sensitive approaches to paranormal investigation are incommensurate with one another. Although teams commonly rely on both approaches, I consistently found that sensitive approaches are subordinated to scientific approaches in the paranormal investigation subculture. At all the paranormal conferences I attended, the majority of speakers reiterated the importance of using the latest technology to prove the existence of ghosts. All but one of the teams I observed and one other that I interviewed were led by men, and both the female team leaders with whom I spoke made a point of telling me that their teams adhered to scientific methods. During investigations I regularly witnessed sensitives' contributions being ignored or at least subordinated to information gathered through technological means. Even Connor, a twenty-one-year-old white male whose team includes multiple sensitives and who himself identifies as an empath, reports that his team values other forms of evidence more highly than psychic impressions:

> We do use the talents and gifts of our psychic mediums, but we have a rule on our team that if you feel anything while investigating, you're not allowed to tell the client; you're only allowed to tell other people on the team. . . . We can't prove it, so basically the only way we're going to actually tell the client . . . [about the psychic impression] is if we can actually prove it through evidence or research.

One psychic, Robin, a thirty-three-year-old white female, was explicitly told by a friend that her interpretations would not be perceived as credible by scientific investigators. In our interview she stated, "When I first started ghost hunting, my friend told me, 'Don't say that you're sensitive. Ghost hunters hate psychics. They hate them because they think that they're full of crap. Just don't even talk about it.' So, I was like, 'All right.'" This advice was not unwarranted, as several of the scientific investigators I know express disdain for people who claim to be sensitive. For example, Matthew claims that "a lot of mediums are looking for attention" and are "just there to make them[selves] feel important," not "actually trying to get evidence of [the] paranormal."

In light of this devaluation, sensitives rely on several strategies for increasing their perceived credibility in the subculture. Some buy into the subordination and minimize the value of their sensitive impressions. Others, however, draw on the legitimacy of science and rationality to buttress their claims.

Disclaiming Sensitive Impressions

Some sensitives express self-doubt about their abilities as a way of disclaiming their sensitive impressions. In an example of what John P. Hewitt and Randall Stokes (1975) call hedging, Christy, a thirty-year-old white female sensitive says, "Any time I give any of my sensitive impressions to clients I'll say, 'I have a disclaimer.' I usually say, 'What I get may or may not be true. It may mean something to you, it may not. So just take it for what it's worth,' you know." Another sensitive, Kathleen, a fifty-one-year-old white female, reports using a cognitive disclaimer—saying, "I know this sounds crazy, but"—as a "deliberate way of making people not think that [she's] a kook." In a variation on this disclaiming technique, a third sensitive investigator, Dennis, a forty-four-year-old white male, expresses concern about being perceived as mentally unstable after he observed what he believes to be the ghost of a little girl:

> I can see there's no person literally there, but overlap[ping] I see this image of this girl. And I'm like, "Am I fucking nuts or what?!" I was so shaken. I'm just like, "What the hell?!" So I went downstairs and was talking to the owner, and he said something like, "What did you see?" I didn't want to say it 'cause it sounds—if someone told me, I'd be like, "You're frickin' crazy."

More common than disclaimers, though, are validation strategies that draw on scientific legitimacy as a way to validate sensitive impressions. Sensitives rely on two distinct strategies: empirical verification and rationality assertion.

Empirical Verification

The most common validation strategy among sensitives is empirical verification. In this strategy, sensitives claim that their psychic impressions are supported by data captured by technological devices. Many point to audio recordings of EVPs as proof that they can truly sense the presence of spirits.

As Raven explained, "I like EVPs because if I say, you know, 'I thought I saw a shadow figure in the corner,' and we happen to capture an EVP shortly before or after me saying so, it's validation that perhaps I did see something." Along with audio recordings, sensitives also appeal to visual evidence in the form of still photographs or video recordings. This strategy is apparent in Kenneth's retelling of an experience he had in the music room at a reportedly haunted high school:

> I went over there and sat next to that one door 'cause I knew in my mind's eye—I felt her, shy and hiding behind that door and peeking out through the window. So I went over there to create a safe space, let her know it's okay, it's safe, you know what I mean? . . . So then, of course, one group that was there . . . got a picture of that girl behind that door right there where I was sitting.

Aside from audio and visual confirmation, sensitives also frame changes in environmental conditions, such as temperature fluctuations, as validation of their clairvoyant abilities. Pattie, a forty-nine-year-old white female investigator, told me of an investigation of a home in which an elderly resident named Karl had passed away several years earlier. The current residents reported footsteps and banging noises in the home. During the investigation, Pattie lacked confidence in the accuracy of her sensitive impressions until a temperature fluctuation confirmed, in her mind, the presence of Karl:

> I felt Karl pretty strongly, and he came through on the equipment as well. And that's always cool for me because I have a wonderful imagination, so sometimes I wonder—because sometimes I just *know* something, and I don't even know how I know it. I knew he was an older man and he looked gaunt. . . . And we held an EVP session, and it got supercold in their living room. It had been about seventy-three degrees when we started, and it dropped down to, like, sixty-five. So I could prove that something was going on.

Regardless of whether they highlight audio, visual, or environmental data, sensitives hope to increase the validity of their interpretations of events by showing how their abilities are, in fact, empirically verified.

Rationality Assertion

A second, less common validation strategy involves explicitly asserting one's rationality as a way to increase the perceived credibility of sensitive impressions. Hannah, a forty-four-year-old white female and self-described empath, resists the notion that sensitive methods make one less rational and also rebuffs the association of rationality with masculinity:

> If you're a serious researcher, whatever hat you're wearing, wear that hat well. It should have nothing to do [with] if you're a man or a woman. And it doesn't mean you're smarter or less smart or you're the psychic or not the psychic—you could be both! I'm scientific, *and* I'm a medium. What does that make me: half man and half woman?

To increase the perceived validity of his sensitive impressions, Dennis emphasizes that he actually debunks many of his own interpretations during investigations:

> We were at a farm, and there was ropes in the attic, and I, like, pictured a guy hanging from a rope. But then again I'm going, "Well, the rope's hanging there. Did that create the image [in my mind] because the rope's hanging there, and we're here for a paranormal investigation?" So I'm realistic enough and objective enough to realize not everything I see [in my mind] is going to be correct.

By pointing out that he does not regard all impressions as equally accurate, Dennis asserts that he is a rational person who does not jump to conclusions on the basis of flawed interpretations. In this strategy, debunking is used not as a way to discount sensitive impressions altogether; rather, it is a means of indicating to others that sensitives are as capable of discerning fantasy from reality as any scientifically minded investigators. The consequence of this debunking of *some* sensitive impressions is that it positions the small number of impressions that withstand debunking efforts as robust examples of genuine clairvoyant abilities.

CONCLUSIONS

Overall, sensitives attempt to validate their approach to investigating by framing their abilities as rational and supported by scientific evidence. While these attempts to draw on the legitimacy of science may increase the perceived validity of sensitive methods in the short run, they ultimately reinforce the dominant belief that empirical data collection is the best way to understand the nature of ghosts. In their desire to be taken seriously, sensitive investigators inadvertently play into the hands of scientific investigators by failing to assert that sensitive abilities are valid *in their own right*. This unintentional reaffirmation of the primacy of science reinforces power imbalances that exist within and beyond the paranormal investigation subculture.

First, by playing into notions of mind-body dualism, sensitives fail to challenge the idea that emotional experiences or intuitive forms of knowing are essentially irrational. They defer to a dominant discourse that devalues such means of accessing truth and therefore implicitly accept their secondary status within the subculture. This strategy has greater consequences for female sensitives because the devaluation of emotionality and intuition is also, in practice, a devaluation of qualities that are culturally encoded as feminine. Female paranormal investigators with sensitive abilities are caught in a double bind (Bartky 1990). If they embrace the essentialist association of intuition with femininity, they can retain a strong feminine self-identity at the cost of being perceived as a legitimate investigator by many in the subculture. On the other hand, if they reject this association and attempt to recast sensitive abilities as simply another form of technological data collection, they may be perceived as more legitimate at the cost of their femininity being questioned. For male sensitives, the risk lies in *not* appealing to technological verification. If they fail to assert the scientific validity of their abilities, they will fail to live up to hegemonic expectations for masculinity—including emotional stoicism and rationality—and fall into a subordinate masculinity (Connell 2005) that severely hinders their ability to be taken seriously. It is to their benefit, then, to assert scientific validation of sensitive abilities so as to protect themselves from challenges to their (masculine) rationality.

Second, the emphasis on scientific validation also marginalizes the voices of investigators who do not have the financial means to procure thousands of dollars of investigative equipment. While this economic marginalization does not exclusively affect sensitive investigators, it presents a special burden to those who, because of their perceived abilities, feel it is unnecessary to use technological gadgets to make contact with spirits. Sensitive investigators who do not use such gadgets are doubted by others because hard evidence, in the form of audio, video, or environmental recordings, is treated as the only truly valid way of determining the presence of a ghost. Some resign themselves to this and investigate without equipment, accepting that their claims are highly unlikely to be perceived as valid by the larger community. Other sensitives purchase and use equipment anyway, despite feeling it is extraneous to their communication abilities. Still others reconcile this conflict by joining groups in which other members have already purchased equipment. This gives them the freedom to conduct investigations unencumbered by equipment while also benefiting from the chance that other members' equipment may help validate their claims. However, this strategy is imperfect in that it leads sensitives to play supportive roles on these teams, advising the placement of equipment or suggesting what questions to ask during EVP sessions. Thus, the financial burden of purchasing equipment forces many sensitives to decide if they are willing to accept marginalization or, in contrast, play along with the subculture's higher valuation of technological means of data collection. Both options end up placing sensitives in a disempowered role relative to those investigators who rely exclusively on expensive gadgetry.

In the end, then, the status conflicts between scientists and sensitives within the paranormal investigation subculture both reflect and reproduce gendered and economic structures of inequality that exist in the larger culture. To counter cultural representations that portray paranormal investigation as childish, pseudoscientific, or mentally ill, leaders within the subculture strive to reframe their practice as pioneering science. In doing so, they marginalize nonscientific claims by those who—by inclination or financial inability—do not play into this narrative. As a consequence, the voices of women and the economically disadvantaged are subordinated to those of middle-class men. Haunted by the specter of invalidation by mainstream scientists—the new priests in this era of scientism—these subcultural elites reproduce within the subculture the historical disadvantages faced by women and the poor in the broader culture. Members of these groups must play along or be cast aside in this scramble for scientific legitimacy.

REFERENCES

Bartky, Sandra. 1990. *Femininity and Domination: Studies in the Phenomenology of Oppression*. New York: Routledge.
Bellah, Robert, Richard Madsen, William M. Sullivan, Ann Swidler, and Steven M. Tipton. 1985. *Habits of the Heart: Individualism and Commitment in American Life*. Berkeley: University of California Press.
Blum, Deborah. 2006. *Ghost Hunters: William James and the Search for Scientific Proof of Life after Death*. New York: Penguin Press.
Braudy, Leo. 2016. *Haunted: On Ghosts, Witches, Vampires, Zombies, and Other Monsters of the Natural and Supernatural Worlds*. New Haven, CT: Yale University Press.
Bruce, Steve. 2002. *God Is Dead: Secularization in the West*. Oxford, UK: Blackwell.
———. 2011. *Secularization: In Defence of an Unfashionable Theory*. Oxford: Oxford University Press.
Clarke, Roger. 2012. *A Natural History of Ghosts: 500 Years of Hunting for Proof*. London: Penguin Books.
Connell, R. W. 2005. *Masculinities*. 2nd ed. Berkeley: University of California Press.
Davie, Grace. 1994. *Religion in Britain since 1945: Believing without Belonging*. Oxford, UK: Blackwell.
Eaton, Marc A. 2015. "'Give Us a Sign of Your Presence': Paranormal Investigation as a Spiritual Practice." *Sociology of Religion* 76 (4): 389–412.
Ellis, Bill. 1989. "Death by Folklore: Ostension, Contemporary Legend, and Murder." *Western Folklore* 48 (3): 201–220.

Finucane, R. C. 1996. *Ghosts: Appearances of the Dead and Cultural Transformation*. Amherst, NY: Prometheus Books.
Fuller, Robert C. 2001. *Spiritual but Not Religious: Understanding Unchurched America*. New York: Oxford University Press.
Goode, Erich. 2013. "Paranormalism and Pseudoscience as Deviance." In *Philosophy of Pseudoscience: Reconsidering the Demarcation Problem*, edited by M. Pigliucci and M. Boudry, 145–163. Chicago: University of Chicago Press.
Heelas, Paul, and Linda Woodhead. 2005. *The Spiritual Revolution: Why Religion Is Giving Way to Spirituality*. Malden, MA: Blackwell.
Hewitt, John P., and Randall Stokes. 1975. "Disclaimers." *American Sociological Review* 40 (1): 1–11.
Hines, Terrence. 2003. *Pseudoscience and the Paranormal*. Amherst, NY: Prometheus Books.
Kaufmann, Eric, Anne Goujon, and Vegard Skirbekk. 2012. "The End of Secularization in Europe? A Socio-demographic Perspective." *Sociology of Religion* 73 (1): 69–91.
Mercadante, Linda A. 2014. *Belief without Borders: Inside the Minds of the Spiritual but Not Religious*. Oxford: Oxford University Press.
Orwell, George. 1946. *Animal Farm*. New York: Harcourt Brace.
Pew Research Center. 2015. "America's Changing Religious Landscape." Available at http://www.pewforum.org/2015/05/12/americas-changing-religious-landscape.
Scruton, Roger. 2016. "Scientism and the Humanities." In *Scientism: The New Orthodoxy*, edited by R. N. Williams and D. N. Robinson, 131–146. London: Bloomsbury Academic.
Thompson, Robert C. 2010. "'Am I Going to See a Ghost Tonight?': Gettysburg Ghost Tours and the Performance of Belief." *Journal of American Culture* 33 (2): 79–91.
Weisberg, Barbara. 2005. *Talking to the Dead: Kate and Maggie Fox and the Rise of Spiritualism*. New York: HarperCollins.
Williams, Richard N. 2016. "Introduction." In *Scientism: The New Orthodoxy*, edited by R. N. Williams and D. N. Robinson, 1–21. London: Bloomsbury Academic.

5

THE ALLURE OF DARK TOURISM

Legend Tripping and Ghost Seeking in Dark Places

RACHAEL IRONSIDE

The Grey Friars Kirk of Edinburgh is the site of one of Scotland's bloodiest battles of the seventeenth century. It is also where the country's most notorious poltergeist is said to lurk and is considered by some to be the "scariest place on earth" (Edwards 2014). The Black Mausoleum in the kirkyard is the resting place of Sir George Mackenzie, nicknamed Bloody Mackenzie for his role in the persecution of the Covenantors under the rule of King Charles II. It is estimated that Bloody Mackenzie was responsible for upward of eighteen thousand deaths of his fellow countrymen, many of whom were tortured before being buried in the same kirkyard in which Mackenzie ultimately found his resting place. Legend tells of an incident in 1998 when a local homeless man broke into the Black Mausoleum to seek shelter from bad weather. During the night the man reportedly began vandalizing the tomb. The ground below him opened up, and he fell into a pit of plague victim remains buried below the structure. Terrified, the man fled the scene, never to be heard from again. A few days later unusual activity started to occur around the mausoleum: one women passing the tomb was blasted backward by a cold force, and another was found unconscious beside the structure with unusual bruising and marks on her neck. Since then there have been over five hundred reported incidents of what is believed to be the disturbed poltergeist of Bloody Mackenzie returning to seek revenge on the living.

Walking down the cobbled streets of the Royal Mile in Edinburgh, it is not unusual to come across several tours offering the opportunity to hear about, and possibly encounter, the city's haunted past. The legend of the Mackenzie poltergeist is, however, somewhat iconic among both locals and visitors. Even before the ghostly activity was reported, the resting place of Bloody Mackenzie was considered to have supernatural properties; local children dared each other to knock on the tomb's door and chant, "Bluidy Mackingie, come oot if ye daur, lift the sneck and draw the bar!" The challenge would be to run away from the tomb before Mackenzie rose from his grave. Fear of visiting the site has been further fueled by reported supernatural attacks, and of the numerous reputedly haunted locations in Edinburgh, the Black Mausoleum is considered the scariest of all. Nevertheless, the site is a popular destination for locals and tourists hoping to experience the poltergeist legend.

The legend of the Mackenzie poltergeist is typical of the supernatural folklore associated with many urban areas. Indeed, people commonly grow up with local legends of the abandoned haunted house at the end of the road, the cave in the woods where a witch was once said to live, or some similar supernatural story that was once told—and perhaps still is. These tales often have an attached warning, accompanied by a story of a victim who dared to question the legend and met a perilous end. As explored by Elizabeth Bird (1994), these legends often develop around particular types of places such as cemeteries, abandoned buildings, bridges, and unusual graves. As observed by several folklorists (Bird 1994; Ellis 1996b; Holly and Cordy 2007), these sites can become a popular attraction for those interested in legend tripping.

Bill Ellis (1996b) defined legend tripping as an excursion to places where something uncanny has allegedly occurred with the intention of experiencing something supernatural. Legend tripping is often associated with adolescents who, after a few drinks and some scary stories, may decide to visit such a site to test the legend's credibility. For example, Bird (1994) describes how youths visiting the Black Angel monument in Iowa City regularly engage in rituals and activities to test the veracity of a legend that warns of death to those who kiss the angel statue. Likewise, Donald H. Holly Jr. and Casey E. Cordy (2007) note that visitors to purported vampire graves in Rhode Island attempt to summon the vampires' spirits by vandalizing and performing sexual acts on the tombs. The Mackenzie poltergeist site has experienced similar forms of legend tripping. Most dramatic was the 2004 arrest of two teenage boys who broke into the tomb and cut the head off a corpse in the mausoleum, before playing with it in the grounds of the kirkyard (Scott 2004). It is perhaps unsurprising then that Mackenzie's ghost remains restless.

The motivations to legend trip vary. In the case of the Black Angel monument and Rhode Island graves, adolescents were testing the legend. As discussed by Holly and Cordy, this often involves activities designed to "invoke supernatural powers," including performing séances, making offerings, and other rituals related to the legend (2007: 345). For young people these activities can be a "ritual of rebellion" (Ellis 1996a: 438) and "rite of passage" (Bird 1994: 203). Legend tripping provides an opportunity to rebel against the rules and laws implied by normality and engage in activities that play with notions of reality. In these instances the legends often pertain to issues such as morality, death, sex, grief, and identity. As discussed by Bird (1994), taking part in these activities may provide an opportunity for young people to confront adult concerns and anxieties through these rituals and forms of play.

For others, participating in legend tripping may have more nefarious motives. In his discussion on adolescents and cult activity, Ellis (1996b), describes how vandalism, graffiti, and the mutilation of animals may have a role in the ostensive play that forms part of the legend trip. Ellis further discusses how such actions can lead to "satanic rumour-panics" as communities and authorities associate such activity with satanic practices—whereas, in reality, youths are rarely engaging in more than hoaxes and role playing (1996b: 168). There are, however, occasions when the vandalism of graves, desecration of burial sites, and exhumation of corpses (such as the mausoleum example previously mentioned) do form part of legend-tripping activities. An unfortunate example of this is provided by Dennis and Michele Waskul (2016), who discuss the vandalism of tombstones in Loon Lake Cemetery. The desecration of the cemetery is said to be due to its being thought of as a "witch's graveyard" and the ghostly legends that have emerged from this.

While these motives suggest a more complex desire to legend trip, it should be acknowledged that recreation and fun are also widely understood to be reasons for participation. Legend tripping may be considered "a form of entertainment" (Ellis 1996b: 438), as individuals engage in a "conscious suspension of reality in the interest of fun" (Holly and Cordy 2007: 346). The potential for a supernatural encounter carries with it exciting and frightening possibilities, much like watching a scary movie or going to a haunted house around the time of Halloween. Moreover, legend tripping offers participants the ability to temporarily escape the mundane and re-enchant the everyday world through the exploration of such legends (see also Chapter 10).

Legend tripping has long been popular in adolescent subcultures and among other thrill seekers. However, the number of organizations that offer the opportunity to engage in this activity through structured, commercialized experiences has recently significantly risen. The City of the Dead Tours in Edinburgh, for instance, offer brave tourists the opportunity to experience the Mackenzie poltergeist for themselves, stating that "an encounter with the poltergeist is the highlight of the tour, with hundreds of people claiming to have been attacked by the entity" (City of the Dead, n.d.). On their digital media sites these tour companies also display photos of some tour participants who have suffered scratching and bruising as a result of their visit. Legend tripping has become big business, with Dracula tourism attracting over 250,000 visitors to Romania annually (Jamal and Tanase 2005), figures suggesting that the Loch Ness monster is worth £25 million to the local economy (32.3 million in US dollars; "Scotland Sets Up" 2014), and ghost tour operators across the United States reporting over 100,000 visitors per year (Saladino 2015).

This chapter explores the commercialization of legend tripping. I first investigate how sites associated with death and tragedy have metamorphosed into dark tourist attractions. Next, I discuss how certain dark destinations use ghost legends as a commercial strategy and examine the reasons that visitors engage in commercial ghost tourism activities. This analysis is informed by a decade of my participation in commercialized legend trips and interviews with ghost tourism participants and organizers. Ultimately, I conclude that the commercialization of dark sites and their ghostly legends provides visitors the opportunity to confront troublesome events of the past and existential questions of the future.

DARK TOURISM

In the winter of 2016 I took a road trip with my husband and a couple of friends to Peterhead, in northeast Scotland. The purpose of our trip was a visit to the newly reopened former Peterhead Prison. Before its closure in December 2013, the prison was well known for incarcerating some of the worst criminals in the country. As we arrived we found ourselves walking through the original reception area, which would have "welcomed" new inmates; our experience, however, was much friendlier. We were greeted by staff who handed each of us an audio guide that gave us a detailed tour of the prison. As we walked the grounds of Peterhead, the guide described prison life and told grisly tales of fights, hostage situations, and murders that had taken place during the prison's 125-year history. We had a chance to hear fascinating accounts of prison life from a former guard who was held hostage during a notorious riot in 1987. Guides also showed us a cell in which an unnamed inmate had a workshop in which he created children's toys. There was something quite sinister about the solitary children's toy placed in the room, and the mystery was heightened by the ambiguity of the prisoner's identity. On the way home, we all spun stories and legends of our own, guessing at the dark memories that were trapped within the cold stone walls of this cell and the many others we toured that day. We were caught up in the macabre history of Peterhead Prison, engaged in the creation of lore about a site that had been anything but fascinating to those who had inhabited it only a few years prior. In short, on this day we were the epitome of "dark tourists."

The definition of "dark tourism" has been debated by several researchers, but it is generally defined as tourism to "sites associated with death, suffering and the seemingly macabre" (Stone 2006: 146). It has also been called "thanotourism" (Seaton 1996: 234), "morbid tourism" (Blom 2000: 29), and "black-spot tourism" (Rojek 1993: 142). The term, while fairly new in academic research, has grown in notoriety in recent years as the popularity of dark tourism sites has increased with the now commonplace commercialization of death and tragedy (Coldwell 2013). Perhaps some of the best-known dark tourism hotspots include Auschwitz-Birkenau, the Cambodian killing fields, and Ground Zero; however, sites may also include places like castles, old hospitals, and graveyards. Around the globe, destinations promote sites of death and suffering to entice visitors. Indeed, as explored in Raymond Powell and Katia Iankova's (2016) study, London's dark sites (including the London Dungeon and Tower Bridge Experience) are some of the most popular in the area and significant boosters for the local economy. Auschwitz-Birkenau has also seen a significant rise in tourism in recent years, attracting over two million visitors in 2016 ("Auschwitz" 2016). Similarly, twenty-three million people have visited the Ground Zero memorial since its opening in 2011 (9/11 Memorial 2015).

As identified by several researchers (Sharpley 2005; Stone 2006), not all dark sites are the same, and they could be considered to exist on a spectrum of darkness, with sites associated with death (such as museums and reenactments) at the lightest end and sites of death (such as concentration camps and locations of genocide) at the darkest end (Stone 2006). As Phillip Stone (2006) discusses further, different forms of dark tourism can be identified along this spectrum. At the lighter end, "Dark Fun Factories" cater to providing entertaining experiences of macabre events, and at the darkest edges "Dark Camps of Genocide" present the opportunity to reflect on events of "genocide, atrocity and catastrophe" (157). Thus, visitors may be motivated to take part in dark tourism for reasons including remembrance (Dunkley Morgan, and Westwood 2011; Yuill 2003), entertainment (Stone 2009; Walby and Piché 2011), and curiosity (Bigley et al. 2010; Yuill 2003).

While the commercialization of death for the consumption of modern-day tourists is a fairly recent phenomenon, the desire to visit places of death and suffering is not new. In fact, bearing witness to suffering and death has long been a form of entertainment, commemoration, and condemnation. The gladiatorial games of ancient Rome, for instance, provided a spectacle of death that attracted a significant audience. As a form of entertainment, these bloody games distracted the audience members from their own hardships and reminded them of the power wielded by their rulers. Pilgrimages to sites of burial and death constitute a second form of witnessing. For thousands of years, humans have made ritualized journeys to sacred burial grounds to honor the dead and reflect on their own mortality. Lastly, public executions have a long history as a method of social control. Whether they were intended to condemn those who violated the most fundamental moral principles of a society or to frighten an entire population into submission, these public displays of deadly force offered witnesses a morality tale about the ultimate cost of deviating from social norms and values. In each of these three forms of bearing witness, the reality of death is openly acknowledged and—in the cases of gladiatorial games and executions—directly observed. This is in stark contrast to today's dark tourism, which maintains a distance between death and the tourist.

For most people in Western society, the thought of witnessing death is now an abhorrent and unthinkable prospect, particularly on the grisly scale often associated with dark sites. Indeed, as discussed by Phillipe Aries (1981), death is somewhat invisible in westernized society. It is hidden away from the public gaze, quietly dealt with behind the doors of medical facilities, religious institutions, and funeral homes. Stone (2012) suggests that these practices have led society into death denying, in which people are preoccupied with preserving life rather than embracing the inevitability of death. Others, such as Bob Pagliari (2004), argue that dark tourism contributes to a state of death deriding, in which entertainment and commercial outlets offer paying customers an opportunity to vicariously experience death. The increasing popularity of dark tourism is considered by some to be a reaction to this increased distance between death and the individual (Stone and Sharpley 2008; Stone 2012). By creating sites that enable tourists to learn about and gaze on the past death of others, dark tourism provides a mechanism through which death in modern society may be both confronted and held at arm's length.

As one might expect, the commercialization of sites of suffering and death is controversial. Critics are especially sensitive to the commercial exploitation of events that could be considered at the darkest end of spectrum (Stone 2006), such as mass atrocities or recent disasters that resulted in massive casualties. An article in *National Geographic*, titled "Is 'Dark Tourism' OK?," frames dark tourism as disrespectful and voyeuristic (Reid 2016). It describes a trend of taking selfies at dark sites and recounts how Justin Bieber referred to Anne Frank as a "Belieber" during his visit to the Anne Frank House. In contrast, Roxanna Magee and Audrey Gilmore (2015) claim that the experience of visiting dark tourist sites is nonetheless important, in that it facilitates personal consideration of the meanings of tragic events. Thus, sites should supply dark history and events to consumers in a way that is sensitive to their context but that also provides the engaging and potentially transformative experience tourists are seeking.

One way that dark tourism is increasingly managed is through engagement with legends attached to the location. Legend tripping at dark sites is not actively recognized as a motivation in the current dark tourism literature, but supernatural stories are regularly used by certain sites to attract tourists. Dark legend tripping could be considered at the lighter end of Phillip Stone's (2006) dark tourism spectrum, with entertainment often at the forefront of the experience supplied to tourists. Two examples of this include the emergence of Dracula tourism in Romania and the attractions created around the Salem Witch trials in the United States (Bristow and Newman 2004). In both cases, destinations have capitalized on the historic legends and stories attached to place in order to present dark events in a compelling but acceptable way (at least for the tourist). Through the commercialization of legends at dark sites, tourists' experience of encountering the death of others—and reflecting on their own mortality—is mediated through forms of entertainment, education, and a more structured form of legend tripping. During my research, I have observed this strategy being increasingly adopted by dark sites with a particular focus on the commercialization of ghostly legends and encounters.

GHOST SEEKING IN DARK PLACES

Following my visit to Peterhead Prison I learned that in the short time it had been open the attraction had already hosted a Halloween event at which visitors were invited to tour the prison at night.[1] On that Halloween the ghostly potential of the prison was sold to visitors as an opportunity to experience "screams in the night and fleeting images of former inmates now long gone" (Eventbrite, n.d.). A couple of months later I learned that a local paranormal group had investigated the site and that the reality-style ghost hunting television show *Most Haunted* would be filming an episode in the prison. It is apparent that Peterhead Prison has already begun harnessing the economic potential of its dark history.

The association between dark sites and ghost seeking is not unusual and perhaps somewhat expected. After all, throughout history, ghosts have been associated with sites of tragedy, death, and suffering. They are, thus, almost intrinsically linked with sites that are dark in nature. However, in the last ten to fifteen years there has been an increased commercialization of not only

---

1. Peterhead Prison opened its doors to the paying public in June 2016 and hosted its first Halloween event on Friday, October 28, 2016.

the dark heritage of these sites but the resident ghosts that haunt them. Dennis Waskul defines these as "commercial ghosts" (see Chapter 3), and their popularity has led to an increased interest and participation in ghost tourism.

Ghost tourism is defined by Beatriz Rodriguez Garcia as "the desire to encounter ghosts, interest in the supernatural, and visitation of places associated with the spirit world such as cemeteries, haunted houses, castles, and historic towns" (2012: 14). It is worth noting that ghosts as an attraction are not necessarily a new phenomenon; for instance, the case of the Cock Lane Ghost in 1762 drew substantial crowds to a small lane in London. As a result, businesses in the area benefited significantly from the increased trade. Similarly, the Fox sisters—most notable for starting the Spiritualist movement in the United States—attracted many people to their small family home in upstate New York with their claims that they could communicate with the spirit of a murdered peddler via rapping on walls and furniture. This led to a financially lucrative nationwide tour for the three sisters—Maggie, Kate, and Leah—throughout the latter half of the nineteenth century (Weisberg 2005). Historically these cases were fairly infrequent, but in recent years a growing number of businesses and organizations have started offering ghost-related services and experiences (Locker 2014).

The popularization of ghost tourism is undoubtedly influenced by a concurrent supernatural boom in popular culture (see the Introduction). In 2002, the British reality television series *Most Haunted* introduced the notion of amateur paranormal investigation to a broader audience. It was quickly followed by several more shows that focused on the real-life activities of paranormal investigators, including *Ghost Hunters* (debuting in 2004) and *Ghost Adventures* (debuting in 2008). Influenced by these shows, amateur paranormal groups also began to form. Over the past decade the number of paranormal investigation teams has substantially increased, with current figures suggesting that there are approximately 2,500 groups in the United Kingdom (Hill 2010) and upward of 4,000 in the United States as of May 2017 (see http://paranormalsocieties.com; also see Chapter 4). The emergence of television shows dramatizing ghost hunting and the resulting explosion of paranormal investigation groups have driven increased interest in ghost tourism. This broad category actually takes several forms, which I now describe.

Ghost Walks and Tours

Perhaps the best-known and most popular form of ghost tourism is the ghost walks or tours that are offered in many cities and towns. The cities of York, England, and Edinburgh, Scotland, each have five tours operating under different organizations. As observed by Garcia (2012), ghost walks offer a similar structure, often involving up to thirty guests being taken on a guided walking route and being told ghost stories at landmarks. It should be noted, however, that the ghost tour experience has now evolved beyond just walking tours, with businesses providing ghost boat tours (such as the Dell's Ghost Boat in Wisconsin) and haunted bus tours (such as the Ghost Bus Tours in York).

During ghost tours there is often an emphasis on humor and, as discussed by Robert Thompson, a "nip and bite" of playfulness in the stories that are told (2010: 82). On the ghost walks I attended, guides would regularly recruit an audience member to humorously reenact the gruesome final moments of characters from their stories. For instance, one tour guide illustrated the details of a grisly death by pulling fake guts from an audience member's stomach while asking another to hold them, much to the amusement of the crowd. By engaging audiences in this way guides present serious stories (often associated with death and suffering) in a not-so-serious way. The performative elements of the ghost walks and tours are important because they enable guests to engage with the dark history of a place in ways that are lighthearted and unthreatening (Gentry 2007).

Ghost Hunting

Following the success of popular paranormal investigating television shows in Britain and the United States, numerous organizations began offering public ghost hunting experiences—for a price. These events usually involve participants taking part in ghost vigils, using paranormal equipment, conducting séances, and staying overnight in a reputedly haunted building. While several organizations have come and gone over the past ten to fifteen years, some of the longer-standing and successful businesses in the United Kingdom and United States include Haunted Happenings, Fright Nights, and Ghost Hunts USA.

When I first started my research, a visitor interested in attending a ghost hunt would have been charged between $90 and $130 per person to stay overnight in a supposedly haunted building and take part in ghost hunting activities. However, over the last ten years the number of businesses offering these services has increased significantly, leading to increased competition. As a result, it could be argued that the distinction once offered by selling a ghost experience has been reduced, and in line with this, the cost of attending such events has also decreased. Currently, you might pay $30–$50 to attend, perhaps more if an overnight stay is involved. Furthermore, because of the high number of ghost hunts that are now available, the experience itself is somewhat standardized, reducing the mystery and intrigue one might expect from participating. In fact, Garcia (2012) argues it is the predictability and repeatability of paranormal experiences that make them commercially viable to begin with. Through the commercialization and standardization of ghost hunts, ghosts and their stories are now a commodified item.

In addition to commercial ghost hunting events, paranormal investigation teams may also offer the public the opportunity to join them on a ghost hunt. These teams often distance themselves from the commercial and entertainment side of ghost hunting to present themselves as serious researchers. However, particularly around Halloween, some teams may charge the public between $20 and $40 to join an investigation, with proceeds going to purchasing additional research equipment or paying for travel expenses. To celebrate and recognize the heightened interest in ghost hunting, a worldwide National Ghost Hunting Day was also established on October 1, 2016.

Haunted Accommodations

It is now common for accommodation providers to capitalize on the haunted reputation engendered by folklore, the media, or the findings generated from ghost hunting groups. Indeed, the status of being the most-haunted accommodation in an area is used frequently as a marketing strategy. Perhaps one of the most famous examples of this in America is the Stanley Hotel, the setting for Stephen King's *The Shining*. Inspired by the rumored haunting of the Stanley Hotel, *The Shining* novel and subsequent film continue to attract to the hotel visitors interested in experiencing one of its resident ghosts. The hotel actively promotes its haunted reputation and claims its haunted rooms are "among our most-requested rooms, [so] availability is limited" (Stanley Hotel 2017). The hotel also offers guests the opportunity to take part in paid theatrical séances ($20), paranormal investigations ($55), and evening ghost tours ($25) (Saladino 2015). Other examples of accommodations capitalizing on their alleged hauntings include the Golden Fleece Inn in York, England, which actively promotes itself as "York's most haunted pub," (Haunted Rooms, n.d.) and the 1886 Crescent Hotel and Spa in Eureka Springs, Arkansas, which markets itself as "America's Most Haunted Hotel."[2] Websites and guides such as http://hauntedrooms.com and the *Telegraph*'s "The World's Most Haunted Hotels" (2017) guide also help visitors find haunted accommodations. In these instances, ghosts are seen by accommodation providers as enhancing their desirability while offering distinction in a competitive market (Mathe-Soulek, Aguirre, and Dallinger 2016). Rather than deter guests, as Frances Kermeen discusses in her reflection on buying a haunted inn, "Ghosts turned out to be the greatest possible attraction" (2002: 1).

---

2. See its website, at http://www.americasmosthauntedhotel.com.

Haunted Attractions

In contrast to ghost walks that take tourists to haunted sites and tell spooky stories, other attractions allow visitors to interact with the supernatural in a museum setting. For instance, tourists can visit Lorraine and Edward Warren's Occult Museum, Zak Bagans's Haunted Museum, and John Zaffis's Museum of the Paranormal—all of which feature artifacts believed to be haunted or possessed by spirits. These objects are often sourced by the museums' curators or donated by their previous owners and come with their own haunted stories. The museums offer visitors tours of haunted objects in addition to selling merchandise such as clothing, books, and videos related to the collections and owners. Collections such as the *Traveling Museum of the Paranormal and the Occult* can also be booked by event organizers to "enhance your event," providing guests with the opportunity to hold and interact with notorious haunted objects (Traveling Museum of the Paranormal and the Occult 2017).

Films such as *The Conjuring* (2013), *Annabelle* (2014), and *The Possession* (2012) and television shows like *Haunted Collector* (2011–2013) and *Deadly Possessions* (2016–present) have further stoked interest in haunted objects. These shows elevate some objects to celebrity status, making the ability to see them in person an event akin to meeting the stars of these shows. To capitalize on this public interest, Zak Bagans—host of *Ghost Adventures*—has opened a Haunted Museum in Las Vegas. This museum houses some of the most renowned haunted objects popularized by film and television. Opened in 2017, the museum generated much excitement, as expressed by one social media user, who wrote, "Holy Mary Mother of God!! First Peggy the Doll now the Dybbuk Box!! Please OPEN SOON!! #RoadTrip" (Grace 2017). These collections allow visitors to experience the supernatural firsthand, to directly engage with physical artifacts that make the ghostly legends with which they are associated seem all the more real.

Haunted Places

Increasingly, cities and towns are marketing themselves as paranormal hotspots. York, England, claimed the title of Most Haunted City in the World in 2014, with over 504 recorded hauntings (BBC 2014), and Pluckley's status as the Most Haunted Village in England rests on a claimed twelve to sixteen resident ghosts in 2008 (Hoyles 2008). The most-haunted status of these destinations has become a central element of their tourism strategy; rather than hiding or explaining away their haunted histories, these cities and towns advertise and promote tourist attractions related to this ghoulish lore.

As discussed by Jeannie Thomas, ghost legends may play a role in presenting the dark and sometimes shameful history of locations by "amplifying historical events by using the supernatural to indicate how these events (and the institutions from which they stemmed) continue to haunt a whole city" (2015: 45). Destinations such as New Orleans use ghost legends to present narratives about slavery (Thomas 2015), and Gettysburg actively promotes its haunted past as a mechanism to discuss the horrors of the battles that took place there (Thompson 2010). Thus, ghosts act as a marketing tool for destinations and also provide visitors and locals alike a means by which they can confront the horrors of such tragic events.

Self-Guided Supernatural Tours

A fairly new addition to the ghost tourism field is the concept of self-guided supernatural tours. These involve road trips or destination visits based on recommended routes that string together multiple supernatural hot spots. For instance, you can now access haunted travel guides through the America's Haunted Road Trip website (http://americashauntedroadtrip.com) and Roadtrippers Ghost Guide (Roadtrippers 2017). These sites provide visitors with information and advice for the self-guided ghost hunter. The America's Haunted Road Trip website has twenty-nine books for sale, each featuring stories on haunted sites within a given city, state, or region in the United States. The books are aimed at travelers interested in exploring the supernatural, and as the back cover of one guidebook states, "[Travelers] don't need to be a professional ghosthunter to explore the scariest spots in Colorado" (Lamb 2016). Similarly, the Roadtrippers Ghost Guide offers free online advice for visiting haunted locations in the United States, including ghost cities, haunted graves, and haunted roads. These more formal resources are in addition to an abundance of blogs and articles that provide information on ghostly locations to visit. In essence, self-guided tours offer tourists packaged forms of legend tripping akin to the ghost tours described above but with the added excitement of feeling as though you are blazing your own trail in search of the supernatural.

VISITOR MOTIVATIONS AND THE GHOST TOURISM EXPERIENCE

It is evident that ghost tourism has been adopted as a commercial strategy by dark sites and destinations. However, to fully understand the success of ghost tourism we should also consider why visitors are motivated to spend money on such experiences. During the last ten years, I attended over twenty paid ghost hunting events as a customer; for three years I have helped host and orchestrate ghost walks and hunts. Throughout this experience, I was always struck by not only their popularity but also the broad demographics that take part in these activities. Allow me to illustrate with an ethnographic description of one such experience during a typical ghost hunt.

The day starts as it does for any normal ghost hunting event. The regular trip to the supermarket to collect essentials, including cookies and soft drinks to keep up through the early hours and a late-night sandwich—everything I need to host an event at a reputedly haunted property in York, at 35 Stonegate. The property is well known for its haunted reputation and during the day invites visitors for a spooky audio tour, including its notorious séance room.[3] I am particularly excited about this opportunity. The building is fairly iconic in York for its ghost stories and, while I had been on the daytime audio tour, the prospect of spending the night is exciting.

I arrive at the venue in late afternoon and am met by representatives of the events company and the main host for the evening, a well-known medium. After getting to know the venue, we start setting up the tea and coffee facilities for the fifteen or so guests arriving at 7:00 P.M.—a mix of both male and female, young and old, believers and skeptics. To start the event the host gathers everyone for an opening-up and protection session: guests are asked to close their eyes and imagine a white light around them, and afterward the host invites the spirits of the house to communicate with the group. Following this ritual, the lights are turned off and we split into two groups. The group I am with heads up to the séance room, while the other group continues exploring downstairs. When we are all seated around the séance table the medium continues to ask for any communication from spirits in the building and encourages guests to speak up if they feel anything. A few people report feeling cold, sensing someone walking behind them around the table, or hearing mysterious taps and bangs. Throughout the night we spend time in each room in the property, inviting the spirits to communicate with us. Guests continue to report unusual sounds or feelings and occasionally claim they see figures or shadows in their peripheral vision. At one point, a guest even feels like the cupboard doors that she is standing in front of open and hit her on the back. The medium confirms and substantiates these claims, offering explanations and a description of the ghost that might have caused it. Although a full apparition did not appear to the group, by the end

---

3. Since my doctoral studies I have been keen to continue my involvement in paranormal events to ensure I am up to date with changes in the ghost hunting culture, and I managed to get involved with a paranormal events company that hosts ghost hunting evenings across the United Kingdom. It has proved to be an excellent opportunity to meet people participating in these events and to also observe supernatural experiences taking place.

of the event, collectively we had seemingly encountered several ghosts, and the guests seemed content with that.

This experience is typical of the ghost hunting events I observed during my research. Often participants also attempt to capture evidence of ghosts using electromagnetic frequency (EMF) meters, dowsing rods, audio recorders, and cameras. These activities are very much akin to the methods shown on supernatural television shows and used by paranormal investigation teams (see Chapter 4). At one event, I witnessed the host trying out a new method of spirit communication involving the group standing in a circle and holding a copper wire, with crystals hanging from it. The group was told that this helped generate energy and invited spirits into the circle. The activity was particularly immersive, and as the host asked the spirit to lift the copper wire, several of the group members' hands started to rise. Eventually, the wire was being held above the group's head as if influenced by a mysterious spiritual force.

The most striking feature of these events is the unreliability of having a ghostly encounter. As David Inglis and Mary Holmes (2003) observe, ghosts rarely appear on cue, and thus ghost hunts arguably sell an experience to visitors that cannot be guaranteed. Other forms of tourism, such as whale watching, also offer participants the possibility—but not the promise—of seeing something extraordinary. What makes ghost hunting different from these forms of sightseeing is that the ontological status of whales and other similar creatures is not in question. In contrast, ghost hunt participants must will themselves into believing in the very thing they are supposedly hunting despite being very unlikely to have an experience that confirms (in their minds, at least) the existence of ghosts. Nevertheless, I regularly saw repeat visitors on ghost hunts. Many guests are content with simply experiencing the exciting potential for something uncanny to occur, while others infer from cold spots or unexplained noises that they have indeed been in the presence of spirits.

Although a ghostly experience is not guaranteed, visitors and hosts I interviewed mention several reasons for their interest in such events. Many appreciate the opportunity to pay for an experience that lasts a short time but allows them to explore issues of spiritual significance. Ghost hunting events provide an environment to explore unconventional belief systems, particularly for those who feel disillusioned by traditional religious institutions and practices. As one interviewee who had been on numerous ghost hunts stated, "A lot of people are trying to find some sort of meaning to life and perhaps aren't seeing that or don't any longer follow conventional religion and therefore are looking for explanations in a different context." These spiritual motivations parallel Marc Eaton's findings in which he recognizes the rise of a spiritual "quest culture" and the increase in individuals who associate themselves as "spiritual but not religious" (2015: 390). Similar to the paranormal investigation groups that Eaton investigates, paid ghost hunting events present the opportunity to seek spirituality in a nonconventional way with the limited commitment that paying for a structured experience requires.

Frequently guests also say that ghost hunting events and walks give them a chance to consider deep moral questions. Ghost stories often present listeners with an opportunity to learn from their inherent moral lessons. One interviewee, Anna, says, "There's those traditional ghost stories that you get everywhere; every country's got one. It's a morality tale. . . . It's the murdered bride on her wedding day coming back to point the finger of blame at her husband, that sort of thing." James reinforces the same moral sentiment: "[Ghost] stories are reminders about how to live now rather than leave things unsaid or undone." Thus, ghost hunts and walks provide tourists an opportunity to reflect on their moral identities by considering the stories that are told to be a reminder, Amanda says, of the "tragic aspects of humanity" and a "warning . . . about how to live."

Taking part in ghost tourism is also considered an educational experience. These tours enable participants to connect with the past, to make "a human link to things which have happened," as James put it. Indeed, as Michelle Hanks (2011) observes, tourists will often recount historical tales they heard on ghost walks, and ghost tour guides consider the sharing of history to be an important part of their role. In this way, ghosts and their stories can act as a form of social memory (Richardson 2003) or mythicohistory (Malkki 1995). As Amanda stated, ghost tours offer "another fictionalization of history, another medium of telling a story about other people, about us, our ancestors." Ironically, the dead help history come alive for those who participate in ghost tourism.

In addition, beyond the benefits of storytelling, the prospect of actually seeing a ghost affords participants the ability to affirm deeper questions and validate prior experiences. The mixture of apprehension and anticipation felt by many visitors to ghost tourism attractions was expressed by George, who said he was "partly there to be entertained, to learn stuff" but also had "the slight thing in the back of [my] head that maybe I will see a ghost." For people like George, the potential of a ghostly encounter was simultaneously frightening and exciting, as it would be undeniable proof of some form of life after death. For others, ghost tourism offers a chance to better understand previous experiences. When asked why she attended a ghost hunt, Louise answered, "A few weird things have happened through my life . . . unexplained feelings, sensations, noises, that sort of thing, that makes you realize that there are things that we do not understand." For Louise and others like her, ghost tourism facilitates a shared experience of spiritual exploration.

During my time observing ghost hunts and ghost walks, it became evident that the creation of a successful ghost tourism experience is not solely based on the stories told. Of particular importance is the physical environment. Dark sites are often rich with history that is seemingly imprinted on the physical environment of these locations. The cobbled streets, ancient buildings, and winding paths of cities such as York or Edinburgh add potency to the ghostly tales told by tour guides. As one guide I interviewed in York said:

> Literally, ghost walks are not about driving from one battlefield many miles away to the other, but it is actually to walk in these historic surroundings, and I think this adds to the sensory advantages of the city—that you've got people that are in the dark, walking around, touching and feeling the atmosphere, listening with their other senses to the stories or in some cases the truth of what is being told.

The historic setting of ghost tourism lends an air of authenticity to the accounts retold by guides. The notion that a ghost might haunt a battlefield or look for its head at the site of a former guillotine is believable to many because these stories of violence and death align with our cultural constructions of why a location may be haunted. Likewise, claims that a ghost haunts a building with a dark history, such as Peterhead Prison, feel genuine for the same reason. Visitors to such locations often comment on features such as creaky floorboards, old furniture, and the original use of rooms still being apparent as indicators of a genuine ghostly location.[4]

During the ghost hunts and tours that I attended, the physical atmosphere of a place was frequently drawn on to reinforce its ghostly potential. The séance room that I previously mentioned is considered, due in part to the feeling engendered by the props in the room, the most supernaturally active at the location. These props include a crystal ball placed in the center of the table, Ouija boards scattered around the room, and red velvet curtains that engulf the room in darkness when drawn. Along with the stories told about the location, the presence of these occult-oriented objects in the séance room primed visitors to read supernatural causation into potentially natural phenomena like a cold breeze or creaking floor. Moreover, by adding to the perception that a place is haunted, these props also validate the historical importance of supposedly haunted locations (Inglis and Holmes 2003). As Sarah told me at a ghost hunting event, "My belief is that all old build-

---

4. There is also often a temporal dimension to ghost hunts, which are regularly scheduled at night because this is when we expect ghostly activity to occur.

ings hold history, including paranormal history. I don't think there would be many old buildings in York that don't have a ghost or two, whether that's recorded in their walls or drifting spirits."

In addition to the physical environment, the qualities of the guides and hosts of ghost tourism attractions are also an important factor in creating a successful experience. During the ghost walks and hunts I experienced, the hosts or guides are always present and adopt a prominent leadership role. They create a spooky atmosphere that facilitates sensory experiences of the supernatural through storytelling and costuming. Guides wear clothing appropriate to the era they are representing (frequently Victorian) and often carry props such as lanterns or walking sticks. Others carry photos containing orbs and wispy images that had been sent in by previous guests on the tours. The guides use these props to authenticate their stories and set the scene for a potential experience. Of the guides and hosts that I met, all were aware of the impact that their performance had on the experience and understood that they needed to appear genuine in their role. As reported by Thompson (2010), many ghost walk guides position themselves as genuinely interested in the possibility of ghosts while presenting stories that edged on humor. In doing so, they adopt a liminal position of both entertainer and supernatural enthusiast.

Alternatively, some hosts adopt a more serious role, presenting themselves as knowledgeable about the supernatural and, in the case of mediums, able to communicate with the spirit world. Performances taking this tack often include a demonstration of investigative equipment or a walk-around with mediums who demonstrate their clairvoyant abilities. Hosts encourage guests to open up their senses to the environment around them and, as one host said, occasionally lead guests into a "light hypnosis." The majority of events that I attended involved guests taking part in a protection ritual at the start of the evening in which they would be taken through a visual meditation, often involving the visualization of a white light surrounding their bodies (for a similar practice among paranormal investigators, see Eaton 2015).

The mind-set induced by a genuinely ghostly atmosphere and performance enables visitors to entertain the possibility that they may encounter the supernatural. By providing an environment in which disbelief is suspended, hosts and guides encourage visitors to immerse themselves in the legend trip and explore the "extraordinary possibility of place" (Holloway 2010: 628). My research made it apparent that darker legends increase the anticipation of this possibility and make sites with dark histories the biggest draws for ghost tourists. Sites associated with demonic hauntings or witchcraft are especially popular. For many years, the Ancient Ram Inn in Gloucestershire, England, hosted sold-out ghost hunting events after popular media reported that evidence of devil worship and the presence of a demonic force had been discovered at the inn. Likewise, sites such as the Hellfire Caves (England), Rolling Hills Asylum (United States), and the Edinburgh Vaults (Scotland) are popular ghost hunting venues because of their darker past. Even my visit to Peterhead Prison was enhanced by the darkness and mystery associated with the prison's history. For me and other ghost tourists, the dark—even evil—nature of these stories heightens the excitement as well as the perceived authenticity of alleged hauntings.

CONCLUSIONS

Legend tripping is a common activity that has traditionally been characterized by adolescent exploration of supernatural folklore for the purpose of testing the legends' credibility and demonstrating the adolescents' bravery in the face of supernatural danger. For others, legend tripping may entail more nefarious motives, as they seek to vandalize and desecrate places associated with these stories. Recently, legend tripping has been commercialized, perhaps most notably in the form of ghost tourism. For businesses and sometimes entire cities, local ghostly legends offer an opportunity to differentiate themselves in the market while also providing visitors with an opportunity to engage with these dark histories in ways that are exciting, experiential, and educational. For those participating in ghost hunts and tours, these activities are a unique way to explore issues of mortality, spirituality, and morality. Ghosts and their legends allow us to confront complex and potentially troubling questions about life and death. In a society so preoccupied with hiding the reality of death from public view, ghosts and dark places are a means by which we can engage with this reality as though witnessing it through a veil. In ghost tourism, death is right before our eyes and yet somehow just beyond our grasp.

REFERENCES

Aries, Phillipe. 1981. *The Hour of Our Death.* Translated by H. Weaver. Oxford: Oxford University Press.

"Auschwitz Sees Record Two Million Visitors in 2016." 2016. *Jewish News*, December 29. Available at http://jewishnews.timesofisrael.com/auschwitz-sees-record-two-million-visitors.

BBC. 2014. "York: Most Haunted City in the World!" Available at http://www.bbc.co.uk/northyorkshire/uncovered/ghost/most_haunted.shtml.

Bigley, James D., Choong-Ki Lee, Jinhyung Chon, and Yooshik Yoon. 2010. "Motivations for War-Related Tourism: A Case of DMZ Visitors in Korea." *Tourism Geographies* 12 (3): 371–394.

Bird, Elizabeth. 1994. "Playing with Fear: Interpreting the Adolescent Legend Trip." *Western Folklore* 53 (3): 191–209.
Blom, Thomas. 2000. "Morbid Tourism—a Postmodern Market Niche with an Example from Althorp." *Norsk Geografisk Tidsskrift* 54 (1): 29–36.
Bristow, Robert, and Mirella Newman. 2004. "Myth vs. Fact: An Exploration of Fright Tourism." In *Proceedings of the 2004 Northeastern Recreation Research Symposium*, edited by K. Bricker, 215–221. Bolton Landing, NY: U.S. Department of Agriculture.
City of the Dead. n.d. "City of the Dead Haunted Graveyard Tour." Available at http://www.cityofthedeadtours.com/tours/city-of-the-dead-haunted-graveyard-tour.
Coldwell, Will. 2013. "Dark Tourism: Why Murder Sites and Disaster Zones Are Proving Popular." *The Guardian*, October 31. Available at https://www.theguardian.com/travel/2013/oct/31/dark-tourism-murder-sites-disaster-zones.
Dunkley, Ria, Nigel Morgan, and Sheena Westwood. 2011. "Visiting the Trenches: Exploring Meanings and Motivations in Battlefield Tourism." *Tourism Management* 32 (4): 860–868.
Eaton, Marc. 2015. "'Give Us a Sign of Your Presence': Paranormal Investigation as a Spiritual Practice." *Sociology of Religion* 76 (4): 389–412.
Edwards, Garreth. 2014. "Edinburgh's Most Haunted: Mackenzie Poltergeist." *Edinburgh News*, October 31. Available at http://www.edinburghnews.scotsman.com/news/edinburgh-s-most-haunted-mackenzie-poltergeist-1-3590047.
Ellis, Bill. 1996a. "Legend Trip." In *American Folklore: An Encyclopedia*, edited by Jan Harold Brunvand, 438–440. New York: Garland.
———. 1996b. "Legend-Trips and Satanism: Adolescents' Ostensive Traditions as 'Cult' Activity." In *Contemporary Legend: A Reader*, edited by G. Bennet and P. Smith, 167–186. New York: Routledge.
Eventbrite. n.d. "Peterhead Prison Museum—Halloween Tour." Available at https://www.eventbrite.com/e/peterhead-prison-museum-halloween-tour-tickets-27540985830#.
Garcia, Beatriz Rodriguez. 2012. "Management Issues in Dark Tourism Attractions: The Case of Ghost Tours in Edinburgh and Toledo." *Journal of Unconventional Parks* 4 (1): 14–19.
Gentry, Glenn W. 2007. "Walking with the Dead: The Place of Ghost Walk Tourism in Savannah, Georgia." *Southeastern Geographer* 47 (2): 222–238.
Grace, Sookie. 2017. Twitter post, March 4. Available at https://twitter.com/hauntedmuseum.
Hanks, Michelle. 2011. "Re-imagining the National Past: Negotiating the Roles of Science, Religion, and History in Contemporary British Ghost Tourism." In *Contested Cultural Heritage*, edited by H. Silverman, 125–139. New York: Springer.
Haunted Rooms. n.d. "The Golden Fleece, York." Available at https://www.hauntedrooms.co.uk/product/the-golden-fleece-pub-york (accessed March 15, 2018).
Hill, Annette. 2010. *Paranormal Media: Audiences, Spirits and Magic in Popular Culture*. New York: Routledge.
Holloway, Julian. 2010. "Legend-Tripping in Spooky Spaces: Ghost Tourism and Infrastructures of Enchantment." *Environment and Planning D: Society and Space* 28 (4): 618–637.
Holly, Donald H., Jr., and Casey E. Cordy. 2007. "What's in a Coin? Reading the Material Culture of Legend Tripping and Other Activities." *Journal of American Folklore* 120 (477): 335–354.

Hoyles, Francesca. 2008. "Pluckley: The Most Haunted Village in England?" *The Telegraph*, October 30. Available at http://www.telegraph.co.uk/travel/destinations/europe/uk/3278642/Pluckley-the-most-haunted-village-in-England.html.
Inglis, David, and Mary Holmes. 2003. "Highland and Other Haunts: Ghosts in Scottish Tourism." *Annals of Tourism Research* 30 (1): 50–63.
Jamal, Tazim, and Aniela Tanase. 2005. "Impacts and Conflicts Surrounding Dracula Park, Romania: The Role of Sustainable Tourism Principles." *Journal of Sustainable Tourism* 13 (5): 440–455.
Kermeen, Frances. 2002. *Ghostly Encounters: True Stories of America's Haunted Inns and Hotels*. New York: Warner Books.
Lamb, Kailyn. 2016. *Ghost Hunting Colorado*. Covington, KY: Clerisy Press.
Locker, Melissa. 2014. "The Boo-tiful Business of Ghost Tourism." *Fortune*, October 31. Available at http://fortune.com/2014/10/31/the-boo-tiful-business-of-ghost-tourism.
Magee, Roxanna, and Audrey Gilmore. 2015. "Heritage Site Management: From Dark Tourism to Transformative Service Experience?" *Service Industries Journal* 35 (15–16): 898–917.
Malkki, Liisa. 1995. *Purity and Exile: Violence, Memory and National Cosmology among Hutu Refugees in Tanzania*. Chicago: University of Chicago Press.
Mathe-Soulek, Kimberley, Grant Aguirre, and Ioana Dallinger. 2016. "You Look like You've Seen a Ghost: A Preliminary Exploration in Price and Customer Satisfaction Differences at Haunted Hotel Properties." *Journal of Tourism Insights* 7 (1): 1–13.
9/11 Memorial. 2015. "Year in Review." Available at http://2015.911memorial.org.
Pagliari, Bob. 2004. "From a Death-Denying to a Death-Defying to a Death-Deriding Society." *Catholic New York*, April 1. Available at http://cny.org/stories/From-a-Death-Denying-to-a-Death-Defying-to-a-Death-Deriding-Society,450.
Powell, Raymond, and Katia Iankova. 2016. "Dark London: Dimensions and Characteristics of Dark Tourism Supply in the UK Capital." *Anatolia* 27 (3): 339–351.
Reid, Robert. 2016. "Is 'Dark Tourism' OK?" *National Geographic*, April 26. Available at http://www.nationalgeographic.com/travel/features/is-dark-tourism-ok-chernobyl-pripyat-disaster-sites.
Richardson, Judith. 2003. *Possessions: The History and Uses of Haunting in the Hudson Valley*. Cambridge, MA: Harvard University Press.
Roadtrippers. 2017. "Ghost Guides." Available at https://roadtrippers.com/collections/ghost-guides-and-tours-11.
Rojek, Chris. 1993. *Ways of Escape: Modern Transformations in Leisure and Travel*. London: Palgrave Macmillan UK.
Saladino, Emily. 2015. "How Haunted Hotels Turn Terror into Cash." *Bloomberg*, October 5. Available at https://www.bloomberg.com/news/articles/2015-10-05/how-haunted-hotels-turn-terror-into-cash.
"Scotland Sets Up Seminar to Assess How Much Money It Makes from the Mystery of the Loch Ness Monster." 2014. *Daily Mail*, April 24. Available at http://www.dailymail.co.uk/travel/article-2612305/Value-Loch-Ness-monster-tourism-industry-assessed-Scottish-seminar.html.
Scott, Kirsty. 2004. "Boys Avoid Jail for 'Violating' Tomb and Beheading Corpse." *The Guardian*, April 23. Available at https://www.theguardian.com/uk/2004/apr/24/ukcrime.scotland.
Seaton, Anthony. 1996. "Guided by the Dark: From Thanatopsis to Thanatourism." *International Journal of Heritage Studies* 2 (4): 234–244.

Sharpley, Richard. 2005. "Travels to the Edge of Darkness: Towards a Typology of Dark Tourism." In *Taking Tourism to the Limits: Issues, Concepts and Managerial Perspectives*, edited by M. Aitken, S. Page, and C. Ryan, 217–228. Oxford, UK: Elsevier.

Stanley Hotel. 2017. "Stanley Hotel." Available at http://www.stanleyhotel.com/hotel.html.

Stone, Phillip. 2006. "A Dark Tourism Spectrum: Towards a Typology of Death and Macabre Related Tourist Sites, Attractions and Exhibitions." *Turizam: Znanstveno-stručni časopis* 54 (2): 145–160.

———. 2009 "'It's Bloody Guide': Fun, Fear and a Lighter Side of Dark Tourism at the Dungeon Visitor Attractions, UK." In *The Darker Side of Travel: The Theory and Practice of Dark Tourism*, edited by R. Sharpley and P. Stone, 167–185. Bristol, UK: Channel View.

———. 2012. "Dark Tourism and Significant Other Death: Towards a Model of Mortality Mediation." *Annals of Tourism Research* 39 (3): 1565–1587.

Stone, Phillip, and Richard Sharpley. 2008. "Consuming Dark Tourism: A Thanatological Perspective." *Annals of Tourism Research* 35 (2): 574–595.

Thomas, Jeannie. 2015. *Putting the Supernatural in Its Place: Folklore, the Hypermodern and the Ethereal*. Salt Lake City: University of Utah Press.

Thompson, Robert. 2010. "'Am I Going to See a Ghost Tonight?' Gettysburg Ghost Tours and the Performance of Belief." *Journal of American Culture* 33 (2): 79–91.

Traveling Museum of the Paranormal and the Occult. 2017. "Booking the Traveling Museum." Available at http://paramuseum.com/booking-paranormal-museum.

Walby, Kevin, and Justin Piché. 2011. "The Polysemy of Punishment Memorialization: Dark Tourism and Ontario's Penal History Museums." *Punishment and Society* 13 (4): 451–472.

Waskul, Dennis, with Michele Waskul. 2016. *Ghostly Encounters: The Hauntings of Everyday Life*. Philadelphia: Temple University Press.

"The World's Most Haunted Hotels." 2017. *The Telegraph*, October 4. Available at http://www.telegraph.co.uk/travel/hotels/galleries/The-worlds-most-haunted-hotels.

Yuill, Stephanie Marie. 2003. "Dark Tourism: Understanding Visitor Motivation at Sites of Death and Disaster." Master's thesis, Texas A&M University, College Station.

6

"THE SPIRITS TELL ME THAT YOU'RE SEEKING HELP"

Fortune-Telling in Late Capitalism

Stephen L. Muzzatti

Emma M. Smith

In contemporary America people are inundated with mediated images of dizzying hyperwealth, a proliferation of rags-to-riches narratives, and relentless inducements to gamble on weekly lotteries with prizes in the tens of millions of dollars. Yet daily we are also confronted with the harsh realities of endless corporate cost cutting, the growing precariousness of work, an inadequate infrastructure, and a quickly eroding social safety net. Anxieties about employment and financial stability, health and wellness, personal safety, and international peace and security abound. At the mercy of global structural forces that few understand and even fewer can control, people desperately strive to bring a sense of order and tranquility to their lives. Thus, a growing number of people seek allies and answers in the supernatural world of fortune-telling and spiritual advising. This upsurge is reflected in IBISWorld's Psychic Services Market Research Report (2016), which outlines a 2.4 percent annual increase in revenue in the fortune-telling industry between 2011 and 2016.

This chapter examines the resurgence and expansion of fortune-telling as a supernatural industry under the prevailing conditions of late capitalism. Particular attention is paid to the role of the fortune-teller as a source of support, guidance, and aid in the context of liquid modernity. This chapter seeks to neither validate nor debunk the practice of fortune-telling. Rather, we contextualize fortune-telling, its practitioners, and those who seek their guidance within the framework of late capitalism in twenty-first-century America. To accomplish this, we begin with a brief overview of fortune-telling before turning to the social construction and history of the fortune-teller. Particular attention is paid to the Anglo-American sphere between the mid-late nineteenth and the late twentieth centuries. Our focus then shifts to the intersecting worlds of work and consumption under late capitalism, with due consideration given to the instability and anxiety of liquid modernity and how this fuels the demand for certainties about the future. This includes an exploration of consumer practices as the entry point to a critical evaluation of the positions of the fortune-teller as service provider and the seeker as a consumer.

LIQUID DREAMS AND UNCERTAIN FUTURES

Although incarnations of the capitalist economic system have existed for a few hundred years, the final decades of the twentieth century marked the true globalization of capitalism and the transformation of social life. This stage, termed "late capitalism" by Fredric Jameson (1991), saw new forms of transnational business and the mediatization of culture across the globe. It also brought with it doubt and uncertainty, as instability—economic, political, and social—ironically became one of the few remaining constants in life.

Building on Jameson's work, with a heavy emphasis on the impact of these economic and cultural shifts on the everyday worlds of ordinary people, Zygmunt Bauman (2000) coined the term "liquid modernity" to describe the unsettled character of life in the new millennium. According to Bauman (2000), modern life shifts so quickly that organization and stability are difficult to achieve and virtually impossible to sustain. This malaise of liquid modernity is characterized by feelings of uncertainty and insecurity about our daily interactions and future existence (Jock Young 2007). Liquid modernity offers little on which people can moor themselves. Our examination of the fortune-telling industry is informed by this societal reality, as people search for assurance and verification on the state of their lives.

Dreams of prosperity are liquefying and becoming less tangible. The Bureau of Labor Statistics reveals that real wages for people near the top of the income distribution in the United States increased 9.7 percent in 2014, whereas wages for the lowest earners continued to fall, by 3 percent (DeSilver 2014). In fact, for most workers, real wages have hardly increased for decades. The decline in living wage jobs, the precariousness of work and growing economic inequality over the past thirty years have reversed many of the economic and social gains made by ordinary Americans during the twentieth century. In many respects, as America charges through the second decade of the twenty-first century, its social, cultural, economic, and political conditions resemble the dangerous and uncertain landscape of the late nineteenth and early twentieth centuries (Alvaredo et al. 2013). Given these conditions, it is not surprising that our levels of collective uncertainty and social angst rival those of that earlier time, which equally saw a rise in the supernatural industry (Bauman 2007; Jock Young 2007).

THE FORTUNE-TELLER: A GUIDING VOICE

Fortune-telling involves the practices of prediction and counseling in areas of importance, concern, and uncertainty in a person's life. Although these services are not officially recognized as accredited mental health or social service initiatives, they do attempt to appease career, familial, and relationship woes as well as other fears about general well-being. The fortune-teller functions as an outlet for people to voice their most significant anxieties in exchange for immediate comfort. Practitioners and clients often subscribe to supernatural beliefs about mystic and spiritual powers, including communicating with the dead and predictive readings (Johnstone 2004). Those who seek the services of fortune-tellers are not unusual in this regard, as more than six in ten adults (65 percent) in the United States believe in the supernatural or have had experiences of engaging with psychic practices (Pew Research Center 2009).

Themes from conventional religious traditions (e.g., Judeo-Christian) are not necessarily incorporated into fortune-telling, as practitioners can conduct their readings in multiple venues, such as in private residences, at carnivals, or at public events. The channeling of future projections can be exercised in forms including astrology, dream analysis, numerology, palmistry, and phrenology (Johnstone 2004). Depending on the client's needs, multiple methods of prediction can be performed during one sitting. Spirit boards, crystal balls, cups, and tarot cards (see Chapter 7) are traditional tools used in fortune-telling.

As we soon address more fully, fortune-telling is commonly associated with the practices of the Roma people and the resurgence of Renaissance magic. Labeled as a pastime for the lower class, fortune-telling's many practitioners would adopt occult knowledge as a guiding principle in their daily lives. Over the centuries, fortune-telling methods have continued to expand and embrace cultural influences from Asia, Africa, and the Caribbean. Tasseography (reading the leaves), conducted for thousands of years in China, and voodoo (a spiritual observance common in West Africa, the Caribbean, and Louisiana; see Chapter 8) are examples of global predictive and mystical practices that are common among U.S. fortune-tellers (Johnstone 2004).

During their fieldwork, in a large Western city, Danny Jorgensen and Lin Jorgensen encountered what they termed an "esoteric community" (1982:

373) of diverse occult seekers, clients, and practitioners encompassing an array of beliefs and practices. Their study alone identified approximately a hundred groups involving as many as fifteen thousand people (Jorgensen and Jorgensen 1982). The intervening decades since Jorgensen and Jorgensen's research have seen a significant professionalization of fortune-telling services and service providers. This professionalization has included formalization through the creation of professional associations, complete with codes of ethics, in-service training programs, and pro bono outreach. One example of this formalization is the Association of Independent Readers and Rootworkers (AIRR). Convened in 2006, the AIRR consists of individuals who practice African American folk magic (hoodoo, conjure, rootwork, etc.). All members are required to graduate from a rootwork course and have two years of experience practicing in the field (AIRR 2017). Like the National Association of Psychic Practitioners, the American Association of Psychics and Psychic Mediums, and similar associations, the AIRR (2017) works to uphold an ethical standard within their profession and spread blessings, healings, and cleansings through different types of readings. Similar to law firms, the AIRR (2017) has established a Pro Bono Fund that distributes spiritual supplies (such as natural and handmade herbal teas, sprays, and oils) and services (free psychic readings) to low-income populations.

FORTUNE-TELLING IN HISTORY

The mysterious but wise fortune-teller, equipped with ancient knowledge, the gift of foresight, and magical healing powers—complete with a silky head covering and peculiar foreign accent—is a common trope of popular culture. Fortune-tellers are regularly caricatured in feature films (e.g., *Sherlock Holmes: A Game of Shadows* [2013], *Drag Me to Hell* [2009]), television programs (e.g., *Game of Thrones*, *Gotham*), comics and graphic novels (e.g., *Madame Xanadu*, *Starman*), and videogames (e.g., *Final Fantasy VII* [2013]). Common representations include the old, haggard, ambiguously Eastern European woman; the youthful, exotic beauty with highly problematic allusions to Gypsies (i.e., the Roma); or conversely, the middle-aged, vaguely racialized man with clipped-English speech, kind eyes, and other traits liberally borrowed from the plethora of stereotypes about servile colonial subjects from the Middle East or South Asia (Leland 2007). Irrespective of gender and ethnicity, seers are almost uniformly presented as marginal, both socially and economically, precariously earning their living through occult powers or stagecraft and sometimes both. Distinctly unsavory and borderline disreputable, the fortune-tellers of popular culture are frequently presented as playing on the fears of those who seek their counsel and providing deliberate misdirection. In other, somewhat more benign representations, fortune-tellers are portrayed as good-hearted and genuine—but ultimately unreliable—allies whose aid comes in the form of opaque half-truths and barely decipherable riddles.

While the fortune-teller character occasionally features prominently in the media's myriad fictionalized lifeworlds, as seen in Disney's *The Hunchback of Notre Dame* (1996) and *The Princess and the Frog* (2009), her or his presence is typically ancillary. In popular culture's storytelling the soothsayer is usually little more than a plot device, serving as a foreshadowing source within a predictive narrative of conflict and resolution. In these representations, seers are conventionally located either in carnivalesque environments or in eerie, isolated settings requiring the lead character to trespass into surreal and possibly dangerous territories.

These cartoonish figures are stock characters in popular culture, but their circumstances and locations bear little resemblance to the diverse realities of traditional or contemporary fortune-telling practices. Indeed, these representations draw on a long history of popular misconception and distrust of fortune-tellers that began to emerge in the 1600s. As Jane Duran (1990) contends, the systematic discrediting of fortune-tellers and other supernatural practitioners by secular and religious authorities in the seventeenth century was integral to the process of rationalizing the newly emerging social order and its ideological justifications. For example, although the practice of fortune-telling was broadly linked to the cultural traditions and routines of the Roma diaspora in Scotland since the fourteenth century, it was not until the sixteenth century that fortune-telling and other forms of clairvoyance began to be labeled as the devil's work by both religious and secular authorities (Cressy 2016).

Christian churches throughout Europe condemned the Roma people and their spiritual practices. The religious establishment was concerned that Roma fortune-tellers would lead parishioners astray—ultimately threatening its authority and influence. In *Book of Vagabonds*, German Protestant reformer Martin Luther refers to the Roma as "fake friars, wandering Jews and rogues" (Duna 2014). Swedish archbishop Laurentius Petri decreed that Roma children were not to be baptized and the Roma dead not buried in sacred ground (Kenrick and Puxon 1972). French Catholics who had their palms read faced the threat of excommunication, and the Catholic clergy in several European countries declared that even people who sheltered or otherwise aided the Roma were themselves subject to sanction (Kenrick and Puxon 1972).

As they did in many Continental nations, the Roma resided near the bottom of England's social hierarchy and were deemed suspect for a host of reasons. Although they had lived and traveled throughout what later became Great Britain for generations, their language and cultural practices—particularly their piecemeal laboring and nomadic lifestyle—were markedly different from those of the Britons and violated vagrancy laws dating back to the fourteenth century (Chambliss 1964). In addition to accusations of kidnapping and murder, the Roma endured charges of heresy, deception, and theft for their fortune-telling. Believing that the Roma's supernatural practices were filled with deceit and trickery, the British Parliament relentlessly produced legislation that forced punishments of deportation, exile, or death on these spiritual practitioners (Cressy 2016). Fears of religious belief cessation and the collapse of social order served as the primary motivation behind the persecution of the Roma and the forbidding of fortune-telling practices. Indeed, constructing and reifying the distinctions between the natural and the supernatural was a prerequisite for new ways of knowing (such as rationality and the physical sciences) to establish themselves as value-free and universal touchstones of truth (Duran 1990).

The secularization of the European mind, perhaps a victim of its own success, reached a crisis stage in England during the Victorian era. Although the place of Christianity in England's cultural fabric had been less than secure for some time, the approaching millennium exacerbated religious uncertainty and cultural angst (Oppenheim 1988). In an effort to allay their fears and counter anxiety, people turned to the supernatural. By this time, magic and superstition were supposed to have been left behind in favor of empirical evidence and scientific methodology. However, "instead of superstition being expunged from the world, it maintained its hold on human emotions, where kinds of knowledge other than the theological or scientific were welcome" (Braudy 2016: 61). Fortune-telling, spiritualism, and psychical research promised answers that conventional science and religion could not or would not provide. As Janet Oppenheim's (1988) comprehensive survey of the Victorian and Edwardian periods illustrates, people from all walks of life turned to the supernatural for evidence of a cosmic balance and purpose in life. Hence, like that of Dennis Waskul and Marc Eaton (see the Introduction), Oppenheim's (1988) research challenges the earlier claims by some psychologists, sociologists, and anthropologists that it was marginalized groups such as women, the poor, and those with low educational attainment who disproportionately sought out—or provided—fortune-telling and related supernatural services.

Supernatural beliefs and practices were never monopolized by any one social class or gender. Both men and women, ranging from the landed gentry to lawyers and teachers, to factory workers and miners sought out trance speakers to communicate with the dead and fortune-tellers to divine the future (Oppenheim 1988). In fact, even President Abraham Lincoln sought advice and guidance from spiritualists after the untimely death of his son, Willie (Maynard 1891). Rumors have also circulated that even Queen Victoria herself sought to communicate with the spirit of her late husband, Prince Albert (Oppenheim 1988).

In contrast to the view of fortune-tellers and other supernatural practitioners in early twentieth-century England, their treatment in Australia in the first decades of the twentieth century reflected deep-seated class tensions, gender biases, and animosity. Foreshadowing some of what can be observed in the contemporary American context, fortune-tellers in Australia during the early 1900s were characterized as, at best, misguided cranks and, at worst, coldhearted con artists. Typically seen as the purview of lower-class women, fortune-telling was considered a national blight (Piper 2014). These underprivileged laborers were quickly categorized as sources of entertainment and amusement for the elite. Popular news publications, such as *Western Mail* and *Queenslander*, also adopted this perspective by publishing jokes and editorial cartoons that mocked the validity of fortune-telling and ridiculed its adherents and practitioners. Because the women conducting psychic readings were not upholding traditional gendered duties associated with a proper home life, they were often exaggeratedly depicted as sideshow performers or sinners. The mediated portrayals of women fortune-tellers as an evil menace clearly contributed to the selective enforcement of long-dormant laws against the practice (including those of criminal status and vagrancy), as well as the creation of new ones. For example, the 1901 Post and Telegraph Act forbade the practice of fortune-telling conducted through the mail system (Piper 2014).

In the United States, predictive practices were the subject of much scrutiny over matters of dishonesty and lack of transparency. The chicaneries of Eusapia Palladino's (1854–1918) nonexistent powers to connect with the dead and the career hoax of the Fox sisters (Maggie, Kate, and Leah; 1830s–1890s) from New York served as ample fuel for public distrust. The inexorable testimony of Harry Houdini, the famed illusionist, during the 1926 Fortune Telling Hearing in Congress also worked to ignite disputes about the validity of spiritual practices and gender roles in the post–World War I years. This hearing centered on the introduction of bill H.R. 8989, in the winter of 1926, which proposed the criminalization of predictive practices. Identifying Houdini's perspective as a threat to gender values and asserting their function within society, women spiritualists successfully defended their position at this hearing and secured a congressional decision to protect their profession (Jeremy Young 2014). This historical event illuminates the tensions affiliated with gender and performance surrounding the observance of the supernatural, a theme widely emphasized throughout the media over time.

Fortune-telling began to develop into its current form in America during the economic boom and cultural transformations that occurred in the decades following World War II. Demographic changes resulting in shifting immigration patterns contributed to this transformation. As immigrants—first from Europe but then from throughout the world—began to populate the American landscape, they brought with them supernatural beliefs and practices. Assimilating over time, the Americanization of these immigrant groups included both their adoption of American values and practices and the integration of some immigrant beliefs into America's transforming cultural fabric. A critical element in the evolution of fortune-telling in America was the growth and expansion of the culture industries, particularly the proliferation of television and advances in communications technologies. For example, in 1962 American audiences watched as upper-middle-class housewife Donna Stone (actor Donna Reid) played at fortune-telling in a town festival (*The Donna Reed Show*, season 4, episode 31). Likewise, though not explicitly portraying fortune-tellers, two popular TV sitcoms from the mid-1960s, *Bewitched* (1964–1972) and *I Dream of Jeannie* (1965–1970), played on similar supernatural themes. The former featured actor Elizabeth Montgomery as Samantha (a witch), and the latter cast actor Barbara Eden as Jeannie (a genie). Both women lived in relative domestic bliss as seemingly normal middle-class suburban housewives.

Last, the changing nature of work and increased consumer spending also contributed to the transformation in the practices of fortune-telling. As in previous centuries, scientific advances in industry and public faith in better living through technology drove a new wave of secularization in America. This shift altered the perception and practice of fortune-telling, which was increasingly seen as a type of service profession or a form of popular entertainment. These changes affected who told fortunes and how they did it, as well as who patronized fortune-tellers and how the public and the authorities responded to it. Fortune-telling was no longer seen as the exclusive purview of suspect foreigners in scary rural or gritty urban settings. Instead, fortune-telling and those who practiced it experienced an image makeover. It was seen as less ethnic, marginal, and suspect. While not yet at the level of apple pie, baseball, and cookouts, fortune-telling was becoming safe, suburban, and ultimately more American.

Probably best described as a period of scientific-spiritual-legal détente, the decades of the 1950s through the 1970s saw gradual but ultimately significant changes in the practices of fortune-telling and the discourses surrounding it. At this time, some state laws and city ordinances still prohibited fortune-telling and what the legislation referred to as occult or crafty sciences, but these laws were all but ignored. Ontological debates about the legitimacy of fortune-telling continued to some degree but were waged with far less intensity and frequency than in the past. When these debates occurred, the stakes—such as intellectual accolades or the moral high ground—were considerably lower. There were no major public debates over fortune-telling, let alone congressional hearings. Instead, as detailed elsewhere in this volume, along with other supernatural beliefs and practices such as crystal power, faith healing, and psychic surgery, fortune-telling—from alectromancy through xylomancy—became far more commonplace (Goode 2000).

In the middle of the twentieth century a larger paradigm shift began occurring in the United States. According to Robert Wuthnow (1998), during the latter half of the century Americans shifted away from institutionalized religious practice toward a more individualized spirituality. As a consequence of this shift, more people found that the old intermediaries between themselves and the divine—such as priests—were no longer part of their lives. Instead, they found the divine within themselves or, alternatively, turned to noninstitutionalized intermediaries like shamans and fortune-tellers. Indeed, fortune-tellers played to the spiritual eclecticism of this New Age seeker crowd (Wuthnow 1998) by drawing from diverse ethnocultural traditions, including aboriginal and indigenous spirituality, Greek mythology, Indian mysticism, paganism, and a host of Eastern belief systems. By the end of the 1970s, fortune-telling was no longer seen as a milieu of weirdoes and fraudsters. It had become mainstream in the form of horoscopes in daily newspapers, psychic readings available in storefronts across the country, New Age reading rooms, and shops selling crystal balls, tarot cards, and other ephemera of the fortune-telling practice.

By the early 1980s, fortune-telling was solidly middle class. Most fortune-tellers presented themselves as professionals who borrowed language not only from the "esoteric cultic milieu" but also from the worlds of small-business entrepreneurship, psychological counseling, and traditional religious ministering (Jorgenson and Jorgenson 1982: 377). This professionalization prompted respected scientist Carl Sagan to quip that by 1980 the country had more professional astrologers than professional astronomers (Goode 2000). In some respects, the transformation of these practices marked the "whitening" of fortune-telling. Constructed as creepy and suspicious when it was the sole purview of Eastern European immigrants, fortune-telling's appropriation by the baby boomer hippie counterculture and the New Age movement normalized the practice. Its transformation was facilitated by its legitimation by young, predominantly white, middle-class (or above), largely college-educated Americans who had the purchasing power and cultural dominance to make their preferences mainstream (Jorgenson and Jorgenson 1982). This quarter-century-long process of recuperating fortune-tellers culminated with the creation of professional associations such as the National Association of Psychic Practitioners and the Union of Independent Spiritual Practitioners.

WORK IN LATE MODERNITY AND THE SUPERNATURAL INDUSTRY

Fortune-telling's unabated expansion in the twenty-first century—totaling $2 billion in revenue as of 2016 (IBISWorld 2016)—is undoubtedly built on the cultural and economic foundations laid a generation ago. However, it is the tectonic nature of liquid modernity that creates today's demand for the certitude fortune-telling seemingly provides. Today we live in a world where secure full-time employment is being replaced by deskilled, temporary, and contract work that offers few if any benefits or, indeed, even a living wage. According to recent statistics, more than 62 percent of people work in the tertiary sector of the economy, more commonly known as the service industry (U.S. Department of Labor 2016). This sector of the economy includes some relatively well-compensated and secure jobs in the financial, professional, and educational fields; however, it is overwhelmingly populated by poorly paid and precariously employed people working in retail, food service, low-level office jobs, and other low-paying service jobs.

Sociologists of work point to at least two fundamental shifts in labor that have occurred in this postindustrial economy. First, information has become a commodity. Although this shift came with the promise of tremendous growth in high-paying tech-sector jobs, the reality is that much of this work, if it ever materialized domestically, was quickly sent offshore. The *Business News Daily* reports research conducted by BDO USA, an accounting and consulting firm, that reveals 63 percent of technology companies outsource outside the United States (Brooks 2013). One example of these trends is Facebook, which is so unfathomably profitable in part because its labor costs are so low (it employs fewer than 17,048 people worldwide) and its product (demographic information on consumers) is of great value to advertisers and other industries (Statistica 2017).

Second, the boundaries that traditionally separated our work lives from other aspects of our existence (such as home and leisure) are rapidly eroding. While traditional work experiences—forty hours a week in a physical workplace of some kind—still exist, flexible work hours and decentralized locations are becoming the norm. Although the public faces of this transformation are artisans working in home studios and professionals communicating with their office via FaceTime or Skype from affluent suburban enclaves, the decentralized service industry mostly includes far less glamorous endeavors such as in-home call centers for technical support or telemarketing, order taking and call routing for fast-food delivery, AirBnB hosting, and Uber driving.

This rise of contingent work and the deskilling of labor have occurred simultaneously with real wages becoming the lowest since the 1970s and credit card, auto loan, and student loan debt the highest in history, at an average of $131,431 per household. With the disappearance of work and a growing vortex of unsecured consumer debt for the former middle classes, it is little wonder the United States has seen a dramatic rise in economic inequality (El Issa 2017). Current levels of economic disparity in America rival those of more than a century ago and are in fact the highest in the developed world (Gongloff 2013). The very institutions that promise stability and prosperity, such as banking, government, and the consumer marketplace, are sources of volatility and economic uncertainty. Continuous changes in regulations and policies contribute to an alarming social imbalance. Growing debt and the associated anxiety of being in debt can leave people feeling bereft of options (Gathergood 2012).

Under these circumstances, fortune-telling has the opportunity to flourish. The commodification of information plays to the fortune-teller's primary strength, which is the offering of divinely inspired wisdom—for a price. The growing economic instability of millions of Americans also drives a demand for assurances that ultimately everything will be okay. Of course, because these instabilities are the inevitable product of a capitalist economic system, there are bound to be recurring cycles of crisis into which fortune-tellers can insert themselves, promising spiritual insights that will help the anxious find peace in the midst of an economic storm. Last, fortune-tellers have followed the trend toward decentralized labor. They frequently operate out of their own homes or make their services available via phone calls, Skype, text messages, webchat, and webcams. As any profession should, fortune-telling in the United States is adapting to the needs and methods present in its current sociocultural context.

THE CONSUMER AND SUPERNATURAL CONSUMPTION

In a late-capitalist consumer culture such as ours, consumption serves a variety of purposes. A source of identity, a gateway to social integration, and a problem-solving strategy, consumerism has become the defining activity of life under late capitalism (Bauman 2007). Liquid modernity produces anxiety and then pushes consumption as a panacea. Within this context, fortune-telling has developed into an industry that sells its customers some semblance of control. The fortune-teller serves as an appealing (and appeasing) resource, a kind of life advisor who offers support, council, and assistance for the right price. These prices range from as little as $0.69 per minute for a telephone call through $45 for a half-hour in-person reading and up to several hundred dollars for premier psychics such as Sylvia Browne's son Chris Dufresne ("How Much," n.d.). Neighborhood newspapers and Internet search engines are full of fortune-tellers identifying themselves with honorifics such as "Dr.," "Deacon," "Marabout," "Master," "Mother," "Pandit," "Papa," "Reverend," and "Sister." These practitioners often claim to be available for immediate consultation, thus meeting the increasing demand for instant gratification that is characteristic of this consumer culture.

Fortune-telling has developed into a privatized site of moral authority, spiritual guidance, and emotional assistance. On the supply side of this transaction, modern fortune-tellers advertise themselves as adroit practitioners of customs and techniques: astrology, dream analysis, curse removal, healing, hypnotherapy, palmistry, predictions, and tarot card readings. Regardless of the techniques employed and the traditions from which they are drawn, the fortune-teller strives to infuse themes of well-being and stability throughout her or his practice. On the demand side, expectations placed on fortune-tellers vary depending on motivations. As is explored later, some people visit fortune-tellers—or increasingly, use mediated and virtual forms of fortune-telling—primarily for entertainment purposes. Yet large and growing numbers of people genuinely seek enlightenment by partaking of the services offered by professional fortune-tellers (Bader, Mencken, and Baker 2010; IBISWorld 2016). Like parishioners seeking comfort and guidance from priests or clients seeking answers from legal advisors and medical practitioners, spiritual seekers look to fortune-tellers as sources of knowledge and consolation. These believers seek advanced levels of competence and insight in the predictive functions of fortune-telling.

During his study of the beliefs of a group of Pacific Islanders in the 1950s, Bronislaw Malinowski (1954) found that there were no magical or superstitious beliefs surrounding safe endeavors such as fishing in a lagoon but many pertaining to dangerous activities such as fishing in the open ocean. Contemporary Americans, confronting very different though no less real dangers than those faced by Pacific Islanders half a century ago, likewise turn to fortune-telling for answers and respite. The ongoing horrors of the war on terror (both abroad and at home), unrestrained corporate violence, growing racial strife, polarizing political rhetoric, inadequate health care, the mortgage crisis, and the disappearance of work and its related economic instability all contribute to vigorous and heartfelt angst. This angst, in turn, fuels the search for meaning. As Erich Goode (2000) contends, if conventional methods of dealing with the crisis, threat, or trauma are available, people will use them. However, when experiencing volatile circumstances in which people perceive existing institutions as inadequately prepared to offer comfort and other resources, they turn to what he terms "extra-scientific" problem-solving strategies (Goode 2000: 233; see also Waskul 2016: 58). It is notable, for example, that while some people seek help from fortune-tellers for the "removal of Black Magic, Blockage Evil, Bad Curse, Witchcraft, Voodoo, Obeah, jealousy and all evils" (Shivananda 2016: 30), a large number seek help with the banal evils of "Depression, Love, Family, Exams, Work, Court cases, Business, Divorce, Health, Children, Sexual problems and many more."[1]

This mixture of mystical and mundane reasons for seeking fortune-tellers speaks to the ways that this practice is meeting needs formerly met through sacred institutions such as the church and secular practices like medicine and psychotherapy. In the context of hopelessness and anxiety fueled by liquid modernity, many are turning away from solutions offered by religion and science in the hope that fortune-telling and other supernatural practices will provide a reasonable strategy for dealing with the stresses of late capitalism.

A MACHINE OF THE FUTURE

For more than a century, the modern form of fortune-telling has been practiced in small, private settings ranging from Edwardian sitting rooms in country estates to cramped studios above storefronts in busy urban centers. For those who seek genuine guidance, traditions—if not the supernatural forces themselves—demand some semblance of quiet privacy. A concurrent trend, however, has been the practice of fortune-telling as entertainment. Sometimes referred to as open-air readings, fortune-telling performances such as those that are conducted on carnival stages, broadcast on TV, or spread via social media like YouTube are generally frowned on by serious adherents, who regard these readings as performance art rather than supernatural practice. As of this writing, "Interactive Fortune Teller" has received well over two million views on YouTube. More about stagecraft than witchcraft, these open-air performances transform fortune-telling from a form of guidance to simple public entertainment.

As with most professions, automation has affected the fortune-telling entertainment industry. First seen in the United States in the early years of the twentieth century, fortune-teller machines were ubiquitous in penny arcades, boardwalks, high streets, plazas, casinos, game rooms, and eventually, shopping malls and video arcades well into the 1980s (Namerow, n.d.). Considered a novelty item for audiences titillated by the supernatural industry, the fortune-teller machine is designed to offer immediate, though impersonal, readings to consumers. Standard models of this prophetic technology are

---

1. This list appears on a shop window advertisement for "Psychic Lily-Anna," observed on September 17, 2016, in Toronto, Canada.

freestanding wooden structures with an ornately carved finish. Mounted within glass casing, positioned within the upper half of the apparatus, is a mannequin. Embodying stereotypical characteristics of genies, draped in jewels and sporting a long beard, or soothsayers, wearing a turban-style head covering or veil, these Zoltar and Esmeralda figures are responsible for facilitating quick transactions that offer amusement for the customer.

Notably absent from the fortune-teller machines is human interaction: a card dispenser and—in later models—mechanized recording replaces the practitioner and negates the possibility of a genuine human encounter. Because the cards and recorded messages are mass produced, consumers understandably question the validity of the fortune given. Mechanization also has broad effects on public perception of living fortune-tellers, whose ability to help people gain insight into their lives is undermined by the impersonal, randomized nature of automated fortune-telling. The omission of the fortune-teller also eliminates the possibility of a personalization of predictive services. Practitioners and clients can no longer negotiate about what formats of readings might be best suited to the client's needs. In place of this personal interaction, users of fortune-teller machines interact with these machines like a gambler repeatedly inserting coins at a casino slots game with the hopes of eventually hitting the jackpot. Users can continually interact with fortune-telling machines with minimal interruptions for as long as they like until they receive a fortune that tells them what they want to hear. In short, the fortune-teller machine trivializes the public's connections to the spiritual world and turns what used to be a very personal experience into a solitary, impersonal exchange.

Today, many of the old the fortune-teller machines are highly sought after as ornate collector's items. As fetishized commodities, consumers covet these pieces of technology as forms of treasure. Not unlike African tribal masks, dream catchers, or other pieces of appropriated and mass-produced artifacts, fortune-teller machines function as a form of further exoticizing the mysterious Other. A few companies in the United States still manufacture fortune-teller machines. In addition to the tremendously popular Zoltar and Esmeralda versions, people inclined to part with a few dollars can get novelty fortunes from an assortment of clairvoyant characters, including the Wizard, King Arthur, Truthful Bear, Wise Guy, the Goat Whisperer, and Donald Trump—whose mysterious machine appeared, disappeared, and then reappeared in New York City several times during the final weeks of the 2016 election (see Figures 6.1–6.3).[2] Although the range of characters

---

2. The Donald Trump fortune-telling machine was initially made by Characters Unlimited, the same manufacturer as that of the iconic Zoltar fortune-telling machine. The machine was additionally customized by its four owners, Jon Barco, Andy Dao, Bryan Denman, and Nathaniel Lawlor, whom we are especially grateful to for their assistance in providing us these images.

Figure 6.1 *Donald Trump fortune-telling machine in New York City. Photograph by Nathaniel Lawlor.*

in these more recent models is greater, they have done nothing to diminish the transformation of fortune-telling from a deeply personal experience to a mechanized transaction that further undermines the credibility of the practice. The evolution toward fortune-telling smartphone apps further exacerbates these trends toward isolation and depersonalization.

Figure 6.2 *The all-seeing Trump. Photograph by Nathaniel Lawlor.*

Figure 6.3 *Fortune from Donald Trump fortune-telling machine. Photograph by Nathaniel Lawlor.*

THE APP OF GREAT FORTUNES

Within the fortune-telling industry, multitudes of smartphone apps, such as Ask Fortuna and AstroFate, have been released for public download. Like fortune-telling machines, these apps provide a wide range of supernatural services, a veritable mystic buffet ranging from astrology to tarot reading. Available for a small fee or as a complimentary download, these programs further eliminate human interaction within the fortune-telling exchange, perpetuating the isolation and depersonalization that began with fortune-telling machines. If customers are unhappy with the answers provided in one program, they can readily access other apps on their device. Users can even instantly compare fates or curses across multiple applications, allowing them to self-select the most favorable predictions. By being able to comparison shop for fortunes, users can comfort themselves with promises of personal success and individual prestige, both highly valued qualities in liquid modernity. These apps also make fortune-telling transactions nearly instantaneous, which appeals to a population that has been socialized in the context of late capitalism to value efficiency over quality (Ritzer 1993). When people need comfort and reassurance, life advice is only a few screen taps away. Daily commutes, lunch hour, and even bedtime are all opportunities for fortune-telling check-in moments.

Although these apps are the latest iteration of fortune-telling, they retain many of the same features of existing cultural representations of fortune-tellers. The format and imagery of fortune-teller apps is heavily borrowed from the fortune-teller machines and novelty toys such as the Magic 8-Ball and Ouija board (Occult Blogger 2009). Moreover, the apps traffic in stereotypical caricatures of fortune-tellers that harken back to the Middle Ages. Consumers can learn what lies ahead from the offensively racialized Djinn (The Amazing Fortune Teller 3D), unravel mysteries through the incantations of the wisest wizard in all the land (Fortune Teller), or have life's toughest questions—such as "Is he 'the one'?" and "Will I win the lottery?"—answered by the universe's one true source of wisdom, a crystal ball (Magic Crystal Ball). The persistence of such imagery in these smartphone apps highlights a paradox inherent in the liquid modern consumer's approach to fortune-telling: even as people feel a great need for predictability and control in a rapidly changing world, they draw on cultural representations and forms of technological mediation that further delegitimize and depersonalize these predictive practices. By interacting with fortune-telling as a form of instantaneous entertainment rather than a personal connection with the supernatural, today's consumers undercut the credibility of the very thing that they hope will bring them a sense of comfort in a time of anxiety.

CONCLUSIONS

In his preface to *Heartbreak House*, playwright George Bernard Shaw comments on the years leading up to World War I, writing that the levels of public insecurity have led people to become

> addicted to table-rapping, materialization séances, clairvoyance, palmistry, crystal-gazing and the like to such an extent that it may be doubted whether ever before in the history of the world did soothsayers, astrologers, and unregistered therapeutic specialists of all sorts flourish as they did during this half century of the drift to the abyss. (Quoted in Oppenheim 1988: 28)

This need for immediate answers and projections about the future has only intensified for people in the intervening century. It is unlikely that even the most pessimistic in the early twentieth century could have envisaged the economic uncertainty and global instability that accompanies late capitalism in the twenty-first century. The genuine and highly warranted lack of faith that people have in their political leaders and social institutions only serves to further exacerbate the dire straits of life in contemporary America. As a result, many people turn to predictive forces for a sense of stability and clarity, lest they sink any deeper into a morass of hopelessness.

The social history of fortune-telling illustrates varying degrees of societal receptiveness to occult knowledge. Long identified as the devil's practice and often affiliated with the Roma diaspora, the fortune-telling profession is routinely subjected to debates about legitimacy and accuracy. This chapter argues for the significance of the fortune-teller as a much needed ameliorative to the viciousness of late capitalism. Identified as the "touchstone of truth, reasoning and rationality" (Duran 1990: 236), the revelations of the fortune-teller can provide solace. This chapter also examines the shifts and advancements in the predictive supernatural industry. Drawing on themes of consumption, fortune-telling practices have become readily accessible through mobilized apps and online technologies. These technologies perpetuate two contradictory trends: the rapid consumption of occult knowledge as an ameliorative to the uncertainties of late capitalism *and* the dilution of fortune-telling practices into toylike products that harm the credibility of predictions given. Both patterns are direct results of the pressures of the liquid modern age.

Given the unstable societal and political conditions of our contemporary age, it is little wonder that people are adrift and cling desperately to anything that promises more stability than late capitalism's liquidity. As the forces of neoliberalism exact greater influence, we predict that people's reliance on fortune-telling practices will continue to intensify.

REFERENCES

AIRR (Association of Independent Readers and Rootworkers). 2017. "About the Association of Independent Readers and Rootworkers." Available at http://www.readersandrootworkers.org/wiki/Association_of_Independent_Readers_and_Rootworkers.

Alvaredo, Facundo, Anthony Atkinson, Thomas Piketty, and Emmanuel Saez. 2013. "The Top 1 Percent in International and Historical Perspective." *Journal of Economic Perspectives* 27 (3): 3–21.

Bader, Christopher D., F. Carson Mencken, and Joseph O. Baker. 2010. *Paranormal America: Ghost Encounters, UFO Sightings, Bigfoot Hunts, and Other Curiosities in Religion and Culture.* New York: New York University Press.

Bauman, Zygmunt. 2000. *Liquid Modernity.* Cambridge: Polity Press.

———. 2007. "Collateral Casualties of Consumerism." *Journal of Consumer Culture* 7 (1): 25–56.

Braudy, Leo. 2016. *Haunted: On Ghosts, Witches, Vampires, Zombies, and Other Monsters of the Natural and Supernatural Worlds.* New Haven, CT: Yale University Press.

Brooks, Chad. 2013. "Tech Firms Outsourcing More Jobs than Ever." *Business News Daily*, March 22. Available at http://www.businessnewsdaily.com/4191-more-tech-firms-outsourcing-jobs.html.

Chambliss, William. 1964. "A Sociological Analysis of the Law of Vagrancy." *Social Problems* 12 (1): 67–77.

Cressy, David. 2016. "Trouble with Gypsies in Early Modern England." *Historical Journal* 59 (1): 45–70.

DeSilver, Drew. 2014. "For Most Workers, Real Wages have Barely Budged for Decades." Pew Research Center, October 9. Available at http://www.pewresearch.org/fact-tank/2014/10/09/for-most-workers-real-wages-have-barely-budged-for-decades.

Duna, William A. 2014. *Gypsies: A Persecuted Race.* Minneapolis, MN: Duna Studios. Available at https://web.archive.org/web/20161108041852/http://chgs.umn.edu/histories/victims/romaSinti/gypsies.html.

Duran, Jane. 1990. "Philosophical Difficulties with Paranormal Knowledge Claims." In *Philosophy of Science and the Occult*, edited by P. Grim, 232–242. Albany, NY: State University of New York Press.

El Issa, Erin. 2017. "NerdWallet's 2017 American Household Credit Card Debt Study." Available at https://www.nerdwallet.com/blog/average-credit-card-debt-household.

Gathergood, John. 2012. "Debt and Depression: Causal Links and Social Norm Effects." *Economic Journal* 122 (563): 1094–1114.

Gongloff, Mark. 2013. "The U.S. Has the Worst Income Inequality in the Developed World, Thanks to Wall Street: Study." *Huffington Post*, August 16. Available at http://www.huffingtonpost.com/2013/08/15/income-inequality-wall-street_n_3762422.html.

Goode, Erich. 2000. *Paranormal Beliefs: A Sociological Introduction.* Prospect Heights, IL: Waveland Press.

"How Much Does a Palm Reading Cost?" n.d. *HowMuchIsIt.org*. Available at http://www.howmuchisit.org/palm-reading-cost (accessed January 16, 2018).

Hughes, Matthew, Robert Behanna, and Margaret Signorella. 2001. "Perceived Accuracy of Fortune Telling and Belief in the Paranormal." *Journal of Social Psychology* 141 (1): 159–160.

The Hunchback of Notre Dame. 1996. Directed by Gary Trousdale and Kirk Wise. Burbank, CA: Walt Disney Pictures.

IBISWorld. 2016. "Psychic Services in the US: Market Research Report." Available at https://www.ibisworld.com/industry/psychic-services.html.

Jameson, Fredric. 1991. *Postmodernism; or, The Cultural Logic of Late Capitalism*. Durham, NC: Duke University Press.

Johnstone, Michael. 2004. *The Ultimate Encyclopedia of Fortune Telling*. London: Arcturus.

Jorgensen, Danny L., and Lin Jorgensen. 1982. "Social Meanings of the Occult." *Sociological Quarterly* 23 (3): 373–389.

Kenrick, Donald, and Grattan Puxon. 1972. *The Destiny of Europe's Gypsies*. New York: Basic Books.

Leland, Charles G. 2007. *Gypsy Sorcery and Fortune Telling*. New York: Cosimo, Classics.

Malinowski, Bronislaw. 1954. *Magic, Science and Religion*. Garden City, NY: Doubleday/Anchor.

Maynard, Nettie Colburn. 1891. *Was Abraham Lincoln a Spiritualist? Or, Curious Revelations from the Life of a Trance Medium*. Philadelphia: Rufus C. Hartranft.

Namerow, Wayne. n.d. "Fortune Tellers." Available at http://www.pinballhistory.com/fortunes.html (accessed January 16, 2018).

Occult Blogger. 2009. "Ouija Board—Why Is It Being Sold as a Kids Toy?" Available at http://www.occultblogger.com/ouija-board-why-is-it-being-sold-as-a-kids-toy.

Oppenheim, Janet. 1988. *The Other World: Spiritualism and Psychical Research in England, 1850–1911*. Cambridge: Cambridge University Press.

Pew Research Center. 2009. "Many Americans Mix Multiple Faiths." Available at http://www.pewforum.org/2009/12/09/many-americans-mix-multiple-faiths.

Piper, Alana J. 2014. "'A Menace and an Evil': Fortune-Telling in Australia, 1900–1918." *History Australia* 11 (3): 53–73.

The Princess and the Frog. 2009. Directed by Ron Clements and John Musker. Burbank, CA: Walt Disney Pictures.

Ritzer, George. 1993. *The McDonaldization of Society*. Newbury Park, CA: Pine Forge Press.

Shivananda. 2016. "Unique Astrologer Master Shivananda." *24 Hrs*, November 22, p. 30.

Statistica. 2017. "Number of Facebook Employees from 2004 to 2016." Available at https://www.statista.com/statistics/273563/number-of-facebook-employees.

U.S. Department of Labor. 2016. "The Employment Situation—November 2016." Available at https://www.bls.gov/news.release/archives/empsit_12022016.pdf.

Waskul, Dennis, with Michele Waskul. 2016. *Ghostly Encounters: The Hauntings of Everyday Life*. Philadelphia: Temple University Press.

Wuthnow, Robert. 1998. *After Heaven*. Berkeley: University of California Press.

Young, Jeremy C. 2014. "Empowering Passivity: Women Spiritualists, Houdini, and the 1926 Fortune Telling Hearing." *Journal of Social History* 48 (2): 341–362.

Young, Jock. 2007. *The Vertigo of Late Modernity*. London: Sage.

7

READING TAROT

Telling Fortunes, Telling Friends, and Retelling Everyday Life

JANET BALDWIN

Playing cards and card games can be traced to fourteenth-century Europe, as evidenced by surviving manuscripts that describe the commissioning, use, and even condemnation of handmade cards. An air of mystery, however, surrounds the manufacturing and use of tarot cards. We know that decks were commissioned to honor special occasions, such as the marriage of Francesco Sforza to Bianca Maria Visconti in 1441 in Milan, Italy. Speculation remains that this set of *tarocchi* cards—one of the first sets to be produced—was used not only for games but also for divination (Farley 2009). From at least the fifteenth century to today, "cartomancers"—those who read tarot cards—have used these seventy-eight-card decks as tools of divination, healing, self-reflection, and establishing order in their lives and for those for whom they read. To truly understand the meaning of tarot cards, we must investigate the cultural tensions, interests, and values of specific historical contexts in which they were used. The goal of this chapter is to provide a rich historical overview before turning to an examination of how tarot cards are used in our current sociocultural context.

TAROT IN HISTORICAL CONTEXT

The rich history of tarot is well documented by William Andrew Chatto (1848), Michael Dummett (1980), and Helen Farley (2009). Rather than recounting that history, I highlight only the most significant tarot decks and discuss how tarot transformed from a game of chance into an esoteric medium of divination. The Visconti di Modrone (ca. 1440) from northern Italy is the earliest known deck of tarot cards, closely followed by the Brambilla deck (1442–1445), made for Duke Filippo Maria Visconti. Next came the aforementioned Visconti-Sforza deck that was produced between 1440 and 1470 for the wife of Francesco Sforza, Bianca (Farley 2009). This deck is significant for two main reasons. First, the French invaders who stormed Milan in 1499–1504 likely came into contact with the Visconti-Sforza deck and spread tarot cards to France, where they were known as *tarocchi*. Second, this deck is the only one from this early era to have survived in more or less complete form (Dummett 1980). As a result, the Visconti-Sforza deck has been used as a template for most subsequent decks (Farley 2009). The imagery of modern tarot decks depicts the Visconti coat of arms, their friends, and family members. For example, Farley (2009) speculates that Francesco Sforza is shown as the figure of Fortitude in the Visconti-Sforza deck. This card depicts a cowering lion—associated with Saint Mark, patron saint of Milan—being beaten by a man, who is believed to be Sforza humiliating the city.[1] Aside from the direct influence of the Visconti-Sforza deck, the allegorical imagery of early decks was also influenced by artwork by Dante (Campbell and Roberts 1987) and can even be compared to Jungian (1959) archetypes in that they reflect themes such as birth, death, and separation that are common across cultures and deeply embedded in the human psyche.

Although there are many contemporary variations, most common decks contain twenty-two major arcana and fifty-six minor arcana cards, totaling seventy-eight cards. "Arcana" comes from the Latin *arcanus*, meaning mysterious or secret. The major arcana are often called trumps, derived from Latin *trionfi*, so these twenty-two cards can be regarded as triumphal secrets or mysteries. Each trump is represented by a central image, a title, a number, a Hebrew letter, and an astrological correlation. They are named as follows: the Fool (0), the Magician (1), the High Priestess (2), the Empress (3), the Emperor (4), the Hierophant (5), the Lovers (6), the Charioteer (7), Strength (8), the Hermit (9), the Wheel of Fortune (10), Justice (11), the Hanged Man (12), Death (13), Temperance (14), the Devil (15), the Tower (16), the Star (17), the Moon (18), the Sun (19), Judgment (20), and the World (21).

The minor arcana consist of pip cards subdivided into four elemental suits: Fire (Wands, Rods, or Batons), Earth (Pentacles, Discs, or Coins), Air (Swords), and Water (Cups). Each card is numbered from one (ace) to ten with four court cards: King, Queen, Knight, and Page—the latter also

---

1. Milan rejected Sforza as the successor to Filippo Visconti (d. 1447). However, when an attack from Venice was imminent Visconti was begged to defend Milan, which he did.

named Prince and Princess. The pip cards carry less weight than the trumps but are interpreted in conjunction with the major arcana when used for divination. Traditionally, only the major arcana portrayed an image that was rich in color and symbolism, while the minor arcana showed only schematic designs and emblems. How these images are depicted depends on the designer, producer, or author.

Dummett (1980) traces the development and use of tarot in a cartomantic and occultist manner to Antoine Court de Gébelin (1719–1784). Gébelin was a French archaeologist, Egyptologist, and Freemason who implied in the eighth of his nine-volume work, *Le Monde Primitif*, that the tarot symbols were fragments from an ancient Egyptian text known as *The Book of Thoth*. Gébelin associated the twenty-two tarot trumps with the Egyptian alphabet (although there are fewer letters) and alleged they were common to the Hebrews' alphabet. He was also the first to link the tarot to the Hebrew alphabet and the Qabalah—an association, according to Farley (2009), that was pivotal to the esoteric system. To be consistent with his claims of Egyptian influence, Gébelin removed all Christian symbols from the cards. For example, the pope became the Hierophant, the popess the High Priestess, and the river running in the Moon became the Nile (Farley 2009).

Inspired by the publication of Gébelin's work on tarot in 1781, Etteilla (a reversal of Jean-Baptiste Alliette's surname) also linked the Egyptian principles of divination with the cards.[2] Etteilla claimed he had studied tarot for thirty years or more, though Alfred Douglas (1976) speculates that his emphasis on divination was more likely driven by a desire to profit from the interest in prognostication in Napoleonic France. More so than Gébelin, Etteilla was responsible for popularizing the alleged Egyptian heritage of tarot through several publications in which he claimed his tarot packs were restorations of Egyptian designs that had been distorted through the centuries (Douglas 1976). His "corrected" versions included alterations to the numerical sequence and symbolism of the cards. These Egyptian Tarot packs were commercially successful and made Etteilla a celebrity in France, even though his contemporaries considered him as nothing more than an opportunist.

Interpretations of the cards shifted as the decks were used and developed by people and groups over the centuries. One influential group that adapted tarot for its purposes was the Hermetic Order of the Golden Dawn, which was established circa 1887. According to Gareth Knight (1986), tarot played a

---

2. Farley (2009) disputes the validity of this claim, because Egyptian iconology was radically different from that of the tarot.

substantial part in the curriculum of this organization, whose founding members were prominent figures in occult and literary circles. One Golden Dawn member, Samuel Lidell Mathers (1854–1917)—also known as MacGregor Mathers—published an elementary instruction booklet on divination. In this booklet, he referred to the work of French occult authorities, especially that of Alphonse Louis Constant (1810–1875) better known by the pseudonym Eliphas Lévi. Although he never produced a tarot deck himself, Lévi ordered the tarot into a coherent Qabalahlistic system because he believed the Qabalah could not be understood without the tarot, and vice versa. Lévi's innovations revived interest in ritual magic and influenced many occultists, among them a man named Gérard-Anaclet-Vincent Encausse (1865–1916), better known as Papus (Douglas 1976).

Lévi and Papus used astrological symbolism, the Hebrew alphabet, and other esoteric schemes to transform the tarot trumps into a complex system of correspondences that made them difficult to read (Farley 2009). Another Golden Dawn member, Arthur Edward Waite (1857–1917), introduced tarot occultism to the British public with a selection of translated texts from Lévi (Dummett 1980). Unlike his predecessors—who created tarot cards to be used only by Golden Dawn members—Waite produced a deck that was very accessible and widely available to the public. First published in 1910 after the dissolution of the Golden Dawn, the Rider Waite deck (incorporating the publisher's name) used Qabalahlistic imagery but transformed the traditionally plain minor arcana cards into colorful cards depicting elaborate scenes. Waite also rectified the deck by changing the order of two trumps: Justice (from 8 to 11) and Strength (from 11 to 8). To accompany the deck Waite produced *The Key to the Tarot*, a booklet that explained the history and symbolism of the cards. More importantly, *The Key to the Tarot* also provided instructions for using the tarot deck for purposes of divination (Waite [1910] 1993). Waite reassured users that they did not need specialized knowledge to read the cards and declared that reading tarot was a purely symbolic exercise that did not hold higher significance. This demystification of occult knowledge and practices contrasted dramatically with the Golden Dawn's inaccessible and esoteric use of tarot cards. Waite's approach ultimately proved more successful. Indeed, the Rider Waite deck is still used today, often as a starter pack for people wanting to begin using the tarot for divination for themselves and others.

Tarot is accessible to a wide audience because of the pictorial designs and numbers on all the cards. As Dummett (1980) suggests, tarot packs were popular among the lower social classes in the last quarter of the fifteenth century. This may be partially due to the availability of cheaply manufactured cards at that time and also the symbolism of tarot being readily understood even by illiterate readers.[3] Much like stained glass windows in churches and cathedrals that served as illustrations to narrate biblical stories (Recht 2010), tarot could be interpreted by illiterate people who wanted to tell fortunes or perhaps seek guidance in the face of difficulties. This pattern still holds today: contemporary decks are relatively cheap, and the symbolism—based on Waite's work—enables interpretation by any reader, rich or poor, experienced or neophyte. The Rider Waite deck opened up an infinite treasury of symbolic language that is used today by people who hope to gain a sense of predictability and control in their lives.

In addition to this desire for divination, tarot reading also offers likeminded people an opportunity to commune with one another. In the process, the tarot enables not only insights into the future but also insights into one's own life. Through group participation in the ritualized reading of tarot, cartomancers form bonds of trust and friendship that give their lives meaning beyond any meanings discerned from the cards themselves. It is to this practice that we now turn.

MEANING AND COMMUNITY IN A TAROT READING GROUP

My research into tarot emerged from participating in regular meetings over the course of a decade with a few women who share an interest in astrology. Although not all the women are familiar with tarot, those who are agreed to show the others how tarot can be used to make sense of everyday life. Men are not explicitly excluded from the group, but few men express any interest in joining us, and it is my experience that more women than men read tarot. This is consistent with the findings of Christopher Bader, Carson Mencken, and Joseph Baker, who report that women are more interested in "ephemeral" phenomena, while men are drawn to more "concrete" phenomena like UFOs, aliens, and lake monsters (2010: 108). Members read for each other, and several also read professionally for other people. I join them at their monthly meetings, which rotate among members' homes and usually last about five hours (10:30 A.M.–3:30 P.M.). Readings are relaxed, communal affairs: each person brings a plate of food to share, and cards are often read along with morning tea. On such occasions care is taken to sweep the table clean and lay a new tablecloth before spreading the cards.

---

3. In 1442 a hand-painted tarot pack was sold for twelve *soldi* (a copper coin worth one-twentieth of a lira) and three *denari*; cheap packs were less than one-eighth that amount (Farley 2009). In 2017 Rider Waite cards sell for about twenty-five dollars.

Reading as Ritualized Experience

This cleaning ritual is one of many beliefs and practices that surround tarot use. Ritual, as Victor Turner reminds us, prescribes formal behavior "having reference to beliefs in mystical beings or powers" (1969: 19). While the handling, care, and storage of cards does not significantly affect the ability to perform a reading, rituals add to the mystical aura of tarot and, in some cases, are even believed to charge the cards with magical power. The beliefs and rituals that are most common in the group I observed concern how one receives cards, the handling and reading of cards, and the purification and storage of cards.

One belief in this group is that the first pack of cards a person uses should be a gift. This tradition may stem from a fifteenth-century practice of giving cards as gifts. There is evidence, for example, that in 1449 cards were gifted to Queen Isabella, wife of King René I, Duke of Lorraine (in present-day France).[4] One member of the group, Cathy, told me that she was given her first pack of cards as a gift from a friend who knew she was interested in learning to read tarot. Her friend told her of the belief that the gifted cards are empowered with love, and Cathy would be reminded of this each time she used the cards.

Rituals also shape the shuffling and spreading of tarot cards. The deck is shuffled in a ritualized manner that is intended to have a soothing effect on the shuffler. It is then cut once, twice, or three times and reassembled by the querent (the person seeking a reading) before being handed to the reader. The cards are then laid out in a particular spread selected by the reader and depending on the questions of the querent. There are many spreads, some using as few as one card to those involving all seventy-eight cards. Readers tend to have favorite spreads on the basis of their belief that some are more effective in answering specific questions. For example, one common spread is the three-card spread representing the situation, the task, and the decision. This spread may be used when a person is unsure about a new venture or a way through a difficult situation. Irena, another member of the group, used this spread when she was offered an opportunity to read cards at a birthday event. She did not personally know the people involved and felt uneasy about doing the reading, so she decided to use her cards to clarify the situation. The question she asked was, "Should I accept the invitation?" The answer Irena received was the four of pentacles (the situation), indicating an unsound venture; the three of swords (task), marking a delay, ending, or heartbreak;

---

4. However, Dummett (1980) suggests that these were playing cards rather than tarot.

and the knight of swords (decision), telling her that it was better to pursue other ideas. Consequently, Irena declined the invitation. Some cartomancers also believe that certain spreads should be used only at particular times of the year. For example, at the beginning of the year a spread of twelve cards is used, each representing an astrological house. These cards are read with the astrological signs in mind, thereby adding another dimension to the symbolic meaning of the cards as the reader gives the querent insights into the upcoming year.

Some considerations of the type and timing of spreads are more practical. For example, during professional readings for others, readers usually use what is known as a "short spread" to maximize the efficiency of a reading while still leaving time for dialogue with the querent if desired. A popular short spread is one illustrated by Waite in *The Key to the Tarot* ([1910] 1993), referred to today as the Celtic Cross spread. This spread uses only ten or eleven cards of the seventy-eight-card deck to make quick predictions for the querent while providing the opportunity for reflection on the querent's fears, desires, and experiences. By incorporating the querent's life experiences and psychological states into the reading, cartomancers encourage querents to perceive synchronicity (Jung 1978), or meaningful coincidence, between the random distribution of the shuffled cards and the events in the querent's life. In this regard, these readings—even though they are short—help readers and querents make sense of their lives and the world.

Because the cards are believed to possess sacred knowledge, the readers in the group I observed treat their cards with reverence. Silk is traditionally used to wrap the cards, a practice that may date back to the first tarot decks, which were expensive to produce and often richly embossed with gold. Mary Greer (1984) encourages the cartomancer to wrap cards in black silk because, she claims, this fabric is an especially good psychic insulator that will protect the cards from negative influences in their vicinity. For this reason, Cathy, the woman who received her first pack as a gift from a friend, wraps her cards in silk. For her, it is better to use a plain rather than a patterned piece of silk so that she can see the cards clearly. She also prefers to wrap her cards in brightly colored silk, as these colors tend to lift her spirit. Pure silk also has a couple of practical benefits for readers. It folds easily around the cards, forming a small parcel that is easy to carry and store out of the sight of curious people. Cathy even makes silk-lined drawstring bags for herself and others, using materials that reflect the colors or theme of the tarot cards inside. She told me that an additional benefit of wrapping her cards in silk is that she always has a clean surface on which to spread the cards to do a reading.

Readers also take precautions to prevent what they call psychic contamination or impregnation. These rituals are designed to protect the cards from picking up negative vibrations from the atmosphere. Greer's (1984) encouragement that readers use silk as a psychic insulator is one example of such a practice. Cathy not only abides by this advice; she also uses a specific deck when reading for others and reserves another for her private use. Between readings, Cathy takes extra precautions by reshuffling the cards to release negative energy, thereby purifying the cards so that the next reading is not influenced by the last. In addition to these rituals, Greer (1984) recommends other cleansing methods such as smudging the deck (wafting sage smoke over it), burying it in the earth, or filling the deck with imagined white light. Cathy also cleanses her cards by placing crystals on top of the deck or within the silk wrapping. In particular, she uses rose quartz—which is said to promote love, forgiveness, and compassion—and snowflake obsidian—considered a powerful healing and cleansing stone (Berkovitch 1995). Other practitioners have their own unique ways of caring for and cleansing their cards. Irena, like Cathy, wraps her cards in silk and places a crystal on top—a blue lace agate, said to assist with communication and confidence (Berkovitch 1995). However, Irena also leaves her cards on the windowsill to catch the light of the full moon each month and always stores her cards in a finely crafted wooden box that she received as a gift. Despite idiosyncratic differences in readers' methods, they all share a set of beliefs regarding the importance of ritual purification of their tarot cards.

Reading as Community Building

In a professional context, readings are usually one on one, with the reader and querent engaged in a private financial transaction. This is very different from the communal experience I witnessed in the group readings at the homes of cartomancers. In these readings, one person shuffles and lays the cards, while other members help read the spread, offering insights and advice. As their friends read the cards, querents take personal notes on the advice, explanations, and intuitive insights offered by readers. These are accompanied by a diagram of the spread that the querent can refer to in order to make sense of events that occur between the reading and the next meeting. At the following meeting, group members often discuss spreads from the previous month, especially if an event or incident occurred that seemed to be predicted by a spread. During one reading I observed, for example, Irena could not understand the placement of the three of swords—which signifies an ending, delay, or heartbreak—in a relatively positive spread. However, at the following meeting Irena explained that the spread now made sense to her because during the intervening month she missed a scheduled flight and had to wait many hours for the next one. Everyone agreed with Irena that the three of swords clearly showed the missed flight and was well placed in the previous month's reading.

Care is always taken by members as each offers insights about the spread. Rarely do members openly disagree with each other; rather, they add to the conversation in a way that supports both the querent and other commentators. For example, the seven of swords was drawn during a reading for Sandra. According to Rachel Pollock (1997), this card can indicate an inclination to commit an impulsive act when careful planning is actually required. Everyone in the group knew that Sandra intended to quit her part-time job, and several of us seeing this card and its placement said she should be careful how she did it. However, Irena disagreed and said, "Why not?" Irena's disagreement initiated a discussion of the best plan of action so that there was a good outcome for both Sandra and her manager. During another reading—this time for Cathy—the four of wands and the four of pentacles appeared in significant places in the spread. The four of wands denotes a celebration, while in contrast, the four of pentacles indicates someone being very miserly (Pollock 1997). The members of the group knew that Cathy had been invited to her cousin's wedding but did not want to go because she felt she was expected to buy an expensive present that she could not afford. We interpreted the four of wands as the wedding celebration and the four of pentacles as her desire to save money on the wedding present she purchased. On the basis of this interpretation, the group persuaded Cathy to attend the wedding but inform her cousin that she had a very tight budget. Cathy followed the group's advice and discovered that her cousin welcomed her regardless of the cost of her present. These examples show how supportive and helpful these group readings were, even when group members occasionally disagreed with the interpretation of spreads.

More experienced readers hold a great deal of power in the group, as their interpretations are given more credence. However, rather than using this power to wield control over or frighten other members, the more experienced readers are careful to phrase their interpretations of individual cards or an entire spread in ways that support their fellow group members. This is especially the case when one group member is feeling gloomy or when a spread appears to be negative. In such circumstances, experienced readers will adapt their interpretations to make the querent feel better, while other members intervene with uplifting interpretations of seemingly negative cards. For example, I observed when a member (querent) asked about her partner and turned over the ten of swords (a person with ten swords in their back), meaning an ultimate betrayal and the end of a situation, Irena pointed out that the card also showed the querent moving into a vibrant and positive situation, seen in the light of the sun piercing the dark clouds.

Even the "scary" cards (as named by some members) such as Death, Tower, and Devil are read in a positive way. For example, the Death card is often quite scary when it appears in a spread. Rather than interpreting it as a predictor of physical death, readers characterize it more benignly as simply the end of something, which implies it is also a sign of a new beginning or opportunity. Similarly, although the Tower card depicts destruction, when it appears in a spread the experienced reader will point out that the fall is due to changes already made in the querent's life, so the destruction should not be a surprise. Moreover, these readers interpret this destruction as a positive change in the querent's fundamental worldview, such as transformations in life philosophy, spirituality, or way of seeing things. The Devil card also usually disturbs querents when it appears in a spread. Experienced readers will shift the focus from the dark symbolism of the card to questions about controlling relationships. They inquire about the querent's desire to hold on to something or somebody or interpret the card as a warning that personal boundaries may need to be set or reset in a relationship. For example, if a mother wishes to hold on to a teenager or, alternatively, seems to be allowing the teenager too much freedom, the reader will advise the querent that boundaries need to be set in a firm but not tyrannical manner.

By reading the cards in the context of an individual's life, the group helps each member make sense of everyday decisions and challenges. They are careful to read the spreads in a considerate and compassionate way, so that no one loses face or is upset by the dialogue. In this way, the tarot provides a shared symbolic language that facilitates both communication and communion within the group I studied.

Reading as Self-Empowerment

Beyond their function as tools of divination and community building, tarot decks are also regarded by group members as reflections of each one's identity. Each group member owns multiple packs of cards and will often use the cards at home before bringing them to a meeting and showing them to other group members. To some degree, the symbolic meaning and feeling a deck evokes varies from reader to reader. Some packs may be rejected by one reader, while a second reader feels perfectly comfortable using them. For example, Jill had purchased the Haindl pack,[5] but after using the cards

---

5. The Haindl pack renders traditional archetypes with modern symbols. The designer Hermann Haindl had an extraordinary life: he was a concentration camp survivor who became a well-known artist in Germany and the United States. Haindl incorporated symbolic representations of several cultures, runes, astrological symbols, iChing, mythology, and much more in his tarot deck.

exclusively for several weeks she found she was becoming quite depressed. She recognized that the cards were darker than the more common and vividly colored Rider Waite deck but also perceived the individual cards as morbid and the spreads as very negative. She read the small booklet placed inside the Haindl pack that included a brief biography of the deck designer and explained the symbolic meanings ascribed by the designer to each card. Jill sensed that her gloominess was the consequence of an intense psychic impression left by the designer, who had survived the Nazi concentration camps. In response to her negative experience with the Haindl pack, Jill put the cards away and subsequently noted that her gloomy spirits lifted.

At the next meeting, Jill offered the cards to Irena with a proviso that she be careful and return them if she also had a negative reaction. Unlike Jill, Irena enjoyed the cards and found that they offered her new insights into her life. Rather than experiencing the deck as sad and gloomy, Irena drew new meanings from the dark symbolism used on the cards. For example, Strength in the Haindl deck is a woman kneeling on one knee, one foot on the ground and the other in water. This figure is wrestling a green snake, attempting to get it under control. The card also features the Moon along with the sign of Leo (also resembling a snake) and the number eight. While some may interpret the card negatively, Irena explained that she saw the card as symbolic of feminine power: by wrestling the snake—which she saw as a sign of renewal or new growth—the female figure was accessing inner strength to overcome challenges in a positive way.[6] This dramatic difference between two group members' interpretations of the same deck is illustrative of the important roles played by one's life experiences, knowledge of tarot symbolism, and psychological state in determining the meaning of a deck or spread. In this regard, the meaning of tarot is a reflection of the reader's sense of self more than it is the result of esoteric symbolism developed over the past centuries.

Further confirmation of the importance of life experiences as a lens through which group members interpret the tarot comes from Lydia's story. Lydia told me that she first learned of the tarot during a major life crisis. She had split up with her husband—who was also her business partner—and had moved out of her family home. Suddenly living alone and trying to navigate this period of transition, Lydia began using tarot cards to gain answers and a sense of control over her life. A friend loaned her a set of mythological tarot cards produced by Liz Greene and Juliet Sharman-Burke. Although the major arcana cards in this particular deck are mostly similar to the Rider Waite deck, the minor arcana are quite different and each linked to a par-

---

6. In the Visconti-Sforza deck this image, known then as Fortitude or Courage, shows a man beating a cowering lion with a stick.

ticular myth. Those depicting disturbing images are Judgment—with bandaged, ghoulish figures emerging from the coffins at the feet of Hermes, the psychopomp—and the three of swords, which depicts Clytemnestra and her lover murdering King Agamemnon by piercing his heart with three swords.

Because she was a budding astrologer, Lydia initially thought that a tarot deck that incorporated astrology and mythology would improve her understanding and interpretation of each card. She read the cards in the evenings, using simple spreads and methodically noting the cards and brief meanings derived from the accompanying small booklet. However, after a few days of using the cards Lydia had a terrifying nightmare: she was falling through space, grotesque images meeting her every glance. She awoke, turned on all lights, and sat in a chair until the morning light came. That morning, she placed the cards in their box and set them aside to return to her friend.

Lydia spoke a few days later to Leah, a friend and trusted confidant whose meditation class she attended. From Leah's perspective, it was not the cards that were to blame but rather Lydia's insatiable hunger for knowledge and understanding that had disturbed her equilibrium. Leah's explanation was that, in an effort to come to terms with her change in life circumstances, Lydia had suddenly opened up doors to the unconscious. Nonetheless, Lydia returned the cards to their original owner but did not give up on tarot entirely. She bought a Rider Waite deck and uses it only during daytime and when she is feeling balanced and secure. Looking back on her nightmare experience, Lydia now interprets it more positively. She believes that she is more sensitive than most people to images and symbols, and she accounts for her negative experience as caused by her state of mind and incomplete understanding of mythological symbolism at the time she was using her first deck.

The experiences of Jill, Irena, and Lydia show that readers often initially perceive the symbolic meaning of tarot as an external reality, an established meaning system that they can access—but not alter—in their efforts to make sense of the world. However, as they engage this symbolic meaning and discuss their interpretations with like-minded others, these women gain a sense of control; control over not only their lives but also the very meaning of tarot. Their interpretations reflect the circumstances of their lives at the moment, but on a deeper level they also reflect to the readers an image of an empowered woman who can successfully overcome life's many challenges.

Reading as Introspection

Although reading in a group is a joyful experience and much can be learned from fellow group members, reading alone and for oneself is also insightful and rewarding, especially if a journal or diary is kept. In personal readings, an individual shuffles the cards and selects one card while wondering, "What will this day bring?" This person then writes down in a diary which card was selected and in the evening reflects on the questions "What did the day bring?" and "How did I meet those challenges?" A similar process, in which seven cards are selected and noted in a diary, may be undertaken for an entire week. This practice helps members feel some sense of predictability and control even when unexpected events occur (like those who seek fortune-tellers; see Chapter 6). For example, Sandra used her daily introspection as a way to cope with a sudden loss. On the day she drew the Death card, Sandra phoned her sister Susan, who lived overseas, and found out that her nephew had died unexpectedly while recovering from an illness. Although shocked, she felt as though the event had been predicted by the Death card. A few days later Sandra drew the Hermit card. Reflecting on the meaning of this card, she decided that it was telling her to offer solace to other family members even though she felt isolated and unable to assist Susan in the preparation for the funeral.

Another related practice in which several members engaged was meditating while using a tarot card. This involved randomly or specifically selecting a card, placing it on one's lap or in a prominent position, and focusing intently on the card before slipping into mediation. It was widely understood in the group in which I participated that great creative insights could be gained through this meditation ritual. In some cases, the group meditated together, even though each person was focusing on her own card. One day Sandra offered to lead a guided meditation. She led the group into a safe and pleasant psychic environment and then invited each woman to meditate on the image of her selected card. Sandra fell silent for approximately twenty minutes before calling everyone back from their meditative experience. After meditating, the women shared the insights they had gained. Irena, for example, had chosen the Emperor card. In her meditative state, she was shown into a chamber-like room crowded with many people from all walks of life. A man seated on a throne arose, descended several steps, and sat down to talk to her. In her explanation of this experience, Irena said she believed she had chosen the Emperor because he was powerful but was also able to converse with all people. Before her meditation Sandra had been concerned about an interview with a lawyer that was to take place a few days later. Her meditative tarot experience gave her more confidence in advance of this interview and led her to a realization that the lawyer was only powerful because of his knowledge, which he would use to help her.

Another form of meditation is the practice of coloring tarot cards. The practice of coloring is said to reduce stress levels (Arcturus 2015) and has become popular recently with the trend of adult coloring books. However, in the context of tarot this form of meditation is nothing new. In the early twentieth century, Paul Foster Case (1884–1954) and Jesse Burns Parke (1889–1964), produced a pack of uncolored cards that was based on the Rider Waite deck. Students of the Builders of the Adytum (BOTA) colored these cards as part of their training within the organization and had to adhere to a strict color scheme that was not made available to outsiders. Case (1947) believed that the practice of coloring evoked specific psychic states that could enhance students' intuitive insights.

Although members of the group in which I participated did not adhere to Case and Parke's strict guidelines, they nonetheless reported that coloring the cards produced a meditative state of peace and tranquility. Lydia found the process of coloring the major arcana cards particularly effective. Following an exercise outlined by Sharman-Burke (1991), Lydia believed that coloring allowed her to achieve deeper meaning of the symbolism within the cards—to tap into the myths portrayed therein. Likewise, Jill said she thoroughly enjoyed the process of coloring the Empress (depicted as the Greek goddess Demeter and representing motherhood and creativity, both personal and archetypal). Jill personally identified with the Empress on both a physical and a spiritual level: she was pregnant with creative ideas and was also a mother who took a very down-to-earth approach to childcare. Less experienced members tended to color their cards in ways that corresponded to color schemes on published cards. Even though these members did not take creative liberties with color choices, I argue that coloring helped less experienced practitioners better understand the symbolism of the cards. By selecting the colors to apply to these symbols, members gained a sense of control over this symbolic meaning. Furthermore, by interacting with the cards in a state of peace and tranquility, members were able to meditate on the particular meanings that these symbols held for them. Thus, coloring and other meditative practices provided the women in my group the opportunity to engage in quiet introspection about their relationships to tarot and to each other.

CONCLUSIONS

This chapter briefly shows the journey of the tarot deck from its humble beginnings as playing cards in the fifteenth century to the rich symbolic cards used in contemporary society. Through a combination of historical review and ethnographic investigation, this chapter places the tarot in past and present sociocultural contexts. Much like occultists of previous centuries, ritualized engagement with tarot enabled the women I observed to develop a tight-knit community. In this community, the women share intimate aspects of their lives with one another, without concern about judgment or envy. These group readings form and maintain bonds of friendship among the women, becoming a support network when group members are struggling with difficult life events or tough decisions. Moreover, the symbolism of tarot cards helps members gain introspective understanding of their personal experiences even when they are not able to rely on the interpretations of trusted friends.

I looked forward to meeting with these women each month, not only because of the need to add depth to my ethnographic research but because I genuinely felt excited about sitting around the table, hearing the conversations, watching as the cards were thoughtfully spread and read. I saw this anticipation and excitement in other members of the group as they arrived and greeted each other; the excitement could be heard in their voices, seen in their body language as they eagerly started the reading process by unraveling their individual and intimate rituals, then settling to mindfully shuffle their cards. There is something magical about the use of tarot, and even the plainest pack comes alive when a spread is chosen and then images are described by the reader and interpreted to gain insights. The source of magic is not within the cards, but they certainly facilitate the feeling of magic, awe, and alchemy.

These women are engaging in a centuries-old tradition in search of the same things that intrigued those who first used the tarot as a tool of divination. Like the fifteenth-century Italian royalty and nineteenth-century occultists who preceded them, the women I observed seek answers to some of life's most fundamental questions: How can we find meaning in struggle? What does the future hold? Is there a greater truth that lies above and beyond the realm of human interpretation? Tarot is a mirror that allows users, past and present, to reflect on the divine wisdom both within and beyond themselves.

REFERENCES

Arcturus. 2015. *The Mindfulness Colouring Book*. London: Arcturus.
Bader, Christopher, F. Carson Mencken, and Joseph Baker. 2010. *Paranormal America: Ghost Encounters, UFO Sightings, Bigfoot Hunts, and Other Curiosities in Religion and Culture*. New York: New York University Press.
Berkovitch, Sheril. 1995. *Crystal Workbook*. Burwood, Australia: Gemcraft.
Campbell, Joseph, and Richard Roberts. 1987. *Tarot Revelations*. San Anselmo, CA: Vernal Equinox Press.
Case, Paul Foster. 1947. *The Tarot: A Key to the Wisdom of the Ages*. Richmond, VA: Macoy.
Chatto, William Andrew. 1848. *Facts and Speculation on the Origin and History of Playing Cards*. London: John Russell Smith.
Douglas, Alfred. 1976. *The Tarot: The Origins, Meanings and Uses of the Cards*. Harmondsworth, UK: Penguin.

Dummett, Michael, with Sylvia Mann. 1980. *The Game of Tarot: From Ferrara to Salt Lake City.* London: Duckworth.
Farley, Helen. 2009. *A Cultural History of Tarot: From Entertainment to Esotericism.* London: I. B. Tauris.
Greer, Mary K. 1984. *Tarot for Yourself: A Workbook for Personal Transformation.* North Hollywood, CA: Newcastle.
Jung, Carl Gustav. 1959. *Collected Works of C. G. Jung.* 20 vols. Princeton, NJ: Princeton University Press.
———. 1978. *Man and His Symbols.* London: Aldus Books.
Knight, Gareth. 1986. *The Treasure House of Images.* Wellingborough, UK: Aquarian Press.
Pollock, Rachel. 1997. *Seventy-Eight Degrees of Wisdom.* London: Thorsons.
Recht, Roland. 2010. *Believing and Seeing: The Art of Gothic Cathedrals.* Chicago: University of Chicago Press.
Sharman-Burke, Juliet. 1991. *The Mythic Tarot Workbook.* Brookvale, Australia: Simon and Schuster Australia.
Turner, Victor. 1969. *The Ritual Process.* London: Routledge and Kegan Paul.
Waite, Arthur E. (1910) 1993. *The Key to the Tarot.* London: Random House.

8

TWENTIETH-CENTURY VOODOO

Black Culture, Cultural Geographies, and the Meaning of Place

I'NASAH CROCKETT

In this chapter I explore the intersections between voodoo and the New Orleans tourism industry. More specifically, I am interested in the discursive and social changes over the course of the twentieth century that allowed the popularization of voodoo tourism toward the end of the century. While African Americans throughout the South practiced voodoo, it became uniquely wed to the landscape of New Orleans in ways that demonstrate ties between race and place. Voodoo has a centuries-old presence within the city and enjoyed an early tourist appeal even before there was a New Orleans tourism industry proper. A trade in voodoo and hoodoo ephemera has been part of the New Orleans economy at least since the days of Marie Laveau in the nineteenth century, and to this day voodoo priests and priestesses are afforded local celebrity status. While the popularity of voodoo in New Orleans could be dismissed as a local quirk, I suggest otherwise. Tourism discourses and practices as they intersect with the history of New Orleans make up a loosely organized vocabulary for interpreting the past and the present (Gotham 2007), and studying black cultural forms of the region offers an alternative understanding for how African Americans have negotiated inequality in ways specific to the geographic realities of both time and space. Thus, as I illustrate, an examination of the development of voodoo and voodoo tourism discourses can give insight into how black culture can shape the cultural geographies and meanings of place.

Both culturally and economically, tourism is essential to New Orleans, one of the most visited destinations in the United States. Tourism accounts for about a third of the city's revenue (Jervis 2007), and some sixty-seven thousand New Orleanians work in the tourism industry (Souther 2006). Tourism has been the city's primary driving force of spatial (re)organization during the past forty years and a principal mediator through which New Orleans has understood itself, its culture, and its history—especially considering that New Orleans has predominantly embraced *heritage tourism*.[1] Moreover, New Orleans has been a complex and constantly mutating city in which meanings of place and community have been inexorably intertwined with tourism practices (Gothem 2007); therefore, studying tourism can allow us an alternative understanding of these shifting meanings.

(MIS)CHARACTERIZATIONS OF VOODOO

While voodoo is among the most popular signifiers of New Orleans in the popular national imagination, surprisingly little is written about its presence or role in the city's tourist landscape versus its status as a religious practice. Indeed, it can be difficult to find writings on voodoo, in New Orleans or otherwise, that are not rife with misinformation and cheap sensationalism. Most published works that sincerely engage voodoo are anthropological in approach, meaning that they emphasize the lived experiences of voodoo practitioners instead of the historical context of voodoo. Examples include Maya Deren's *Divine Horsemen: The Living Gods of Haiti* (1953), Zora Neale Hurston's *Tell My Horse: Voodoo and Life in Haiti and Jamaica* (1938), and Karen McCarthy Brown's *Mama Lola: A Vodou Priestess in Brooklyn* (1991). Meanwhile, works on the development of tourism in New Orleans, such as J. Mark Souther's *New Orleans on Parade: Tourism and the Transformation of the Crescent City* (2006), Kevin Fox Gotham's *Authentic New Orleans: Tourism, Culture, and Race in the Big Easy* (2007), and Anthony J. Stanonis's *Creating the Big Easy: New Orleans and the Emergence of Modern Tourism, 1918–1945* (2006), include examinations of the industry's appropriation and utilization of black New Orleans culture (such as jazz funerals and Mardi Gras Indians), but voodoo is generally excluded from the cultural practices they consider.

The general omission of voodoo in published works about New Orleans is undoubtedly partially due to the difficulty of securing reliable sources. Voodoo has been subject to a sustained centuries-old antiblack smear campaign that has cast the practice as a satanic, uncivilized, and superstitious

---

1. Heritage tourism, or what is sometimes called cultural heritage tourism, refers to forms of tourism that are oriented toward the unique cultural heritage of a location and entail an attempt by the market to authentically represent the history, stories, and people of the past and present. Thus, more than just sightseeing, in heritage tourism tourists engage the people of the past and present—and most especially their culture—as a commodity that is central to their travel experience.

practice that brought out the worst in its practitioners, who have historically been black, enslaved, or—when free—disenfranchised. Thus, many articles (journalistic and scholarly), books, and other written works on voodoo are completely erroneous in their description of the faith and are prone to exaggeration in their accounts of interactions with practitioners. In addition, until relatively recently, blatant racism on the part of voodoo's investigators prohibited accurate and productive scholarship.

Furthermore, voodoo is an oral-based religion, meaning that practices are transferred in speech rather than codified in and interpreted from fixed texts. Voodoo is also a closed, initiation-based system, in which a certain depth of knowledge is denied to the uninitiated. It has no formal theology or creed, no strictly defined organizational structure, and no credentialed clergy or ecclesiastical hierarchy (Mohammed 2005). This orality makes for a dynamic religion, in which ritual practices are adapted to the needs of practitioners from different regions and temples. However, it also complicates the tasks of potential historians. Those few who have studied voodoo in New Orleans leave behind a legacy of scholarship that varies widely in both quality and reliability. Robert Tallant's 1946 book *Voodoo in New Orleans* is a prime example. As editor for the Federal Writers' Project of the Works Progress Administration (WPA) in Louisiana, Tallant was genuinely interested in voodoo and had access to hundreds of oral interviews with voodoo practitioners. Nevertheless, *Voodoo in New Orleans* is full of inaccuracies and reads like sensationalistic pulp fiction. Despite its shortcomings, Tallant's book is valuable for being one of a small number of books dedicated entirely to voodoo in New Orleans.

VOODOO AS RELIGIOUS PRACTICE

Voodoo is one of a group of syncretic New World Afro-Caribbean religions that include santería, obeah, and candomblé. Voodoo, and its progenitor Haitian vodou, can be traced back to two African regions: the former kingdom of Dahomey, also known as the Bight of Benin, and the Congo River basin (Fandrich 2005). It is believed that the term "vodun" derives from a word meaning "divine spirit" in Fon, a Dahomean language (Fandrich 2005). Anthropologist and avant-garde filmmaker Maya Deren is credited with writing the first thorough examination of Haitian vodou, *Divine Horsemen*, which remains one of the premier works on vodou spirituality and morality within the context of Haitian society. Deren's description of basic vodou concepts and practices is particularly useful:

> Like all religions, Voudoun is built on certain basic premises. Briefly, it proposes that man has a material body, animated by an *esprit* or

gros-bon-ange—the soul, spirit, psyche or self—which, being non-material, does not share the death of the body. This soul may achieve . . . the status of a *loa*, a divinity, and become the archetypal representative of some natural or moral principle. As such, it has the power to displace temporarily the gros-bon-ange of a living person and become the animating force of his physical body. This psychic phenomenon is known as "possession." The actions and utterances of the possessed person are not the expression of the individual, but are the readily identifiable manifestations of the particular loa or archetype principle. Since it is by such manifestations that the divinities of the pantheon make known their instructions and desires and exercise their authority, this phenomenon is basic to Voudoun, occurs frequently, and is *normal* both to the religion and to Haitians. (Deren 1953: 15–16)

In vodou, the loas work as intermediaries for an all-powerful but distant god, Bon Dieu. Each loa has its own songs, rhythms, and dances that are performed during rituals. Loas also have individual personalities that relate to the areas of human life that they concern themselves with, and they must be appeased at any invocation. For example, the loa of romantic love (among other areas), Erzulie Freda, is popularly depicted as a beautiful coquettish woman with a penchant for the fine things in life; her *servituer* (servant)[2] would leave perfume, champagne, jewelry, or flowers at her altar when seeking her assistance.

New Orleans voodoo, however, differs from Haitian vodou in a few key ways. First, while Haitian vodou recognizes only the loa, New Orleans voodoo recognizes loas and orishas, which can be considered the loas' counterparts in Brazilian candomblé and Cuban santería. Voodoo also recognizes an indigenous American spirit named Black Hawk that is entirely unique to New Orleans and can be considered part of the same Native American and African American cultural syncretism that produced the famous Mardi Gras Indian. Additionally, voodoo has a close relationship with hoodoo, which is a form of African American folk magic that is religiously nonspecific; in vodou, magic is practiced within the confines of voodoo rituals.

VOODOO AND THE HISTORY OF NEW ORLEANS

Voodoo's heavy, lingering presence in New Orleans is an aspect of local culture that has been remarked on for centuries, and its continuity is a testament

---

2. Voodoo practitioners would say they serve, not worship, the loa.

to both its adaptive nature and to New Orleans' history as a crossroads of the Atlantic World. Founded by the French in 1718, New Orleans was a strategic part of France's attempts to control the entire trade of the Mississippi River (Fandrich 2005) and was settled initially by French-Canadian fur traders. The first slave ship arrived in the colony in 1719, and twenty-five slave ships in total came to the colony while it was under French control. In 1763 the Treaty of Paris was signed, which transferred New Orleans from French to Spanish control, and there it remained until it was sold to America in 1803 as part of the Louisiana Purchase.

Under the Spanish, New Orleans blossomed from a scrappy outpost into a proper urban center. They also eliminated import duties on slaves, which dramatically opened up a market that had all but closed by the end of the French period (Sublette 2008). Additionally, the implementation of Spanish law in place of the French Code Noir gave slaves a greater opportunity to purchase their freedom, greatly expanding the numbers of free people of color, which jumped from 165 at the end of the French period to about 1,500 by the end of the Spanish period (Mohammed 2005). The Spanish period also saw the increasing popularity of Congo Square, an area at the edge of the city where both free and enslaved people of color would gather on Sundays to dance and play music. By the time the U.S. authorities were handed New Orleans in 1803, a strong African presence was thriving and defining the city, separating it from other Southern and even Northern cities in the Union.

Many accounts of voodoo in New Orleans were made in the early nineteenth century, when scores of white planters, fleeing the violence in revolutionary Haiti, settled in New Orleans with their slaves, who brought the religion with them. It is estimated that three thousand Haitian refugees arrived in the state between 1809 and 1810 alone (Sumpter 2008). While the exact beginning of voodoo is impossible to ascertain, it is highly likely that these West Indian slaves influenced how voodoo was practiced. However, it would be erroneous to read their migration as the definitive genesis of voodoo in New Orleans. The earliest report of African spiritual practices appears in the writing of French planter Antoine-Simon Le Page du Pratz, whose *Historie de la Louisiane*, written in the 1730s and published in 1758, was the first written history of Louisiana. Le Page du Pratz spends some time outlining the practices of slaves, writing that Africans were "very superstitious and attached . . . to little toys which they call *gris-gris* . . . [and] would believe themselves undone if they were stripped of these trinkets" (quoted in Sumpter 2008: 122). Marcus Christian, head of the Negro Federal Writer's Project in Louisiana, recounted a 1773 famous court case in which two slaves were accused of attempting to poison their overseer with the use of a toxic gris-gris (Sumpter 2008). While it is difficult to get a full picture of the practice from what is available in this written account, it is clear that some form of African religion was being practiced before the nineteenth century.

After 1803, American city officials passed laws and ordinances meant to bring the racial and social order of New Orleans more in line with that of the nation. The transformation from colony to state demanded the end of racial fluidity and the implementation of legislation that restricted political power of both free and enslaved blacks. Between 1806 and 1857 the emancipation of slaves was declared illegal, immigrants of color who arrived after 1825 were required to leave the state, the famous quadroon balls—which facilitated the common-law marriages between free women of color and white men, known as *plaçage*—were banned, and cemeteries became racially segregated (Sumpter 2008). It is in this context of a shifting racial and social terrain, and the increasing marginalization of New Orleans' black citizenry, that voodoo tourism and a voodoo tourist discourse began to take shape.

MARIE LAVEAU—THE "VOODOO QUEEN"— AND SAINT JOHN'S EVE CELEBRATION

Of course, any discussion of New Orleans voodoo must include Marie Laveau, the (in)famous "Voodoo Queen of New Orleans." As one of the most popular and mythologized figures in New Orleans history, the continuing presence of voodoo in the city is in no small part due to her efforts. Her tomb is a testament to her lasting popularity: located in Saint Louis Cemetery No. 1, the oldest cemetery in New Orleans, Laveau's grave is visited by hundreds of people each year. Undoubtedly, the tomb of Laveau is one of New Orleans' most visited gravesites and a major tourist draw. Her lasting legacy is due, in part, to the numerous individuals who have kept her alive in popular memory but is equally a testament to her own business and marketing skills. Indeed, it was Laveau who first popularized New Orleans voodoo on a national level and created discursive and economic space for voodoo as popular entertainment. It is fair to say that voodoo tourism can trace its birth directly to her.

Marie Laveau was born on September 10, 1801, in the twilight of the Spanish period. She was the daughter of a free man of color, Charles Laveau (who was possibly the illegitimate son of a prominent politician), and a free woman of color, Marguerite Darcantel—both New Orleans natives. At the age of seventeen Marie married Jacques Paris, a free quadroon from Haiti. However, their marriage was not happy, and within a year he disappeared from both the city and the historical record. It is widely rumored that, after her husband left, Laveau worked as a hairdresser for wealthy white patrons as a means to support herself, and it was these professional contacts that facilitated her ascendancy to the status of Voodoo Queen of the city. However, contrary to these rumors Laveau was never listed as a hairdresser in the city directory of the U.S. census (Long 2001); the majority of her time was instead spent working as a nurse. Her social and political contacts were probably earned from a combination of both domestic and medicinal work, and—if her father was indeed the son of a politician—he could have greatly assisted in the formation of her political network.

The mid-1800s appear to be when Laveau began her voodoo activities. This early work was practiced in the domestic sphere, on a person-to-person and case-by-case basis. By the 1870s, she began moving voodoo into the public sphere, most notably through her involvement in the Saint John's Eve celebrations. The observance of Saint John's Eve in New Orleans preexisted Laveau; it was most likely brought to the colony by the French and the Spanish and then adopted by enslaved Africans because Haitian vodou practitioners celebrated a similar holiday. At some point, voodooists began to gather on the banks of Lake Pontchartrain on or around June 23 to celebrate the holiday. Beginning in the 1870s, hundreds of visitors took the Pontchartrain Railroad in hopes of witnessing these voodoo ceremonies. Indeed, New Orleans newspapers from 1870 to 1876 made a point to cover the event (Touchstone 1972). Laveau helped neutralize the potential danger voodoo held for whites by transforming the practice from a private rite into a public spectacle. Furthermore, she centered herself in the narrative of the Saint John's Eve festival, further adding to her reputation as the Voodoo Queen of New Orleans. Her (self-)promotion paved the way for voodoo tourism.

The number of attendees varies from account to account, but it is clear that the holiday drew large crowds. One writer from the *New Orleans Times*, after learning the location of the dance from "an old negress, who sells in the market and whom I have known for years to be well posted," described about "two hundred persons—mixed colors—white, black and mulattoes," with another one hundred following his arrival (Touchstone 1972: 376). An account from 1874 numbered the crowd at twelve thousand (Touchstone 1972). The makeup of the voodoo spectacle varied as well. A *New Orleans Times* writer described a midnight ceremony that featured Marie Laveau, a black cauldron, and the sacrifice of a live rooster (Touchstone 1972). Another visitor, after searching for Laveau, found instead her "representative," who initially intended to "inaugurate the festivities on this night, but . . . on account of the large [attendance] of white people, she had determined not to do it" and left. The visitor was then forced to turn his attention to the smaller groups gathered around the lake, where "the negro was in his element—plenty of whiskey, plenty of light and a big crowd" ("African Rites" 1874: 3, 4).

However, as Blake Touchstone (1972) has demonstrated, the majority of the "voodoo ceremonies" that took place at Lake Pontchartrain were not actual rites but were instead gatherings of local African Americans who took advantage of white curiosity and the leisure time afforded by the holiday to both have a good time and earn a little income. For example, after being directed to a "voodoo chapel" one reporter was disappointed; he saw "men, women, and children in all degrees of raggedness, and heard the uneven measure of the meanest music and lowest Negro dance it was ever [our] privilege to witness" (Fandrich 2005: 147). Another reporter in 1875 wrote of a special license obtained so that a building on the Milneburg wharf could hold voodoo ceremonies; policemen served as guards and helped collect money (Touchstone 1972). Actual voodoo ceremonies were more than likely not performed for the white attendees, but the activities described by reporters helped shape public perception of the religious practice.

VOODOO LITERATURE: LYLE SAXON, THE LOUISIANA WRITERS' PROJECT, AND ROBERT TALLANT

Also beginning in the late nineteenth century but reaching full formation by the mid-twentieth century is the growth of what I call "voodoo literature"—books, newspaper and magazine articles, and travelogues that take voodoo as their primary subject matter. While voodoo had been prime fodder for journalists since at least the mid-eighteenth century, the genre shifts of the subject matter from newspapers to magazines to books (and later film) clearly illustrate the firm existence of a significant and avid audience that continues to the present day. Works such as Lyle Saxon's *Fabulous New Orleans* (1928), *New Orleans City Guide* (1938) by the Federal Writers' Project of the WPA, and Tallant's *Voodoo in New Orleans* are perhaps the most representative of this genre. The popularity of these works is hardly due to the quality of the writing, which is comparable to that of pulp fiction, and they are filled with numerous inaccuracies and blatant racism. But in spite of (or perhaps in part because of) these caveats, these books enjoyed enormous popularity upon their publication and have retained a significant readership into the present day.

This popularity becomes increasingly noteworthy when one considers the cultural work that voodoo literature performs, especially its role in determining voodoo tourism practices. Through their writings, Saxon, the WPA, and Tallant played a fundamental role in shaping audiences' and tourists' expectations of what voodoo was, what it looked like, who practiced it, and how it was practiced. These sensationalistic representations of voodoo and its practitioners mainly used a discourse that imbued race and place with spectacular, supernatural meanings. Their repeated images of sinister black folks gathering at midnight to perform frenzied rituals filled with bizarre paraphernalia defined voodoo as a crude practice that was primarily the domain of African Americans but was nonetheless accessible to white outsiders (if one knew whom to ask). In other words, Saxon and his peers normalized the reductive notion of voodoo as a form of entertainment, a spectacle that was not suitable for white *participation* but was an enthralling commodity for white *consumption*.

Fact and fiction are deeply blurred in these three books (and in the newspaper articles, for that matter). Urban legend, myths, and hearsay were all incorporated but with little effort to verify these accounts because the primary goal was to entertain. Fact-based explorations of voodoo were mostly being done by anthropologists such as Zora Neale Hurston. The *New Orleans City Guide* and Tallant's *Voodoo in New Orleans* predominately drew on interviews with black New Orleans residents, but the veracity of these interviews (many of them done by Tallant, who worked as an editor for the Louisiana Writers' Project) has since been questioned (Allured 2006). Regardless of the veracity of these accounts, the discourse about voodoo that they generated greatly contributed to popular understandings of the practice that later informed voodoo tourism in New Orleans.

The headline of one 1933 *Chicago Daily Tribune* article could double as a pithy summarization of how voodoo was approached during this time: "Fanatic Devotees of Voodoo in Deep South Preserve Weird Rites: Superstitious Blacks Cling to Belief in Sorceries and Charms Devised by Vanished 'Kings' and 'Queens'" (Mcnaugh 1933). The article details a voodoo ceremony that readers are led to believe is a firsthand account but is probably cobbled together from previous accounts that were just as filled with inaccuracies. Yet what is most significant here is not the account's accuracy but the language of racialized spectacle:

> The shadowy figures that bore the candles through the woods are transformed at once into men and women, the kind one might expect to meet in the fastness of an African jungle. . . . The black bodies reflect the light of the torches or silhouette in front of the smoking flames to cast fantastic shadows upon the lurid trunks of the trees. (Mcnaugh 1933: G8)

After describing the first half of the ceremony, which includes a rattlesnake and the possession of the voodoo queen, the author goes on:

> Soon everyone is dancing in wild abandonment. The dancers shriek and moan as each tries to outdo the others. Nude girls, white as chalk,

appear among the leaping figures. They are young wenches painted white, or else, as it has been whispered in many places, actually white girls. The dance grows more revolting as it continues. (Mcnaugh 1933: G8)

The appearance of naked, (possibly) white female dancers adds a measure of scandal to this already outrageous scene. Their presence disrupts the notion that voodoo—with its associated barbarity—is limited to African Americans. Moreover, their nudity and femininity play into the white population's fears that "their" women will be seduced by the carnality of black culture. This narrative, then, positions voodoo as a potential threat to the coherence and boundaries of the New Orleans racialized and gendered social order.

Other contemporaneous writings played on similar themes. Saxon's *Fabulous New Orleans* relied on racist representations of voodoo with great success: by 1934 the book had sold fifty thousand copies, was recommended reading in New Orleans public schools, and—most important for voodoo tourism—visitors were reported arriving in New Orleans with copies of the book clutched in their hands (Thomas 1991). The chapter titled "Voodoo" recounts a voodoo ceremony that Saxon claimed to have witnessed, but it employs virtually all the tropes of previous voodoo literature—especially its dependence on racist stereotypes of Negroes:

> To understand properly the workings of this black magic, one must understand something of the negro's characteristics. . . . [H]e is intently emotional, he possesses a childlike credulity . . . his imagination is easily inflamed. (Saxon 1928: 239)

This offensive description is repeated in his description of the African American man who leads Saxon to the ceremony, who is described as "a fullblooded Congo black man . . . very ignorant, very superstitious" (Saxon 1928: 309). Later, Saxon details the beginning of the ritual:

> A new rhythm. Hips are shaking now. Men and women tip bottles to their lips as they sway. The emaciated yellow girl tears at her waist with a shrill scream. A man throws himself upon her and bites her breast. The big negro pulls him away and throws him to one side. There is blood on the girl's breast, but she continues to swing her body, uttering now and then a thin, high cry. (321)

These scenes portray voodoo as a base, repulsive practice that both stems from and fuels the supposed baseness and repulsiveness of black men and women. Voodoo, and by extension black culture as a whole, is made synonymous with *lack*—a lack of morality, value, civilization, decency, and humanity. In these accounts, voodoo is the domain of the racialized bereft.

The *New Orleans City Guide* was one of the WPA's four-hundred-volume American Guide Series, which was published between 1935 and 1941 (Powell 2009). Published by the Federal Writers' Project of the WPA, the guides covered every U.S. state and U.S. territories such as Puerto Rico. The guides came at a time when the country's historical and cultural identity and memory was of foremost concern. They were also designed in part to facilitate automobile tourism across the country and were thus written with a burgeoning national tourist audience in mind (Megraw 2011). Published by the state-based branch of the Federal Writers' Project, known as the Louisiana Writers' Project, the *New Orleans City Guide* was well received upon its publication. It sold nineteen thousand copies, went through five printings, and was reissued three times between 1952 and 2009 (Larson 2009; Powell 2009). The Louisiana Writers' Project was directed by none other than Saxon, who by this time was a fixture in the local literary scene. Saxon was the primary writer and editor of the *New Orleans City Guide*, which consisted of two sections: one on the state's history, folkways, economic industries, and so forth, and a second focused on cities and towns in Louisiana.

Saxon managed to add his distinctive literary touch in the "Folkways" section, which is where voodoo first appears. This section is presented as the narrative account of a nameless traveler who has recently arrived in the French Quarter. The traveler encounters a Creole man who takes him on a tour through the city in search of voodoo. Continuing the discursive tradition of mapping race and belonging onto the cityscape of New Orleans, the two walk toward the "Negro Quarter near Claiborne Street" in search of a particular "voodoo woman" whom the Creole's colored nurse used to consult. As they walk, the Creole man describes voodoo thus:

> My friend, the Voodoo is a thing which has caused much trouble to us from earliest times. The Voodoo was brought here from Africa by the niggers our ancestors bought as slaves. And let me tell you, my friend, those early colonists, they had to keep a sharp eye out for trickery. These Voodoo queens, they knew things no white man ever knew. They could make people die, have them buried, and raise them again two weeks or a month later. (Federal Writers' Project 1938: 58)

However, the actual encounter with the voodoo woman does not live up to the narrator's expectations:

The Voodoo woman, of course, is a disappointment. The Creole never honestly expected she would divulge any of her secrets, but she is very pleasant, and tells you with a flashing smile that *"Zaffaire Cabritt ça pas zaffaire Mouton"* (The goat's business is none of the sheep's concern). (62)

This is a key moment in which Saxon implicitly outlines the discursive work of voodoo literature and the resulting expectations that lie at the heart of voodoo tourism. The traveler's visit to the voodoo woman is worthwhile only if she divulges her secrets regarding the inner workings and practices of voodoo. Otherwise the trip is a "disappointment," meaning the value lies not in the interaction with the woman but in acquisition of this secret knowledge. Although Saxon himself was certainly unconcerned with dispelling misconceptions, his writings normalized the idea that encounters with voodoo should be both entertaining and informative.

Perhaps the most popular example of voodoo literature is Tallant's *Voodoo in New Orleans*. Born in New Orleans in 1909, Tallant was eventually tapped by Lyle Saxon to assist him with the Louisiana Writers' Project. Much of Tallant's effort was spent gathering oral history interviews that make their way into the *New Orleans City Guide* and *Voodoo in New Orleans*, as well as his other writings. As a novel, *Voodoo in New Orleans* straddles a blurry line between fiction and ethnography that more than once flirts with outright plagiarism. While a bibliography at the end of the book includes works by Saxon, George W. Cable, and Henry C. Castellanos and a number of newspaper articles, the text itself has no citations or footnotes, and thus there is no way to tell where Tallant's writing ends and someone else's writing begins. This is in line with the patchwork approach taken by the Louisiana Writers' Project and Lyle Saxon, which may explain why Saxon wrote an enthusiastic foreword to the book, calling it a "truthful and definitive picture" of voodoo and proclaiming himself highly pleased with the "accuracy and integrity" of Tallant's work. Tallant continued the work of his forebears by using voodoo to reinforce racial, spatial, and social differences in the cityscape. Similarly to the *City Guide*, in Tallant's account race makes an early and central appearance:

Sometimes a white man in New Orleans takes a walk along South Rampart Street, one of the famous Negro thoroughfares of America. He turns at Canal Street, the city's most important business street, and immediately finds himself in a new world, with its own particular sights and sounds and smells. (Tallant 1946: 3)

Once again, the encounter with voodoo is framed through the experience of a tour through an otherworldly African American neighborhood, one so distant from white New Orleans that "the white man walking on South Rampart Street is a foreigner" (Tallant 1946: 4). This difference is further highlighted in his description of street vendors, many of whom sell voodoo "novelties":

> If the white man inspects these he will see candles of various sizes and colors, incense and strange-looking roots and herbs, usually reduced to brown powders. He will see the empty vials and small bottles these vendors sell, and he will wonder at the sight of the queer old women who stop to buy them. He may even speculate on whether or not these people are Voodoos. He will get no satisfaction asking questions. Here he has reached a barrier. . . . Everyone will be polite, but they will tell him nothing—unless he is known to be a white Voodoo. (Tallant 1946: 4)

As in Saxon's and the WPA's works, the narrative begins with a strict color-knowledge barrier being set. The authors then temporarily cross this barrier with the help of local black voodoo practitioners or those familiar with voodoo (who might not be black, as with the Creole interloper, but are definitely not white). This narrative gives potential visitors to the city a road map for having their own encounter with the spectacle: go to this neighborhood, find someone who knows, and have her or him show you. Still to this day this is the model for voodoo tourism, in which tourists are safely guided through the voodoo landscape of New Orleans by either voodoo practitioners or those who are—or claim to be—intimately familiar with the workings and magic of voodoo.

THE PERSECUTION OF VOODOO

At the same time that this particular discourse of voodoo was solidified and made fit for popular consumption, actual voodoo practitioners were subject to increased persecution from local and national authorities—specifically, the New Orleans police, the State Board of Health, and federal postal authorities (Long 2001). Between the early 1900s and into the 1950s, voodoo practitioners who operated a business either through long-distance mail order or local community channels were arrested and fined, typically on charges of mail fraud, practicing medicine without a license, or both.

One of the most publicized cases was that of Dr. Lewis Rockford, who owned a hoodoo drugstore in the Lower Ninth Ward and also held church services several times a week in an auditorium flanking his house. Accused of "doing a large business in voodoo charms, thereby defrauding the customers of the U.S. Post Office Department of their rights to expect everything they ordered and paid for," Rockford was sentenced to two years at an Atlanta federal penitentiary for mail fraud (Long 2001: 134). Another famous case was that of the Cracker Jack Drug Store, which was owned by a white physician and pharmacist named George A. Thomas and located on South Rampart Street, a black commercial and entertainment district. The federal investigation of Dr. Thomas for selling "hoodoo supplies" made the front page of both the *New Orleans Morning Tribune* and the *Times-Picayune* in the mid-1930s (Long 2001: 147). Although it appears that Dr. Thomas was lucky enough to escape indictment (perhaps due in part to his race), other business owners were not so fortunate. Much like accusations of deception and trickery leveled at fortune-tellers (see Chapter 6), the alleged connection between fraud and voodoo underscored the illicit status of voodoo in the New Orleans imaginary.

While antivoodoo attitudes drove much of the crackdown on black-owned voodoo businesses, the crackdown was also motivated by Jim Crow–fueled desire to limit African American economic attainment. Scholars such as Glenda Elizabeth Gilmore (1996) have discussed how the visible display of black wealth irritated whites during the early years of Jim Crow. This envy of wealthy black citizens had a chilling effect on the business of voodoo, which could indeed be quite lucrative. One report from the Louisiana Writers' Project noted that "queens and doctors" made a salary of over $50,000 annually (Long 2006: 133). A separate Louisiana Writers' Project article details how Dr. Rockford Lewis "[employed] five secretaries to handle his ever growing out-of-town correspondence, sported a huge diamond ring and rode around in a Pierce Arrow auto, driven by a liveried chauffeur" (Breaux and McKinney 1937). By the second half of the twentieth century, voodoo stores had been effectively banished to segregated African American neighborhoods. A 1960 article titled "Voodoo Vendors" noted that most of the "voodoo novelty shops" were located "in the negro sections" of New Orleans and most of the customers were African American (Zinman 1960: 15). Unsurprisingly, tourists were discouraged from visiting these predominately black neighborhoods, resulting in financial troubles for many voodoo shop owners.

THE CIVIL RIGHTS MOVEMENT AND THE SHIFTING VIEWS OF VOODOO

The catalyst for New Orleans' shifting views of voodoo can be traced back to the social upheavals of the 1960s and 1970s and the concomitant realignment of racial power. In the South, the civil rights movement successfully dismantled the legal structures of social segregation, although New Orleans (like other southern cities) initially resisted these changes. However, after several high-profile incidents, including Ruby Bridges's historic 1960 attempt to attend William Frantz School, the resulting damage to the city's image forced city leaders to realize that segregation was no longer a sustainable option. The backlash from resistance to school desegregation was especially felt by the tourism industry: hotel and restaurant sales fell more than 30 percent, Bourbon Street business and taxi fares slumped, and French Quarter hotels and restaurants reported empty rooms and tables in the week before the Sugar Bowl (Souther 2006).

Despite the backlash, New Orleans experienced further progress toward racial justice in the latter half of the 1960s and into the 1970s. The Voting Rights Act of 1965 paved the way for black involvement in Southern municipal politics for the first time since Reconstruction. By 1970, African Americans had grown to nearly half the city's total residents (Souther 2006), and they made up nearly three-tenths of the city's electorate. The black community proved its political power in 1970 by casting a significant number of the votes for Moon Landrieu, the successful Democratic candidate for mayor of New Orleans that year. Before the Landrieu administration, tourism was primarily seen as a means to attract further investment in other areas of the city's economy. It was concentrated around Mardi Gras (which was tightly controlled by elite, all-white krewes) and preservationists' displays of the French Quarter, along with local restaurants, hotels, and shops (Souther 2006). Landrieu wholeheartedly embraced tourism as a means of economic growth and a source of employment for the city's increasingly impoverished black population.

Black New Orleanians' growing political power transferred over to the tourist industry as well. In 1965, the rule barring blacks from the Association of Commerce was lifted (Gotham 2007), which allowed black-owned businesses to receive the same level of promotion as white-owned businesses. The black community's impact on the tourist landscape would accelerate after the second half of the 1980s, when the preservation of the city's African American heritage became a principal concern. For example, percussionist Luther Gray founded the Congo Square Foundation in 1989 and lobbied for Congo Square (the nineteenth-century gathering spot for enslaved and free blacks) to be listed on the National Register of Historic Places, which it was in 1997 (Souther 2006). In 1990, the Greater New Orleans Black Tourism Network was founded as an arm of the Greater New Orleans Tourism and Convention Commission and with the mandate of crafting a distinctive experience for African American tourists. It was this organization that worked with *Essence* magazine in 1995 to make New Orleans the permanent home of the annual Essence Music Festival, which remains one of the city's largest annual events to date.

The black New Orleanian cultural practices of second lines, brass bands, jazz funerals, and Mardi Gras Indians also enjoyed increased attention from city boosters and became commonplace images in tourism brochures, travel guides, and promotions (Gotham 2007). Whereas previous understandings of the city associated local culture with whiteness and nonblack Creoles, post-1970 tourism discourse created a new space for African and Afro-Creole within the definition of "New Orleans culture." Most importantly, this black culture was seen as not only valuable but essential to the New Orleans experience. Visiting Preservation Hall, eating Afro-Creole food, and watching second lines became integral to the authentic tourist experience.

The founding of the New Orleans Historic Voodoo Museum (NOHVM) in 1972 is yet another testament to how views of black culture changed after the demise of Jim Crow. By the end of the 1990s several voodoo institutions negotiated tourism in ways denied to their early twentieth-century predecessors. This group includes the NOHVM, voodoo stores such as Marie Laveau's House of Voodoo, and personalities like the Chicken Man, who traveled through the French Quarter selling gris-gris, calculating lottery numbers, and posing for pictures with tourists. Other establishments, such as the Island of Salvation Botanica, founded by Ukrainian-Jewish vodou initiate Sallie Ann Glassman, dedicate themselves largely to voodoo as a religious practice—although they welcome tourists. The Voodoo Spiritual Temple was founded in 1990 by New Orleans transplants Oswan and Miriam Chimani; the temple is home to a community of voodoo practitioners and also hosts a number of voodoo tours on a near-daily basis. Then there are individual figures such as Priestess Ava Kay Jones, who is an initiated *mambo* (Haitian vodou priestess) and regularly presides over vodou ceremonies. She also lectures about voodoo for tourists and tourist industry workers. She founded the Voodoo Macumba Dance Troupe, an African dance company that performs for both voodoo and nonvoodoo audiences (Davis 1999).

As African American culture became part of the tourist landscape, it also became acceptable to explore voodoo as a legitimate aspect of that heritage. Voodoo thus underwent a decriminalization process that transformed it from a presumed satanic illustration of black inferiority into a recognized religion of the African diaspora. Released from their marginalized status, practitioners could openly pursue both the religious and economic side of voodoo without fear of reprisal. Voodoo practitioners were then able to contribute to the discourse surrounding voodoo to a greater degree than they ever had before, both in New Orleans and across the nation.

This recent neutral stance toward voodoo in New Orleans can also be seen in media depictions that sharply contrast with earlier accounts. For example, in 1989 the *Chicago Tribune* reported:

> Voodoo, however, seems to hold a special place in the cash register of the New Orleans pilgrimage business. Like Dixieland, the religion suffers (or perhaps benefits) from a lack of definition. Most tourists know only that voodoo derives from West African religious rites that became mixed with Roman Catholicism in the West Indies and came to America with the slaves. The neophytes also have been given to understand that, outside Louisiana, few U.S. citizens practice voodoo on any organized basis. (Cross 1989: 31)

Given that this is the same newspaper that in 1933 told of "negroes in the South" preserving "weird rites," the anthropological ordinariness of this passage is significantly more remarkable than it otherwise seems. Voodoo is now understood as a unique and historically grounded aspect of New Orleanian culture versus its previous representation as a degenerate practice carried over from darkest Africa.

Yet at the same time, this newfound freedom does not indicate that an entirely new discourse has been developed. Previous understandings and imaginings of voodoo remain, even in this moment of renaissance and in fact help mold the contours of modern voodoo tourism. It can be argued, for example, that education and exploration are the organizing principles for both voodoo shops and voodoo tours, just as it was for early twentieth-century voodoo literature. Choices regarding the products sold in stores, the areas visited on tours, and the images used to advertise and entice are all shaped by the tourist's desire to understand voodoo. As in earlier eras, today's producers of voodoo tourism frequently engage with earlier, often inaccurate discursive understandings of voodoo as a means of satisfying this desire. Thus, popular misconceptions about voodoo are retained in the current tourist industry, and critical inquiry into the unequal power relationships that formed these misrepresentations are sidestepped in favor of offering tourists experiences that are more pleasurable.

CONCLUSIONS

While it is impossible to determine the exact origins of voodoo, it is clearly an eclectic mix of religious practices—mostly of African and Haitian origin—along with distinctive elements that are uniquely New Orleanian. These historical and cultural ties to voodoo are now a large part of the city's heritage tourism, though not that long ago voodoo—along with its African American practitioners—was marginalized and maligned. Some of the most popular classic depictions of voodoo are overtly racist and portray the practice as base and repulsive, reflecting the white perception of black culture on the whole during this period. Perhaps most ironically, just as voodoo was being molded into a tourist commodity in the 1930s and 1940s, practitioners of voodoo were facing persecution by local, state, and federal authorities. This persecution continued until the tidal wave of the civil rights movement marked a new era in which voodoo—and African American cultural contributions more generally—would be recast as an integral part of the New Orleans tourist landscape.

Clearly, voodoo's place in the New Orleans tourist imaginary is both a product of and a response to New Orleans' particular history of race, geography, and power. By examining the interactions between voodoo and the tourism industry, we can better understand the impact of popular discourse on New Orleans' African American population as well as broader understandings of American history. Though fraught, the city's development of voodoo tourism is a testament to the dynamic history of black cultural life in New Orleans and to the interdependent relationship between race and place. As a cultural product, voodoo tells us part of the story of New Orleans, which in turn helps us grapple with the uniquely racialized history of the United States.

REFERENCES

"African Rites on American Soil: The Voudous First Night." 1874. *New Orleans Bulletin*, June 25. Reel 8, Robert Tallant Papers, Amistad Research Center, New Orleans, LA.

Allured, Janet L. 2006. Review of *The Mysterious Voodoo Queen, Marie Laveaux: A Study of Powerful Female Leadership in Nineteenth-Century New Orleans*, by Ina Johanna Fandrich, and *Voodoo Queen: The Spirited Lives of Marie Laveau*, by Martha Ward. *Humanities and Social Sciences Net*, March. Available at http://www.h-net.org/reviews/showrev.php?id=11484.

Breaux, Hazel, and Robert McKinney. 1937. "Dr. Rockford Lewis." April 6. Reel 8, Robert Tallant Papers, Amistad Research Center, New Orleans, LA.

Brown, Karen McCarthy. 1991. *Mama Lola: A Vodou Priestess in Brooklyn*. Berkeley: University of California Press.

Cross, Robert. 1989. "Hoodoo Voodoo?" *Chicago Tribune*, August 16. Available at http://articles.chicagotribune.com/1989-08-16/entertainment/8901050551_1_voodoo-dolls-mardi-gras-bourbon-street.

Davis, Rod. 1999. *American Voudou: Journey to a Hidden World*. Denton: University of North Texas Press.

Deren, Maya. 1953. *Divine Horsemen: The Living Gods of Haiti*. New York: McPherson.

Fandrich, Ina Johanna. 2005. *The Mysterious Voodoo Queen, Marie Laveaux: Leadership in Nineteenth-Century New Orleans*. New York: Routledge.

Federal Writers' Project. 1938. *New Orleans City Guide*. Boston: Houghton Mifflin. Available at https://archive.org/details/neworleanscity00writmiss.

Gilmore, Glenda Elizabeth. 1996. *Gender and Jim Crow: Women and the Politics of White Supremacy in North Carolina, 1896–1920*. Chapel Hill: University of North Carolina Press.

Gotham, Kevin Fox. 2007. *Authentic New Orleans: Tourism, Culture, and Race in the Big Easy*. New York: New York University Press.

Hurston, Zora Neale. 1938. *Tell My Horse: Voodoo and Life in Haiti and Jamaica*. New York: Harper and Row.

Jervis, Rick. 2007. "Tourists Return as City Mends." *USA Today*, October 12, p. 1A.

Larson, Susan. 2009. "WPA City Guide Still Draws New Orleans Readers." *Times-Picayune*, May 22. Available at http://blog.nola.com/susanlarson/2009/05/wpa_city_guide_still_draws_new.html.

Long, Carolyn Morrow. 2001. *Spiritual Merchants: Religion, Magic, and Commerce*. Knoxville: University of Tennessee Press.

———. 2006. *A New Orleans Voudou Priestess: The Legend and Reality of Marie Laveau*. Gainesville: University Press of Florida.

Mcnaugh, John A. 1933. "Fanatic Devotees of Voodoo in Deep South Preserve Weird Rites." *Chicago Daily Tribune*, December 24, p. G8.

Megraw, Richard. 2011. "Federal Writers Project." In *Know Louisiana: The Digital Encyclopedia of Louisiana*, edited by David Johnson. New Orleans: Louisiana Endowment for the Humanities, 2010– . Available at http://www.knowlouisiana.org/entry/federal-writers-project.

Mohammed, Patricia. 2005. "The Sign of the Loa." *Small Axe* 9 (2): 124–149.

Powell, Lawrence N. 2009. "Lyle Saxon and the WPA Guide to New Orleans." *Southern Spaces*, July 29. Available at http://www.southernspaces.org/2009/lyle-saxon-and-wpa-guide-new-orleans.

Saxon, Lyle. 1928. *Fabulous New Orleans*. New York: Century Company.

Souther, J. Mark. 2006. *New Orleans on Parade: Tourism and the Transformation of the Crescent City*. Baton Rouge: Louisiana State University Press.

Stanonis, Anthony J. 2006. *Creating the Big Easy: New Orleans and the Emergence of Modern Tourism, 1918–1945*. Athens: University of Georgia Press.

Sublette, Ned. 2008. *The World That Made New Orleans: From Spanish Silver to Congo Square*. Chicago: Lawrence Hill.

Sumpter, Amy R. 2008. "Segregation of the Free People of Color and the Construction of Race in Antebellum New Orleans." *Southeastern Geographer* 48 (1): 19–37.

Tallant, Robert. (1946) 1984. *Voodoo in New Orleans*. Gretna, LA: Pelican.

Thomas, James W. 1991. *Lyle Saxon: A Critical Biography*. Birmingham, AL: Summa.

Touchstone, Blake. 1972. "Voodoo in New Orleans." *Louisiana History* 13 (4): 371–386.

Zinman, David. 1960. "Voodoo Vendors: Old Black Magic Still Practiced." *Spokesman-Review*, November 5, p. 15. Available at http://news.google.com/newspapers?id=bjJWAAAAIBAJ&sjid=iecDAAAAIBAJ&pg=5276,1919841&hl=en.

9

VAMPIRISM

Modern Vampires and Embattled Identity Claims

Joseph P. Laycock

If you live in the United States or Canada, there is a good chance you have crossed paths with someone who identifies as a vampire. The so-called real-vampire community consists of individuals who feel they must feed on the blood or vital energy of others to maintain their physical, mental, and spiritual well-being. Having studied this community since 2007, I have met vampires from many walks of life, including information technology specialists, medical professionals, and law enforcement. In most cases, acquaintances and coworkers were unaware of the individual's identity as a vampire. However, the last few years have seen an increasing awareness of the real-vampire community among the general public. In the wake of Stephenie Meyer's *Twilight* series and its film adaptations and HBO's *True Blood* series based on the novels of Charlaine Harris, there was a media rush for shows and specials featuring real vampires. One of my research contacts in the vampire community described receiving e-mails from television producers at least once a month.

Out of this sensationalism, a more serious conversation has begun to emerge. Since about 2015, there have been several articles by doctors and other helping professionals discussing encounters with self-identified vampires and attempting to make sense of their identity claims. Awareness of the vampire community has coincided with larger cultural battles concerning LGBTQ issues and what kinds of identity claims society should accommodate. In this political climate, some have expressed derision and even outrage that researchers and helping professionals would give any consideration to individuals claiming to be vampires. Such critics feel that self-identified vampires are clearly delusional or indulging in a puerile fantasy and that researchers and helping professionals are enabling them by taking their identity claims seriously.

This chapter seeks to render the controversy surrounding vampire identity claims understandable by locating it within a historical and social context. I argue that *modernity*—by which I mean the sociocultural norms, attitudes, and practices associated with the modern world—entails an ever-expanding array of possible identity claims. At the same time, modernity places ever-greater pressure on individuals to discover who they are and locate themselves within and among these claims. With this in mind, the idea of someone wrestling with the question of whether they are a normal human or something *other* or *more* than human can be regarded as a foreseeable progression in a pattern of increasing categories of identity. This situation also helps explain the cultural evolution of the vampire in folklore and fiction as well as the current cultural fascination with vampires. As modernity causes people to feel like outsiders, the vampire has come to be seen less as a demonic enemy of society and more as a sympathetic character or even a fellow outcast.

Finally, the reactionary response to vampires and their identity claims can also be seen as an acknowledgment—albeit a hostile one—of the conditions of modernity. Those who mock vampires seem to understand instinctively that identities are socially constructed and rendered viable through discourse. Thus, even as they scoff at researchers who examine vampires (especially those in the helping professions), these critics paradoxically concede that real vampires need not be dismissed out of hand as delusional or freakish and could one day receive social recognition as a new category of identity.

WHAT DO YOU MEAN YOU'RE A VAMPIRE?

The statement "I am a vampire" can signify many different and even contradictory claims. There is also not a complete consensus within the vampire community about what defines a vampire. One widely recognized distinction is between so-called lifestyle vampires and real vampires. Lifestyle vampires admire the vampire of folklore and fiction as a cultural archetype and enjoy emulating it. This interest may include participating in a subculture of vampire-themed societies and events held at nightclubs. The vampire lifestyle also has a heavy sartorial element that may include Goth or Victorian clothing, special jewelry (often featuring variations on an Egyptian ankh, made famous by the film *The Hunger* [1983]), and prosthetic fangs. "Fangsmiths" run small businesses producing fangs for the vampire community. Fangsmiths often have some training in dentistry and their products are usually quite sophisticated. In rare cases, lifestyle vampires may have porcelain fangs that are installed permanently. But no matter how dedicated lifestyle vampires are, they generally concede that they are more or less ordinary people participating in an unusual subculture.

By contrast, "real vampires" believe they are different from ordinary people in a more fundamental way that goes beyond affiliation with a subculture. There is not a consensus as to whether real vampirism is supernatural in nature or a naturally occurring phenomenon not yet understood by medical science, but real vampires generally agree that one cannot choose whether to become a vampire. In most cases, the real-vampire community does not believe that otherwise normal persons can be turned into a vampire as they are in fiction. Instead, the majority of real vampires describe coming to a realization that they have always been a vampire and that encountering the real-vampire community simply provided them with the vocabulary to express that condition. This process is sometimes referred to in the community as an "awakening." Real vampires may or may not participate in the vampire lifestyle. Those who do, often describe wearing fangs and other forms of participation in the subculture as an outer cultural expression of an identity they were born into.

Real vampires do not believe that they are undead or immortal. Some real vampires feel they have unusually sharp senses or heightened levels of empathy and intuition but generally do not claim to have any superhuman abilities associated with fictional vampires such as shape-shifting. Most real vampires do not describe having the traditional weaknesses of the folkloric vampire (garlic, silver, etc.), although a sizable minority claim to have a sensitivity or an aversion to sunlight. The feature that most defines real vampirism is a need to consume either the blood or vital energy of others. This need is typically framed as a health issue in which the vampire's well-being deteriorates the longer the time without feeding. A universal set of symptoms is not associated with the need for feeding, but vampires have reported experiencing migraines, anxiety, nightmares, and other physical, mental, or emotional problems. Vampires feed in different ways, but the most common feeding types are known as sanguinarian vampires (blood consumers) and psychic vampires (energy consumers).

Sanguinarian vampires generally consume human blood, although there is precedent for consuming animal blood. There is anecdotal evidence that in the past sanguinarian vampires used many techniques to acquire blood, including such methods as saving used adhesive bandages (Laycock 2009). However, since the vampire community became more organized in the 1990s, there has been a focus on finding the most sanitary and ethical methods of acquiring blood. Sanguinarians rarely consume more than a few drops of blood released from small cuts. Some sanguinarians prefer to use disposable lancets designed for testing blood sugar. Blood is acquired from consenting donors, and the community has produced a donor's bill of rights outlining an ethical relationship between donors and vampires.[1] The vampire community believes in self-policing, and abuse of donors appears to be very rare.

Psychic vampires believe they feed on the life force, or subtle energy, of other people. The existence of subtle energy cannot be scientifically proved, but this idea has precedent in traditional Asian health practices such as tai chi and yoga as well as Western metaphysical traditions such as mesmerism. The idea that certain people are vampires who drain the psychic energy of others is also described in numerous occult texts of the nineteenth century. Writings produced by occult groups such as the Theosophical Society (Olcott 2004) and the Golden Dawn (Fortune 1997) describe ways to detect and thwart such individuals. Psychic vampire and writer Michelle Belanger describes reading this material and concluding that she was the sort of entity described in it. Self-identified psychic vampires believe that while they cannot eliminate their need for the vital energy of others, they can find ethical ways to feed. This might entail asking permission to feed or feeding in areas where a great deal of ambient psychic energy is believed to be present, such as rock concerts or Pentecostal church services. Some psychic vampires have argued that their feeding can even benefit others—for example, by helping calm someone suffering from hyperactivity. Psychic vampires have significant cultural overlap with holistic health systems such as Reiki that also posit the existence of subtle energies linked to health.

So-called hybrid vampires may engage in both feeding modalities as opportunity presents. Some vampires have also raised the possibility of other forms of feeding, such as sexual, or Eros, vampires, who feed through sexual interactions (Carré and Gray 2016). Exactly what types of feeding constitute vampirism and what sort of energy vampires are feeding *on* has been an ongoing topic of discussion and debate within the real-vampire community.

It is unknown how many self-identified vampires exist. Some within the community estimate the total population to be several thousand. From 2006 to 2009, a research group called the Atlanta Vampire Alliance conducted the Vampire and Energy Work Research Study, which surveyed real vampires and other individuals who believe they work with vital energy. Over 1,450 individuals completed the global survey (Suscitatio Enterprises 2017). Some

---

1. Belfazaar Ashantison (2004), a sanguinarian from New Orleans, composed what is most likely the first donor's bill of rights. It outlines a relationship of mutual cooperation and respect between vampire and donor. In addition to discussing physical safety, the document also ensures the donor's right to be safe and free from stress while engaged in the vampire-donor relationship.

vampires known to the researchers did not take the survey, and it is unclear whether the study sample of 1,450 represented the majority of the community or a smaller portion. While it seems unlikely that real vampires will ever be a sizable minority, it seems equally unlikely that this community will disappear any time soon.

(MIS)UNDERSTANDING VAMPIRES

It is difficult for outsiders to make sense of the identity claims of vampires. The most common assumption when people first learn about self-identified vampires is that vampirism is either a kind of mental illness or an alternative form of religion. In my experience, both these ways of categorizing claims of vampire identity are inadequate, but there is not an obvious commonplace third category in which to locate them.

There is a small body of psychiatric literature on "vampirism" (Vanden Bergh and Kelly 1964; Jaffe and DiCataldo 1998; Noll 1992; Oppawsky 2010; Olry and Haines 2011). Psychiatric diagnoses have been proposed, such as clinical vampirism and Renfield's syndrome, in which individuals feel compelled to consume blood, although these are not official diagnoses found in the *Diagnostic and Statistical Manual of Mental Disorders (DSM-5)*. Significantly, this psychiatric literature is not based on studying members of the real-vampire community but rather on people who have been institutionalized following incidents in which they became a danger to themselves or others. While these individuals *did* exhibit a compulsion to consume blood, they usually did not claim they craved blood because they were vampires. Often, these patients were incapable of explaining why they did the things they did. Consequently, it was usually the psychiatrists themselves, rather than the patients, who connected this behavior to vampirism.

I have no training in psychiatry, but for what it is worth, I do not think any of the vampires I have met are mentally ill. I do not know how to evaluate their claims that they require blood or energy to be well, because they are describing subjective experiences that I cannot measure. But other than reporting these experiences, vampires do not seem substantially different from anyone else. The problem is not that their thinking is disordered but rather that they begin with a different set of premises and experiences in how they understand themselves.

The other common assumption is that vampirism is a religion. It is true that many self-identified vampires participate in a "cultic milieu" (Campbell 1972: 199). That is, real vampires are often interested in ideas drawn from the occult, metaphysics, and holistic health practices. There are also true vampire religions, complete with sacred texts, rituals, and religious hierarchies. A prime example of such a group would be the Temple of the Vampire, founded in 1989. The Temple of the Vampire maintains a roster of active members, offers correspondence classes in vampire rituals and philosophy, and publishes a document called *The Vampire Bible*.[2] However, only a small portion of the overall vampire community has any affiliation with the Temple of the Vampire or similar groups. Question 155 of the Vampire and Energy Work Research Study presents a list of fifty-one religions as well as Pagan and esoteric traditions. It asks, "Which faith, discipline, paradigm (spiritual/fraternal), or religion do you identify with? (Check all that apply.)" (Suscitatio Enterprises 2017). The top seven responses are (1) magick, (2) Wicca, (3) neo-Paganism, (4) occultism, (5) Christianity, (6) shamanism, and (7) agnostic/atheist/humanist/irreligious. Only a handful selected vampirism as their religion.

There are good arguments that vampirism might be regarded as a religious phenomenon, given the metaphysical beliefs associated with vampirism. Vampires also sometimes employ religious terms to describe the experience of feeding. For example, describing the sensation of feeding, one informant said, "[It's] like the universal 'ohm' resides in my head, vibrating through every atom I possess" (Riccardo 1996: 202). However, referring to the vampire community as a religion obscures more than it reveals because it implies elements like an institutional hierarchy, a prescribed body of rituals, and a catechism of shared beliefs—none of which are found across the community of vampires as a whole.

This leaves us without any ready-made framework with which to understand how vampires are different from nonvampires. For their part, vampires often compare vampirism to sexual orientation. Like advocates of the LGBTQ community (with which the vampire community has significant overlap),[3] vampires typically reject claims that their identity is a mental illness or a lifestyle choice. Belanger has described how her choice to publicly write about her experiences of vampirism has come with consequences, espe-

---

2. *The Vampire Bible* (Temple of the Vampire, 1989) was once available on Amazon but now can be purchased only through the Temple of the Vampire's website. Primarily, it describes a ritual for communing with "the Undead Gods," who are described as ancient disembodied entities that feed on human life force. The final section, titled "The Coming Apocalypse," tells how human civilization was first created by vampire gods in the ancient Near East. Younger vampires rebelled against their disembodied creators and destroyed the portals they used to enter our world. However, the Undead Gods will soon return and slaughter most of humanity in a "great harvest." As allies of the Undead Gods, the Temple of the Vampire will be spared and rule over humanity. *The Vampire Bible* begins with the epitaph "Within lies fact and fancy, truth and metaphor. Discriminate with care." Thus, the significance of the "great harvest" myth is left deliberately vague.

3. On the survey, 55 percent of respondents identified as heterosexual, 6 percent as homosexual, 32 percent as bisexual, and 6 percent as pansexual. One percent declined to respond (Suscitatio Enterprises 2017).

cially for a potential career as a professor. She writes that the progress of the gay rights movement has provided her with hope that the identity claims of vampires may not be as stigmatized in the future (Belanger 2005). Looking at the history of the LGBTQ community, there is evidence that Belanger's hope is not misplaced. The current backlash against the identity claims of vampires appears to be a reactionary response; in general, discourse about this community has become increasingly less sensationalistic.

It is unknown how long the real-vampire community has existed. While there seems to have been activity in the 1970s, the movement became prominent in the 1990s. This shift was supported by both wider access to the Internet and a surge of vampires in popular culture with films such as *Interview with the Vampire* (1994) and television series such as *Forever Knight* (1992–1996). White Wolf's role-playing game *Vampire: The Masquerade* was published in 1991. Live-action versions of the game helped bring self-identified vampires together and shaped an emerging subculture.

Unfortunately, a gruesome double homicide initially drew media attention to this community. In 1996, sixteen-year-old Rod Ferrell murdered Naomi Ruth Queen and Richard Wendorf of Eustis, Florida. Ferrell had been leading a coterie of teenagers described as "the vampire clan" from Murray, Kentucky, to New Orleans and had stopped in Eustis to pick up Heather Wendorf, a clan member and the daughter of the victims. Ferrell sometimes described himself as a five-hundred-year-old vampire named Vassago and had assigned similar vampiric names to his friends. The decision to attack the Wendorfs appears to have been a spontaneous action by Ferrell in which his associates did not participate. There was no clear motive for the murders, and it seems likely that Ferrell's identity as a vampire was play that became serious, resulting in irreversible consequences (Sato 1991).

The murders made national news and inspired a minor moral panic over vampires. Multiple true crime books were published about the case and several college campuses banned *Vampire: The Masquerade*. Psychological literature on this case did not frame it as an isolated incident but rather as a "case study" that demonstrated the existence of a widespread "vampire cult" (Miller et al. 1999; White and Hatim 2010).[4] Thomas Miller and colleagues even suggested that Ferrell had been "indoctrinated" into "the vampire cult" by "a stranger who appeared in the community about a year prior" (1999: 214). No citation is given for this detail, and I am unaware of any other literature on the case describing such an individual. By using words like "cult" and "occult" in imprecise and

---

4. Of the seven authors that contributed to these two articles, nearly all of them were from either the University of Kentucky or Murray State University, the latter being where Ferrell briefly played *Vampire: The Masquerade*.

uncritical ways, these articles framed identification as a vampire as a heretical and dangerous religion. Simultaneously, they offered a medicalized explanation in which everything from weak family bonds to role-playing games, and even exposure to *Sesame Street*'s "The Count" as a child (211), contributed to mental disturbances that drove adolescents to join "the vampire cult."

In addition to psychologists, the murders drew the attention of self-described occult crime experts who claimed that the Wendorf murders were part of a widespread pattern of vampire and occult-inspired crime. Unfortunately, the work of these "experts" became some of the first pseudoscholarly material published on the vampire community. A key figure in this material was Dawn Perlmutter (1999–2000, 2003, 2004), whose writings framed the vampire subculture as a deviant religion that is hostile to Christianity and bent on violence and murder. Perlmutter did not interview any self-identified vampires, and her research relied heavily on news reports and websites. This fear-driven view of the vampire community essentially reiterated the satanic panic of the 1980s, when an older generation of occult crime investigators alleged that all levels of American society had been infiltrated by a vast satanic conspiracy that murdered people with impunity.[5]

The public's next encounter with vampire culture came with the rise of reality television. In 2004, the Syfy channel aired *Mad Mad House*, in which so-called normal people were made to live in a house with so-called alternative people, including Don Henrie, a vampire. In one episode, viewers watch Henrie consume a brandy glass full of human blood. After 2004, demand increased for real vampires to appear on talk shows, news segments, and reality television series. Most vampires avoided this attention, not wanting to be outed to their friends and neighbors. A few, such as Henrie, had numerous appearances and even parlayed this attention into an acting career.

These patterns intensified after 2009, a high-water mark in popular demand for vampires, with *Twilight* and *True Blood*. After the publication of my book *Vampires Today* (2009), I started to receive regular solicitations from television producers seeking vampires to appear in their shows and documentaries.[6] Moral entrepreneurs also sought to capitalize on this craze.

---

5. Ironically, Ferrell himself later appealed to the satanic panic mythology in an interview given from prison. Ferrell alleged that he was not fully responsible for his crimes because he had been exposed to a satanic human sacrifice as a child. Even though Ferrell had never publicly told anyone this story before 2010 and it lacked any specific names, places, or corroborating evidence of any kind, the documentarians still found the story compelling (MSNBC 2014).

6. At the height of the calls, I received one from producers for the talk show *Dr. Phil*. In essence, they wanted to me to appear as an expert to explain why *Twilight* was inspiring teenagers to bite each other on the neck. I expressed skepticism and asked whether Dr. Phil understood what hickeys are. The producer did not call me again.

When fifteen-year-old Danielle Black convinced a friend to murder her father in Hampton Roads, Virginia, the event was connected to *Twilight*. In an interview with a local news channel, Don Rimer, a local detective and self-described occult crime expert, explained that Black had orchestrated her father's death for "trying to intervene in her new *Twilight*, vampire behavior" (Laycock 2012).

Conservative evangelicals piled on, and books such as Steve Wohlberg's *The Trouble with Twilight* (2010) and William Schnoebelen's *Romancing Death* (2012) attempted to link the popularity of *Twilight* with the Ferrell murders. In the sociology of moral panics, this is known as convergence, in which a frightening but atypical event (a murder) is linked to a widespread but harmless phenomenon (*Twilight* fandom) to imply a threat that is both serious and ubiquitous (Hall et al. 1978: 226). These writers also added a healthy dose of demonology and supernaturalism to their narratives. Wohlberg implied that Meyer's novel was demonically inspired, while Schnoebelen outrageously claimed to have once been a literal vampire who subsisted entirely on human blood before converting to evangelical Protestantism.

Amid all this fearmongering and sensationalism, a new generation of academics began to research the real-vampire community and to employ serious ethnography in an attempt to understand their object of study. This scholarship gave vampires a chance to explain themselves in their own words while also providing critical analysis. In addition to my work in religious studies (Laycock 2009, 2010), the English scholar John Edgar Browning (2015), professor of social work D. J. Williams (Williams and Prior 2015; Williams and Browning 2016), psychologist Emyr Williams (Perry 2014), and others have contributed to this body of research.

In 2015 the discourse about self-identified vampires underwent a sudden shift. In March, Archana Reddy, an ER doctor, described an encounter with an anemic patient who she learned was a self-described vampire (Reddy, n.d.). Rather than speculating on whether her patient was dangerous or delusional, her article simply acknowledges the existence of the vampire community and advocates learning more about them. In June 2015, D. J. Williams and Emily Prior (2015) coauthored an article titled "Do We Always Practice What We Preach? Real Vampires' Fears of Coming Out of the Coffin to Social Workers and Helping Professionals" and published in the journal *Critical Social Work*. The authors discuss how individuals in the helping professions can best assist people who identify as vampires and note that many self-identified vampires fear discussing their identity and lifestyle with medical professionals. Williams and Prior do not suggest that helping professionals need to accept these identity claims at face value, but they advocate reserving judgment to maintain a "therapeutic alliance" (80) with those they seek to aid.

The article triggered a chain reaction as numerous media outlets scrambled to report on it (Kutner 2015; McKenna 2015; M. Taylor 2015). The *Christian Science Monitor* covered the article with the headline "Is 'Vampire' a Genuine Identity?" (Caspari 2015). Journalists seeking to build on the story interviewed medical professionals, several of whom also conceded that vampires seeking medical help should not be dismissed out of hand as mentally ill. In an interview for the BBC, a professor of medicine at the University of California, Los Angeles, Tomas Ganz, remarked, "We have a collective tendency to label unconventional behaviors as psychiatric abnormalities. But I have no basis for describing it as such if the individual and their donor are comfortable with their unconventional nutrient choice" (Robson 2015). Similarly, Simon Rego, a professor of clinical psychiatry, stated:

> The relationship between any patient and her doctor, nurse, or therapist will touch on the belief system the health professional brings into the room. It wouldn't matter if it was mysticism, or belief in UFOs, or an alternative lifestyle that's outside the mainstream. I try to be respectful and non-judgmental—to focus on what's causing the patient psychological distress. You can't build trust without taking risks. Take risks and watch to see what the response is. See if it can open doors. (Quoted in Brown 2015).

Seemingly overnight, people were listening to vampires. Perhaps more significantly, fewer voices expressed certainty that experts could easily reduce vampire identity claims to medical or religious explanations. Instead, helping professionals were conceding that treating vampires was an unprecedented situation.

This shift did not come without resistance. A substantial backlash against Williams and Prior's article came with a heavy dose of anti-intellectualism that was aimed not at the vampires but at the academics who wanted to learn about them and at the universities that would support that research. One individual sent Williams an e-mail informing him that he was "JUST ANOTHER LIBERAL IDIOT INFESTING AMERICAN UNIVERSITIES WITH JUNK STUDIES" (Williams 2015). The *Daily Caller* ran the facetious headline "Take People Who Think They Are VAMPIRES Seriously, Taxpayer Funded Professor Urges" (Owens 2015).

Fueling this reaction was the larger context of a culture war surrounding issues of identity. In April of 2015, celebrity Bruce Jenner came out as Caitlyn Jenner, a transgender woman, in an interview on *20/20*. In June, a controversy broke surrounding Rachel Dolezal, a professor and activist who identifies as black despite having two white parents. Williams and Prior's article was published only days after the *Obergefell v. Hodges* decision, which legalized gay marriage across the country. Many Americans likely felt disoriented by these rapid developments. In a *New York Times* op-ed titled "The Year We Obsessed over Identity," Wesley Morris (2015) suggests that the rise of Donald Trump represented a conservative backlash against changing attitudes about identity claims.

Some of the attacks against Williams and Prior suggest that these critics are actually upset about much broader issues of identity politics, especially LGBTQ rights. Consider the following editorial written in response to Williams and Prior's article in the traditionalist Catholic newspaper *The Remnant*:

> If I decide to start identifying as a werewolf you'd better get ready to defend my inalienable right to be treated as such. After all, this is America! I can demand my own special werewolf public restrooms, Congress will enact new laws forcing barbers to give me the full-body werewolf treatment, and you WILL bake me a were-cake!
>
> Buy [sic] if we continue down Lunacy Lane here, I wonder how we will ultimately ascertain who is mentally ill in our society and who is not; who needs treatment and who does not; who's dangerous and who isn't; who is, well, quite frankly, nuts and who's sane. Or will it even matter anymore, now that the inmates are clearly running the asylum. (Matt 2015)

The author of the editorial begins by parodying political correctness, but in closing he betrays a fear that the categories that make up the structure of his world could be changed and that he might suddenly find himself in a society that no longer makes sense.

A similar concern is expressed in a 2015 editorial in the *Guardian* written by the ethicist Matthew Beard in response to Williams and Prior's article: "OK, So You Think You're a Vampire. Whose Job Is It to Tell You You're Not?" Whereas Williams and Prior do not regard identifying as a vampire as an inherent problem, Beard seems to assume that it is. Whether vampire identity claims are a problem for the vampires themselves or for others is not stated. Unlike *The Remnant*, Beard is not hostile toward the gay rights movement. However, he expresses his concern that it is difficult to support gay rights while rejecting the identity claims of vampires. He writes:

> The reason it is hard is because we lack a coherent, objective framework that builds on an amalgamation of historical, cultural, philosophical, artistic, and scientific accounts of what it means to be a human being, and what it is to live in human community.

Instead, society determines legitimate forms of self-determination or identity on the basis of consensus. If sufficient numbers of people demand recognition, they are rewarded it, but until then, they won't be treated legitimately. (Beard 2015)

While Beard does not medicalize vampires as mentally ill or incite moral panic by framing them as a dangerous cult, he also rejects the idea that helping professionals should try to work with their identity claims. Beard continues:

The solution isn't—as the authors of the study argue—to be careful not to proliferate traditional vampire mythology—garlic, stakes, coffins and all the rest—which is likely to lead to microaggressions that could traumatize "real vampires." Rather, it's to recognise that the quest for self-identity and meaning is one that is best done with some guidance. (Beard 2015)

Exactly who should be empowered to give such guidance in determining which identity claims should be accepted and which should be dismissed is not stated. I am doubtful that the "objective framework" that Beard proposes as a basis for acceptable identity claims would ever actually be objective.

In summary, in only two decades we have seen public discourse evolve from imagining vampires as mentally ill and dangerous cultists to viewing them as a vulnerable minority. A great deal of anxiety has come with this shift. Paradoxically, many people seem to have found vampires less disturbing when it was generally assumed they wanted to kill us. As I have argued elsewhere (Laycock 2016), the critics of Williams and Prior are responding to a much more fundamental fear: that the categories we use to order our society—even such fundamental categories as "sane" and "insane"—cannot be taken for granted, because they are socially constructed.

The sociologist Peter Berger (1967) argues that human beings cannot function without a socially constructed framework for understanding the world. Without such a framework, "the individual is submerged in a world of disorder, senselessness and madness" (Berger 1967: 23). Borrowing from Émile Durkheim ([1897] 1951), Berger dubs such a condition anomie and calls it "the nightmare *par excellence*." Normally, the legitimacy of this framework, which Berger calls a nomos, is taken for granted. However, the threat of anomie is still raised by "marginal situations" in which we experience "haunting suspicions that the world may have another aspect than its 'normal' one, that is, that the previously accepted definitions of reality may be fragile or even fraudulent" (23). Thus, society provides numerous tools to keep people oriented toward an official version of reality. Religion has historically served as the primary institution for keeping people reality focused.

Berger's theory of anomie largely explains critics' disproportionate reaction to the identity claims of vampires. Vampires are dangerous not because they are violent but because they confront us with a marginal situation: if someone can declare herself a vampire and not be declared insane, then our entire nomos can suddenly seem constructed rather than self-evident. Compared to this, some people might find it preferable to believe that vampires are merely deranged criminals and cultists.

WHY VAMPIRES? WHY NOW?

In her classic book *Our Vampires, Ourselves* (1995), Nina Auerbach argues that we can study the history of Anglo-American culture by studying the way vampires have been imagined and reimagined. Before the Romantics resurrected the vampire as a seductive aristocrat, the vampires of folklore were inhuman monsters. The term "vampire" appears to have conflated entities found in Slavic, Germanic, and Greek folklore, including revenants that rose at night to drain the blood of the living, werewolf-like creatures and other shape-shifters, and nocturnal witches and demons. All these entities were considered unquestionably demonic and inimical, and—for the cultures that imagined these beings—vampires reinforced these cultures' values and social norms. Someone might become a vampire through practicing sorcery, committing incest or suicide, or breaking similar social taboos. The Slavic studies scholar Bruce McClelland states of the folkloric vampire, "In the broadest terms, the vampire represents the consequence of succumbing to forces that remove the individual from the ordered, productive life of the community" (2006: 56). This function is hardly unique to folkloric vampires: monster stories are used to reinforce social taboos in cultures around the world. But as early as the nineteenth century, there was an alternative reading of the vampire, not as a demonic foil for society, but as a tragic figure that society was incapable of tolerating. Lord Byron's 1813 poem *The Giaour* describes a vampire driven to kill his own daughter and drink her blood. Byron was not portraying the horror of the vampire so much as the horror of *being* the vampire. Only six years later, John Polidori, Byron's personal physician, wrote *The Vampyre*, generally considered to be the first modern vampire story.

I propose that it is not a coincidence that vampires have gained popularity at the same time that our once taken-for-granted understanding of our place in society has been increasingly called into question. The social conditions that make it possible for self-identified vampires to question whether they are normal humans like everyone else are the same ones that compelled fictional vampires to be portrayed as a tragic or sympathetic figure rather than a demonic opponent. They are also the same social conditions that reactionaries are responding to when they claim scholars like Williams and Prior have gone too far in taking self-identified vampires seriously.

In his book *The Heretical Imperative*, Peter Berger (1979) suggests that modernity entails an ever-widening range of identities and lifestyle choices in which fewer dimensions of our personhood can be taken for granted and more must be discovered, defined, or chosen ("heresy" comes from the Greek *hairesis*, meaning "choice"). It is an "imperative" because however much we may like to default to an identity ascribed by our culture, this is increasingly not an option. As Jean-Paul Sartre stated, we are "condemned to be free" (1966: 186).

Not only must modern people locate themselves in relation to emerging concepts of political, religious, and cultural orientation (e.g., Am I feminist? Am I a fundamentalist? Am I a hipster?), but historians such as Michel Foucault (1990) and Ian Hacking (1986) have argued that we have effectively invented new kinds of people. Foucault suggests that "the homosexual" was one of a series of concepts created by psychiatrists to transform what had previously been understood as a type of sexual activity into a category of person (1990: 101). But paradoxically, this category enabled "the homosexuals" to speak for themselves, thereby facilitating the gay rights movement. Furthermore, everyone now had to decide how this new binary of homosexual-heterosexual applied to them, further exacerbating the "heretical imperative" described by Berger.

This situation has several implications for the vampire. The folkloric vampire served as a foil and a cautionary tale to enforce conformity and group cohesion. But by the time of Byron, many modern people increasingly found themselves identifying not with the villagers but with the monster they had previously ostracized. It is hardly surprising, then, that we increasingly see vampires presented in popular culture not as evil but as beautiful, rebellious, and tragic. This connection between the vampire and the heretical imperative is best displayed in Anne Rice's *Interview with the Vampire*, in which Lestat, an older vampire, explains to Louis why he has made him immortal:

"I must make contact with the age. And I can do this through you. You are the spirit, you are the heart."

"Don't you see? I'm not the spirit of any age. I'm at odds with everything and always have been! I have never belonged anywhere with anyone at any time!"

"Louis," he said softly. "This is the very spirit of your age. Don't you see that? Everyone else feels as you feel. Your fall from grace and faith has been the fall of a century." (Rice 1976: 286)

The message here is clear: modernity has made Louises of us all. We are all vampires; we are all damned.

CONCLUSIONS

Within the context of the heretical imperative, the emergence of self-identified vampires seems unsurprising. It would certainly not have surprised Foucault that discourse continues to generate new types of people. A new binary of vampire-nonvampire can be seen as simply one more concept that modern people can now navigate. Much of the scandal surrounding self-identified vampires concerns the health claims associated with this identity. For example: Do vampires *really* need human blood to be well? And if they don't, aren't they mentally ill? But these questions distract from what I think is really happening. Above all, identifying as a vampire is a strategic deployment of vocabulary and concepts to make sense of one's self and one's place in the world. As Charles Taylor wrote in *Sources of the Self*, "To have a sense of who we are, we have to have a notion of how we have become, and of where we are going" (1989: 47). Sociological studies of several identity groups, including alcoholics (Denzin 1993), transgendered people (Mason-Schrock 1996), codependent people (Irvine 1999), and even Christians (Wilkins 2008), have suggested that these identities are possible because society provides narrative tools for thinking about oneself in terms of a particular category of person. In the same way, the real-vampire community, by providing concepts like awakening and theories of energy transfer between self and others, empowers certain people to construct narratives about themselves and to relate experiences that might otherwise be indescribable and uninterpretable.

The impulse to mock real vampires and, especially, those in the helping professions who listen to them can be understood as an attempt to halt this expansion of potential identities. I find it significant that people rarely exert energy attacking those who are clearly delusional or isolated in their alternative beliefs—especially when these beliefs do not appear to affect others. It is only after the realization that the heretofore deluded individuals might not be dismissed out of hand that satire and other strategies are employed to police discourse. It seems to me that what really disturbs these critics is not the vampires themselves but rather the realization that while categories of identity appear to be objectively real, they are for the most part socially constructed. Like Foucault, these critics also seem aware that doctors and helping professionals are uniquely empowered as gatekeepers who can decide which identities are legitimate and illegitimate. When they attack scholars like Williams and Prior as "liberal" academics they simultaneously concede the power these individuals have to shape the categories we have available to talk about ourselves.

It seems to me that we cannot mock self-identified vampires out of existence any more than we can reverse the conditions of modernity. Furthermore, when frustrated communities empower individuals who promise to return to a simpler time or to eliminate deviants, the results are often immoral and gruesome. We do not have to accept the claim that human beings produce psychic energy that nourishes vampires or that sanguinarian vampires actually require human blood to survive. But we do have to think seriously about how to productively coexist with individuals who see the world very differently than we do. If nothing else, the presence of self-identified vampires is an index of a healthy democracy. When even vampires feel they can live among us with relative safety and dignity, how much more secure will be the safety and dignity of everyone else?

REFERENCES

Ashantison, Belfazaar. 2004. "Donor Bill of Rights." New Orleans Vampire Association. Available at http://www.neworleansvampireassociation.org/donor-bill-of-rights.html.

Auerbach, Nina. 1995. *Our Vampires, Ourselves*. Chicago: University of Chicago Press.

Beard, Matthew. 2015. "OK, So You Think You're a Vampire. Whose Job Is It to Tell You You're Not?" *The Guardian*, July 30. Available at http://www.theguardian.com/commentisfree/2015/jul/31/ok-so-you-think-youre-a-vampire-whose-job-is-it-to-tell-you-youre-not.

Belanger, Michelle. 2005. *Sacred Hunger: The Vampire in Myth and Reality*. Fort Wayne, IN: Dark Moon Press.

Berger, Peter. 1967. *The Sacred Canopy: Elements of a Sociological Theory of Religion*. Garden City, NY: Doubleday.

———. 1979. *The Heretical Imperative: Contemporary Possibilities of Religious Affirmation*. Garden City, NY: Anchor Press.

Brown, Jennifer. 2015. "Why 'Real Vampires' Fear Going to the Doctor." *Everyday Health*, October 28. Available at http://www.everydayhealth.com/news/why-real-vampires-fear-going-doctor.

Browning, John Edgar. 2015. "The Real Vampires of New Orleans and Buffalo: A Research Note towards Comparative Ethnography." *Palgrave Communications* 1 (1): 15006–15014.

Campbell, Colin. 1972. "The Cult, the Cultic Milieu and Secularization." In *A Sociological Yearbook of Religion in Britain*, vol. 5, edited by M. Hill, 119–136. London: SCM Press.

Carré, Suzanne, and Deacon Gray. 2016. "Sexual Vampires: Myths and Motivations." *Journal of Positive Sexuality* 2 (November): 37–45.

Caspari, Sarah. 2015. "Is 'Vampire' a Genuine Identity? A Look at the Surprising World of 'Alternate Identities.'" *Christian Science Monitor*, July 9. Available at http://www.csmonitor.com/USA/USA-Update/2015/0709/Is-vampire-a-genuine-identity-A-look-at-the-surprising-world-of-alternate-identities.

Denzin, Norman K. 1993. *The Alcoholic Society: Addiction and the Recovery of the Self.* New Brunswick, NJ: Transaction.
Durkheim, Émile. (1897) 1951. *Suicide: A Study in Sociology.* Translated by George Simpson. New York: Free Press.
Fortune, Dion. 1997. *Psychic Self-Defense.* York Beach, ME: Samuel Weiser.
Foucault, Michel. 1990. *The History of Sexuality.* Vol. 1, *An Introduction.* New York: Vintage Books.
Hacking, Ian. 1986. "Making Up People." In *Reconstructing Individuality: Autonomy, Individuality, and the Self in Western Thought,* edited by T. C. Heller, M. Sosna, and D. E. Wellbey, 223–236. Stanford, CA: Stanford University Press.
Hall, Stuart, Chris Critcher, Tony Jefferson, John Clarke, and Brian Roberts. 1978. *Policing the Crisis: Mugging, the State, and Law and Order.* London: Macmillan.
Irvine, Leslie. 1999. *Codependent Forevermore: The Invention of Self in a Twelve Step Group.* Chicago: University of Chicago Press.
Jaffe, Philip D., and Frank DiCataldo. 1998. "Clinical Vampirism: Blending Myth and Reality." In *The Vampire: A Casebook,* edited by A. Dundes, 143–158. Madison: University of Wisconsin Press.
Kutner, Max. 2015. "Real Vampires Exist, and They Need Counseling Too." *Newsweek,* July 9. Available at http://www.newsweek.com/real-vampires-exist-and-they-need-counseling-too-351575.
Laycock, Joseph. 2009. *Vampires Today: The Truth about Modern Vampirism.* Westport, CT: Praeger.
———. 2010. "Vampires as an Identity Group: Analyzing Causes and Effects of an Introspective Survey by the Vampire Community." *Nova Religio* 14 (2): 4–23.
———. 2012. "Death of an Occult Crime Expert Reawakens Controversy." *Religion Dispatches,* January 26. Available at http://religiondispatches.org/death-of-an-occult-crime-expert-reawakens-controversy.
———. 2016. "Reply to 'Do We Always Practice What We Preach? Real Vampires' Fears of Coming Out of the Coffin to Social Workers and Helping Professionals.'" *Critical Social Work* 17 (2): 83–89.
Mason-Schrock, Douglas. 1996. "Transsexuals' Narrative Construction of the 'True Self.'" *Social Psychology Quarterly* 59 (4): 176–192.
Matt, Michael. 2015. "Vampire Rights: Better Not Refuse to Bake These Guys a Cake." *The Remnant,* July 15. Available at http://remnantnewspaper.com/web/index.php/fetzen-fliegen/item/1857-real-vampires-we-%20will-overcome-better-not-refuse-to-bake-these-guys-a-cake.
McClelland, Bruce. 2006. *Slayers and Their Vampires: A Cultural History of Killing the Dead.* Ann Arbor: University of Michigan Press.
McKenna, Brittney. 2015. "Some People Identify as Vampires, and Experts Say It's Time to Accept Them." *MTV News,* July 9. Available at http://www.mtv.com/news/2208216/vampire-identity-study-acceptance.
Miller, Thomas W., Lane J. Veltkamp, Robert F. Kraus, Tina Lane, and Tag Heister. 1999. "An Adolescent Vampire Cult in Rural America: Clinical Issues and Case Study." *Child Psychiatry and Human Development* 29 (3): 209–219.
Morris, Wesley. 2015. "The Year We Obsessed over Identity." *New York Times Magazine,* October 6. Available at http://www.nytimes.com/2015/10/11/magazine/the-year-we-obsessed-over-identity.html.

MSNBC. 2014. "Interview with a Vampire." October 22. Available at http://www.msnbc.com/documentaries/watch/interview-with-a-vampire-346331203883.

Noll, Richard. 1992. *Vampires, Werewolves, and Demons: Twentieth Century Reports in the Psychiatric Literature.* New York: Brunner/Mazel.

Olcott, Henry Steel. 2004. "The Vampire." In *The Theosophist: October 1890–April 1891,* edited by H. Olcott, 385–393. Whitefish, MT: Kessinger.

Olry, Régis, and Duane E. Haines. 2011. "Renfield's Syndrome: A Psychiatric Illness Drawn from Bram Stoker's Dracula." *Journal of the History of the Neurosciences* 20 (4): 368–371.

Oppawsky, Jolene. 2010. "Clinical Vampirism-Renfield's Syndrome: A Case Study." *Annals of the American Psychotherapy Association* 13 (4): 58–63.

Owens, Eric. 2015. "Take People Who Think They Are VAMPIRES Seriously, Taxpayer-Funded Professor Urges." *Daily Caller,* June 8. Available at http://dailycaller.com/2015/07/08/take-people-who-think-they-are-vampires-seriously-taxpayer-funded-professor-urges.

Perlmutter, Dawn. 1999–2000. "The Sacrificial Aesthetic: Blood Rituals from Art to Murder." *Anthropoetics* 5 (2). Available at http://www.anthropoetics.ucla.edu/ap0502/blood.htm.

———. 2003. "Vampire Culture." In *Religion and American Cultures: An Encyclopedia of Traditions, Diversity, and Popular Expressions,* edited by G. Laderman, 279–283. Santa Barbara, CA: ABC-CLIO.

———. 2004. "The Forensics of Sacrifice: A Symbolic Analysis of Ritualistic Crime." *Anthropoetics* 9 (2). Available at http://anthropoetics.ucla.edu/ap0902/sacrifice-2.

Perry, Keith. 2014. "Britain Has 'Subculture' of 15,000 Vampires, Says University Lecturer." *The Telegraph,* May 29. Available at http://www.telegraph.co.uk/news/science/10862188/Britain-has-subculture-of-15000-vampires-says-university-lecturer.html.

Reddy, Archana. n.d. "Vampires amongst Us, Even in the ER." *Emergency Care for You.* Available at http://www.emergencycareforyou.org/Health-Tips/Doc-Blog/Vampires-Amongst-Us,-Even-in-the-ER (accessed January 16, 2018).

Riccardo, Martin V. 1996. *Liquid Dreams of Vampires.* St. Paul, MN: Llewellyn.

Rice, Anne. 1976. *Interview with the Vampire.* New York: Alfred A. Knopf.

Robson, David. 2015. "The People Who Drink Human Blood." *BBC,* October 21. Available at http://www.bbc.com/future/story/20151021-the-people-who-drink-human-blood.

Sartre, Jean-Paul. 1966. *Being and Nothingness.* Translated by Hazel Estella Barnes. New York: Washington Square Press.

Sato, Ikuya. 1991. *Kamikaze Biker: Parody and Anomy in Affluent Japan.* Chicago: University of Chicago Press.

Schnoebelen, William J. 2012. *Romancing Death: A True Story of Vampirism, Death, the Occult and Deliverance.* Shippensburg, PA: Destiny Image.

Suscitatio Enterprises. 2017. "Vampire and Energy Work Research Study." Available at http://www.suscitatio.com.

Taylor, Charles. 1989. *Sources of the Self: The Making of Modern Identity.* Cambridge, MA: Harvard University Press.

Taylor, MaryGrace. 2015. "New Study Confirms the Existence of Real-Life 'Vampires.'" *Men's Health,* October 9. Available at http://www.menshealth.com/science-of-real-vampires.

Temple of the Vampire. 1989. *The Vampire Bible.* Lacey, WA: Temple of the Vampire.

Vanden Bergh, Richard L., and John F. Kelly. 1964. "Vampirism: A Review with New Observations." *Archives of General Psychiatry* 11 (5): 543–547.
White, Megan, and Omar Hatim. 2010. "Vampirism, Vampire Cults and the Teenager of Today." *International Journal of Adolescent Medicine and Health* 22 (2): 189–195.
Wilkins, Amy C. 2008. "'Happier than Non-Christians': Collective Emotions and Symbolic Boundaries among Evangelical Christians." *Social Psychology Quarterly* 71 (3): 281–301.
Williams, D. J. 2015. Electronic communication with the author, June 16.
Williams, D. J., and John Edgar Browning. 2016. "Looking Inside the Coffin: An Overview of Contemporary Human Vampirism and Its Relevance for Forensics Professionals." In *The Criminal Humanities: An Introduction*, vol. 2, edited by M. Arntfield and M. Danesi, 117–134. New York: Peter Lang.
Williams, D. J., and Emily E. Prior. 2015. "Do We Always Practice What We Preach? Real Vampires' Fears of Coming Out of the Coffin to Social Workers and Helping Professionals." *Critical Social Work* 16 (1): 79–92.
Wohlberg, Steve. 2010. *The Trouble with Twilight: Why Today's Vampire Craze Is Hazardous to Your Health*. Shippensburg, PA: Destiny Image.

10

CRYPTOZOOLOGY

The Hunt for Hidden Animals and Monsters

TEA KRULOS

The word "cryptozoology" breaks down as *crypto*, meaning "hidden," and *zoology*, the "study of animals." Thus, cryptozoology literally means what the title of this chapter suggests: the study of hidden animals. Ironically, many of the subjects of cryptozoology are more famous than the word itself; almost everyone has heard of the big three of cryptozoology: Bigfoot, the Loch Ness monster, and the Chupacabra. Other subjects of cryptozoological study—Mothman, Ogopogo, the Jersey Devil—are famous among cryptozoologists and locals where the stories originate but not necessarily familiar to the public. These mysterious creatures are collectively referred to by cryptozoologists as "cryptids."[1]

Cryptozoologists regard their field as more aligned with science than the supernatural. Like zoology, cryptozoology focuses on the discovery and taxonomy of new life forms. Cryptozoologists use language that sounds "scientifical," as skeptic Sharon Hill (2010) describes it. That is, cryptozoologists describe themselves as researchers and use terms like "expeditions," "case studies," and "data analysis." They give cryptids more scientific sounding names like "hairy upright hominids" or "flying hominids" to make their subjects sound less spooky or cartoonish. The scientific community, however, often

---

1. This chapter is not an exhaustive study of cryptids. Other examples of commonly recognized cryptids include Manwolves (werewolf-like creatures spotted in the Midwest and beyond), the poisonous Mongolian Death Worms (which allegedly live in the Gobi Desert), and the Bishopville Lizard Man (occasionally reported lurking near the Scape Ore Swamp of South Carolina).

derides the field of cryptozoology as a pseudoscience because the researchers involved are often amateur hobbyists. Few cryptozoologists make a living working in their field and there is little in the way of peer review, published studies in scientific journals, or conventional scientific method and analysis. Cryptozoology also attracts the attention of skeptics, who typically point out the lack of definitive empirical evidence for cryptids and explain away reported sightings as misidentifications, hoaxes, or delusions (Krulos 2015).

In this chapter, I detail the most common varieties of cryptids—from those that have been proved to exist to those that are almost certainly mythological. Next, I turn an inquisitive eye to the cryptozoologists themselves, examining who they are and why they pursue these elusive creatures. Last, I address the threats to cryptozoology's fragile legitimacy by skeptics and hoaxers before touching on cryptozoology's broader social functions.

VARIETIES OF CRYPTIDS

Lazarus Species and Living Fossils

The first category of cryptozoological creatures—animals that have cheated extinction—is the least controversial because it is supported by a couple of notable case examples. The symbol of the International Cryptozoology Museum in Portland, Maine, is a fish called the coelacanth, which museum founder Loren Coleman calls "the darling of cryptozoology" (Krulos 2015: 11) (see Figure 10.1). A lobe-finned fish with large scales, the coelacanth can grow up to five feet long and ranges from bright blue to brownish in color. The case of the coelacanth is important for cryptozoologists because it stands as an example of a time when widely accepted scientific opinion was proved wrong. Thought to be extinct for sixty-five million years, the coelacanth was dubbed a "living fossil" when a living specimen was caught by a fisherman in 1938 off the coast of South Africa. Another example was caught in 1952, and hundreds have been caught and studied since (Coleman and Clark 1999).

Besides the coelacanth, other examples of Lazarus species of animals thought to be extinct have been (re)discovered to be alive. The Lord Howe Island stick insect (also known as the tree lobster) was thought to have been extinct by 1920, but a small colony of about twenty-four insects was found on the islet of Bell's Pyramid in 2001 (Nelson 2009). Likewise, the Javan elephant, a pygmy elephant also reported extinct, was found on the island of Borneo in 2003. It turned out that a sultan had imported some of the elephants to Borneo, where a small population survived in the jungle (Grossman 2012). In addition, impressive new species are discovered all the

Figure 10.1 *A life-size model of a coelacanth and other artifacts related to the discovery of a living coelacanth in 1938. Photograph courtesy of the International Cryptozoology Museum.*

time. In 1976, the first specimen of the megamouth shark was caught off the coast of Hawaii. Growing up to eighteen feet long, the megamouth is a filter feeder with a large mouth equipped with luminous photophores to lure prey (Coleman and Clark 1999). It was a sensational discovery—a completely new species of shark with a giant glow-in-the-dark mouth, entirely hidden from human awareness until the year *Rocky* won best picture at the Oscars and Peter Frampton was at the top of the charts.

These species are important because they prove the fundamental argument of cryptozoology: that it is possible for creatures to exist even when mainstream science is unaware of their existence or even flatly denies that possibility. By leaving open the potential for new discoveries, the coelacanth and other Lazarus species add plausibility to claims about other yet-to-be-discovered species and perhaps even more-folkloric cryptids. For example, one such animal that is theorized to be left over from a prehistoric age is the Mokèlé-mbèmbé, which is described as a living sauropod in central African countries, with most reports from the Congo River basin. A German expedition to the Congo in 1913 met pygmies who described this animal, which they called Mokèlé-mbèmbé, or "one who stops the flow of rivers," as the size of an elephant with a long, flexible neck and a tail like an alligator. Several expeditions have journeyed into the largely unexplored Likouala swamp region in search of the living dinosaur. Researchers have discovered an inconclusive footprint and recorded video of something unclear swimming in Lake Tele, but concrete proof of the Mokèlé-mbèmbé remains elusive (Coleman and Clark 1999).

Lake monsters such as Mokèlé-mbèmbé are the most widely reported examples of living fossils. Most cryptozoologists believe lake monsters are plesiosaurs or another similar dinosaur species that survived extinction, although others argue that they might be an unidentified type of whale or long-necked seal (Krulos 2015). The most famous cryptid in the lake monster category is undoubtedly the Loch Ness monster. Nessie, as the creature is commonly called, first gained popularity in the 1930s when multiple sightings were reported along the shore of Loch Ness. Reports date back as far as the first and second centuries, when the Scottish Picts carved a depiction of a Nessie-like Pictish Beast into their symbol stones. There is also a medieval tale of Scottish Saint Columba confronting a man-killing dragon in the area in A.D. 565 (Coleman and Clark 1999).

The Loch Ness monster truly became an international sensation in the twentieth century, as the advent of photography and other technologies enabled people to support their claimed sightings with seemingly objective evidence. In 1933, the *Inverness Courier* reported a couple saw an "enormous animal" swimming in Loch Ness (Coleman and Clark 1999). This firsthand account was supported the following year with photographic evidence—a now-famous black-and-white photograph known as the surgeon's photo—that seemed to show a head, long neck, and upper body swimming in the lake. Another famous Nessie photo, the Stuart photograph, taken July 14, 1951, appeared to show three large, dark humps rising out of Loch Ness (Loxton and Prothero 2012).[2]

---

2. These two photos were revealed to be hoaxes years later. The surgeon's photo was of a child's toy, and the Stuart photo was created by using three bales of hay covered with tarpaulins and floating in shallow water.

In addition to these famous photographs, the 1960 Dinsdale film—named after Tim Dinsdale, the researcher who filmed the footage and later wrote seven books on the subject—purports to show a hump moving across the loch. Researchers have also used sonar scanners to investigate claims about Nessie's existence. Some of these investigations, such as those conducted by the Loch Ness Investigation Bureau between 1962 and 1972 as well as Operation Deepscan in 1987, found inconclusive evidence of something large living in Loch Ness (Loxton and Prothero 2012). Others, including a 2003 study funded by the BBC that included six hundred sonar beams and satellite tracking devices, found no such evidence (Radford 2015). Despite a lack of conclusive evidence, these continued searches feed public curiosity about Nessie and perhaps contribute to nearly one in four people in Scotland believing the Loch Ness monster is probably real (Edwards 2012).

Although Nessie is the best-known lake monster, it is far from the lone case study. In fact, in terms of folklore it seems like every major lake, river, and bay is home to at least one lake monster story. Some of the most widely known examples include Champ, spotted for hundreds of years in Lake Champlain, which borders New York, Vermont, and Quebec. Ogopogo is described as a horned lake monster spotted in Lake Okanagan in British Columbia. The Flathead Lake monster of Montana has been spotted regularly since its first reported sighting in 1889, and South Bay Bessie is Lake Erie's answer to Nessie. After a string of Bessie sightings in the 1990s, a $100,000 reward was offered by the Huron Lagoons Marina for the beast's capture (Coleman and Huyghe 2003; Willis, Henderson, and Coleman 2005).

This proliferation of sightings around the world is explained differently depending on one's beliefs regarding the ontological status of lake monsters. Cryptozoologists tend to believe at least some of these reports and account for their persistence over hundreds of years as evidence of a breeding population of monsters in these bodies of water. They argue that places like Loch Ness and Lake Champlain have nurtured several generations of an undiscovered population of lake monsters (Krulos 2015). This also helps them explain why some lake monsters that were frequently sighted in the past are no longer seen. One such example is a creature nicknamed Bozho that was spotted frequently in Lake Mendota near Madison, Wisconsin, between the late 1800s and the 1920s before disappearing (Pohlen 2013). This lack of recent reports does not inhibit cryptozoologists because it fits with a biological model that says, quite simply, if a breeding population does not exist, a species—cryptozoological or otherwise—will not persist. In such cases, cryptozoologists merely switch from looking for a population of creatures to searching for evidence of remains.

For those who do not believe in the existence of lake monsters, the explanations are threefold. Some believe that those who report sightings have misinterpreted natural phenomena. Skeptics Benjamin Radford and Joe Nickell (2006), for example, maintain that a purported photo of Champ, which was shot in 1977 by the Mansi family while vacationing on Lake Champlain, merely shows an unusual looking piece of driftwood that floated up to the surface. In other cases, it seems as though sightings are the work of hoaxers who hope to deceive the public for fun, fame, or fortune. The 1934 surgeon's photo of the Loch Ness monster is almost universally known to be a hoax, made from a toy submarine and plastic wood putty (Radford and Nickell 2006). Still others argue that these legends are sustained for the financial benefit of communities near supposed sighting locations. The legend of Nessie drives the local economy of Loch Ness and surrounding communities, as tourists flock to the Scottish Highlands hoping to capture a glimpse of the dinosaur-like creature. The Nessie industry includes places to buy souvenirs, sign up for boat tours, get lodging, and pay to view Nessie-themed items in museums. Two museums in the small town of Drumnadrochit have a bitter rivalry for tourist dollars—one museum owner was even arrested for stealing the other museum's sign (Love 2013). Estimates of Nessie's economic impact on the Scottish highlands is between £25 million and £130 million per year ($31 million–$162 million), and local tourist boards are contemplating how to profit even further from this "monster marketing" strategy (Brown 2014).

Sasquatch and Other Strange Hominids

The pattern of claims and counterclaims that we see with lake monsters repeats itself in the debates about creatures that cryptozoologists commonly refer to as "upright hairy bipedal hominids," colloquially known by their regional names—most notably Bigfoot. As with Nessie and her peers, sightings of such creatures have been reported around the world for hundreds of years. The sightings vary in the reported size, posture, and hair color of the upright hominids but generally describe the beasts as being similar to humans and covered with fur. In the Himalayas, there have long been reports of such a creature, known as the Yeti, covered in white fur. In Brazil and Bolivia, there are similar stories of an apelike creature with red hair called the Mapinguari. Likewise, there is a Chinese legend of a creature known as the Yeren, a humanlike creature also known as the Chinese Wildman or man-monkey (Coleman and Huyghe 2006). The Yowie is the Australian outback's answer to the legend. An apelike creature called the Skunk Ape or Stink Ape is rumored to roam the American South; it is a smaller chimp- or orangutan-sized creature whose name derives from the foul odor said to emanate from its body hair.

In North America, Bigfoot has been reportedly spotted in every state and province except Hawaii but is mostly commonly associated with the Pacific Northwest, where creatures that fit this description can be found in Native American lore. According to Coleman:

> Creatures that are manlike and hairy and said to be part of the real world, not the spirit one, were familiar to the first inhabitants of this land. In the West the creature was known by a variety of names, from *Oh-Mah* to *Skookum*. A few chroniclers and researchers have also liked the Native-sounding nature of Sasquatch, the name that J. W. Burns, Indian-agent teacher of the Chehalis Indian Reserve, coined from Native British Columbian words, including *sokquetal* and *soss-q'tal* for the hairy giants. (2003: 32)

Coleman notes that another source suggests the word is an Anglicization of the word *sésqec* of the Halkomelem language, a member of the Salish language family. Other Pacific Northwest tribes speak of the gigantic hairy *tsiatko* (the Nisqually tribe) and the *tenatco*, who "dug a hole in the ground as a place to sleep and kidnap [human] adults and children," among others (Coleman 2003: 32).

Reports have also emerged from sources other than tribal lore. For example, Theodore Roosevelt mentions a similar murderous creature in his 1893 memoir *The Wilderness Hunter*. According to the description given to Roosevelt by a seasoned hunter, a large bipedal animal that was not a bear destroyed the hunter's camp and terrified his hunting party (Dockett 2017). In an account published in 1924, a group of miners working near Mount Saint Helens in Washington State were threatened by a gang of angry ape-like creatures that pummeled the miners' cabin with rocks. Proving that such tales have cultural staying power, the gorge in which the alleged incident occurred is named Ape Canyon (Coleman 2003). Years later, one of the miners, Fred Beck, published his version of the incident in a book titled *I Fought the Apemen of Mt. St. Helens* (1967).

Modern interest in Bigfoot picked up on the West Coast in the 1950s with sightings and documentation of large footprints. Indeed, the name Bigfoot was coined in 1958 by the *Humboldt Times* after construction worker Jerry Crew made a cast of a giant footprint he found on a job site near Bluff Creek in Humboldt County in Northern California. The footprints were later revealed to be staged by the construction crew subcontractor and known hoaxer Ray Wallace (Coleman 2003). As with lake monsters, in the twentieth century Bigfoot hunters turned to photography and videography to collect what they purport to be concrete evidence of the monster. The most famous alleged Bigfoot footage is known as the Patterson-Gimlin film, shot in 1967, also near Bluff Creek. The film lasts for about a minute and seems to show a giant hairy hominid (dubbed Patty by researchers) strolling through the forest, then turning to look at the filmmaker for a second before disappearing into the forest. Debate still rages about whether the footage is genuine or a hoax perpetrated by Roger Patterson and Bob Gimlin, the two men who shot the film. The footage has been heavily scrutinized with enhanced analysis, restoration, re-creations using costumes, motion-capture sensors, and three-dimensional modeling. People have come forward to claim they were part of the hoax, while others have come forward to say that those claiming to be part of the hoax are liars (Coleman 2003; Krulos 2015).

Since the Patterson-Gimlin film, there have been hundreds of photos, videos, footprint casts, and hair and scat samples collected by what are often called Bigfooters (cryptozoologists who limit their research to the search for Bigfoot evidence). Almost every state in the United States has at least one regional Bigfoot research team, with most teams participating in at least a couple of investigation trips a year. The largest group of Bigfooters is the Bigfoot Field Researchers Organization, founded in 1995. The organization has chapters in many states, an archive of hundreds of reports on its website (http://bfro.net), and received substantial publicity through its reality TV program *Finding Bigfoot* (Krulos 2015). These teams differ in the terminology they use to describe the creature or their methods of collecting evidence. Most divisive is the debate between pro-kill and no-kill teams. The pro-kill camp argues that a body must be harvested and preserved to prove to mainstream scientists that Bigfoot definitively exists. In contrast, no-kill groups view as barbaric the idea of slaughtering such a mystic creature and point out that modern science provides methods of producing proof without killing the animal, such as DNA sampling. Despite these differences, many Bigfooters agree that the creature is likely an unidentified primate or a *Gigantopithicus*, a genus of ape thought to have gone extinct a hundred thousand years ago (Coleman 2003). A smaller subgroup abides by fringe theories that suggest that Bigfoot might be an extraterrestrial or interdimensional being (Lapseritis 2005).

As with lake monsters, claims about Bigfoot are founded on a combination of folklore, personal accounts of encounters, and allegedly objective evidence collected through quasiscientific methods. Likewise, these reports have been undermined by alleged or proven trickery by hoaxers who deceived the public for their own gain. In their efforts to retain some semblance of legitimacy in the face of these controversies, Bigfooters have turned to technology and scientific-sounding language to package their claims in ways that are more palatable to the scientific establishment and members of the public who place great faith in science.

Evil Portents: Mothman, Chupacabras, and the Jersey Devil

Other miscellaneous mystery creatures are too bizarre for conventional explanation. These entities sound like campfire tales of ghouls and goblins. Sometimes they fly, and often they have glowing red eyes. One thing that these creatures frequently have in common is that they are used to explain mysterious, tragic, or evil circumstances for the communities where they are sighted.

Mothman: One of cryptozoology's most frightening cases is the story of Mothman, reported as a gray-skinned, red-eyed, winged humanoid creature spotted by several people in and around Point Pleasant, West Virginia (see Figure 10.2). The first sighting sounds like something straight out of a 1950s sci-fi monster movie. On November 15, 1966, two couples went joyriding in the TNT area, a stretch of forest near an abandoned World War II–era dynamite factory on the outskirts of Point Pleasant. Young people often drove to the TNT area for a private place for romance, to socialize, or to drag race. On this night, however, the young couples encountered a hideous red-eyed creature that chased them as they raced back to town, with the creature reportedly squeaking loudly and swooping down at their car. The terrified couples reported the sighting to police (Wamsley 2005). Shortly thereafter the story spread via newspapers, which named Point Pleasant's frightening monster Mothman and reported on its characteristics—just as newspapers had earlier coined the name Bigfoot and spread the tales and photos of Nessie.[3]

For the following month and into the next year, people claimed to see Mothman on a near-daily basis. There were other reports of strangeness in West Virginia during this time, including sightings of UFOs. Point Pleasant was also supposedly visited by the mysterious Men in Black, who paranormal researchers believe are either government or extraterrestrial agents sent to silence UFO witnesses. Thirteen months later, tragedy struck Point Pleasant when forty-six people died as a result of the collapse of the Silver Bridge, which connected Point Pleasant to Ohio. People connected the disaster to the Mothman mythology, suggesting that the strange sightings were a portent (Keel [1975] 2002). After the tragedy, Mothman sightings all but stopped,

---

3. When cryptozoologists investigate these stories, they often assign more scientific-sounding descriptors to reframe the reports as empirical evidence rather than outlandish, tabloidesque claims. For example, among cryptozoologists, Mothman is classified as a flying hominid.

Figure 10.2 *Mothman statue, located in downtown Point Pleasant, West Virginia, commemorating sightings of the cryptid in 1966–1967. Photograph by the author.*

although people still occasionally claim to have spotted the creature. In 2016, for example, a man driving near Point Pleasant took several photos of a creature similar in appearance to the Mothman that he claimed was jumping from tree to tree along the highway (Pierson 2016).

Today, Point Pleasant attracts cryptozoologists and legend trippers (see Chapter 5) who stop at the Mothman Museum and visit some of the famous locations from the story, such as the TNT area. The most well-known investigation of the incidents was by author John Keel, a researcher of cryptozoological sightings, UFOs, and other strange phenomena. *The Mothman Prophecies*,[4] written in 1975, explores his visits to Point Pleasant in 1966–1967 to interview witnesses and look for evidence. Keel is an obvious believer, and although he did not see the Mothman himself, he reports on other strange encounters he had, including spotting a UFO and receiving odd phone calls.

Chupacabras: Chupacabras rose to fame in the 1990s. These creatures were first reported in Puerto Rico in 1995 after the remains of chickens, goats, and other livestock were discovered with their blood allegedly drained. The mystery deaths were alarming to those whose livelihood depended on raising and selling the animals, and the culprit was soon assigned a name: Chupacabra (which translates as "goat sucker"). As word of this mysterious bloodsucking beast began to spread, an eyewitness came forward to describe a bizarre gargoyle creature with large black eyes, bat-like wings, a kangaroo posture, and a row of spines down its back. After being featured on a popular Spanish-language daytime talk show, *Cristina*, Chupacabra sightings spread through Latin America and eventually to the southern United States. Adventure-seeking cryptozoologists have self-financed investigations of these sightings but so far have searched the jungles of Puerto Rico without finding definitive evidence. The most in-depth investigation was carried out not by cryptozoologists but by a skeptic, Benjamin Radford, who laid out a compelling case that no such creatures exist in his book *Tracking the Chupacabra* (2011).

Both Mothman and the Chupacabras are somewhat similar in that they are a Rorschach test of supernatural studies: people have described them as ghosts, demons, extraterrestrials, government experiments gone wrong, interdimensional beings, or cryptids. Skeptics tend to dismiss cases like the Mothman as one of mistaken entity—perhaps a crane or barn owl—and some believe that people such as jumpy West Virginians were simply letting their imaginations run wild. Likewise, skeptics dismiss Chupacabras as misidentified mangy dogs or other animals that—when perceived through the lens of public hysteria—turn into demonic bloodsucking beasts in the eyes of witnesses.

---

4. The book was adapted as a 2002 movie starring Richard Gere.

The Jersey Devil: A similarly odd and terrifying creature is the Jersey Devil (originally referred to as the Leeds Devil). First reported in the Pine Barrens forests of New Jersey as far back as the 1700s, witnesses described the creature as a horse-faced, bat-winged, devil-tailed creature. According to folkloric accounts from the hyper-religious days of colonial America, a woman named Deborah Leeds was giving birth to her thirteenth child when she invoked the devil to stop the pain of childbirth. Other versions of the story say there was a family curse or that Leeds had been damned by not converting from the Quaker faith to her husband's Episcopalianism after marriage. She gave birth to a devil baby, who soon escaped into the forest near her home. This folkloric creature appeared in haunting stories told to children for generations, usually with a cautionary moral lesson about the consequences of losing faith in God (see McCrann 2000).

In January and February of 1909, a string of sightings of a strange beast was reported from Pennsylvania and New Jersey. The beast was named by newspapers—as with most cryptids—the Jersey Devil. There was such a panic that some schools and businesses closed. Two hoaxers cashed in on the alarm by charging people at a Philadelphia museum to see a Jersey Devil they claimed to have captured. As was later discovered, their "devil" was an unfortunate kangaroo that they had painted green and adorned with wings. Jersey Devils are still occasionally reported in the Pine Barrens; however, the term has come to refer to any strange sighting of any kind, not necessarily the strange winged creature reported in 1909 (Coleman and Clark 1999).

Although these creatures may have fascinated the public because of their association with horrifying events, they nonetheless have been converted into marketable commodities that now serve as tourist attractions or nonthreatening symbols of local pride. Point Pleasant attracts tourists every year for an annual Mothman Festival, which draws thousands of people. Year around, visitors pose for photos in front of a terrifying Mothman statue in a plaza downtown and look at artifacts in the Mothman Museum, which also offers a Mothman tour. Like the region surrounding Loch Ness, the small town of Point Pleasant greatly benefits from this tourism. One study reports that approximately 70 percent of Point Pleasant's tourism results from the Mothman lore, and much of the small town's income is generated from selling Mothman-themed tchotchkes, including coffee mugs, plush animals, and even "Mothman pancakes" (Krulos 2015: 128). Chupacabras have become a pop culture hit, too. Commercialized uses of the Chupacabra include a cartoonish monster featured in low-budget movies made for the Syfy channel, story lines on shows like *The X-Files* and *The Venture Brothers*, a caricatured visage on the label of Chupacabra Pale Ale from Cupaca Beer Company, and prominent display on logos for the Milwaukee Paranormal Conference. The Jersey Devil was a plot device in a *Scooby-Doo!* comic book and—a special honor for any Jersey native—the focus of a Bruce Springsteen song (2009's "A Night with the Jersey Devil"). Indeed, in 1993 the Jersey Devil became the namesake mascot of New Jersey's National Hockey League team.

Along with Nessie and Bigfoot, these examples show how cryptids are frequently viewed as marketable commodities in the regions most closely associated with sightings of the beasts. In these instances, questions of whether they actually exist are secondary to locals' desire to profit from the mystery. Although these opportunistic marketing ploys are not intended to delegitimize cryptozoology as a practice, they undermine researchers' efforts to be taken seriously. When cryptozoologists talk about Bigfoot, the media and general public are more likely to conjure up a cartoonish character in a beef jerky commercial than to think of an upright hairy hominid unknown to science. The ubiquity of such farcical representations hinders cryptozoologists' attempts to receive at least a modicum of respect for what they do.

CRYPTOZOOLOGY'S STRUGGLE FOR LEGITIMACY

As mentioned at the outset of this chapter, cryptozoologists view their endeavors as a pioneering form of scientific discovery. At the same time, they are aware that this claim to scientific legitimacy is fragile for a number of reasons. One reason for its fragility is that cryptozoology is not integrated into mainstream science as a formal discipline with rigorous training, funding, and representation in peer-reviewed journals or at academic conferences. No major university offers accredited courses in cryptozoology. This means that those who are interested must find online courses and nonaccredited classes or—most commonly—self-educate by reading books, following websites, listening to radio shows and podcasts, and watching documentaries. A few have a postsecondary education or are even college or university professors; however, many have no secondary education, live in rural areas, and are merely interested in discovering Bigfoot or some other specific cryptid.

No grant-writing programs or institutions fund cryptozoological research (Krulos 2015). As a result, cryptozoologists usually fund their studies out of their own pocket, investing in their research as a personal passion. In rare cases cryptozoologists have the ability to personally fund multiple expeditions. Such was the case with Tom Slick, a Texas millionaire and an heir to an oil business, who bankrolled expeditions in the late 1950s and early 1960s to look for the Yeti in the Himalayas, the Sasquatch in the Pacific

Northwest, and the Orang Pendek (a cryptid primate reported in Sumatra; Coleman 2002). However, most cryptozoologists are forced by financial circumstances to treat their research as a hobby rather than an occupation. A Bigfoot researcher I met who is a Michigan field representative for the Bigfoot Field Researchers Organization has self-published a book and was paid a small amount for leading a field expedition sponsored by the Bigfoot Field Researchers Organization. However, the amount of money he has spent on his own equipment, gasoline, and other expenses far exceeds the amount he has made as a Bigfooter, and his day job is working as a high school history teacher. Another cryptozoologist I met lived for many years in Burlington, Vermont, where he focused on researching reports of Champ, the lake monster. He has a day job as a clerk in a convenience store and spends his spare time researching at the library, interviewing eyewitnesses, and spending countless hours scanning the lake with a pair of binoculars (Krulos 2015).

As a consequence of the lack of funding, cryptozoologists support their research through selling books, charging for tours or expeditions, and earning appearance fees on television or the cryptozoological conference circuit. The most prominent cryptozoologists write magazine articles and books about their research; however, authorship money depends entirely on book sales, the marketing efforts of the publisher, and how prolific the writer is. Book advances typically range from $5,000 to $25,000, depending on the publisher. Some cryptozoology-themed books have been successful: *The Mothman Prophecies* ([1975] 2002) by John Keel was on the *New York Times* best-seller list, *Mysterious America* (2007) by Loren Coleman has consistently stayed in print, and cryptozoology author Linda S. Godfrey (2012, 2014, 2016) has published three books through a division of Penguin Books.

In terms of special attraction or expedition services, museums like the Mothman Museum or the International Cryptozoology Museum charge admittance fees that generate income ($3 per adult for the former, $10 for the latter). The Bigfoot Field Researchers Organization raises funds by offering expeditions in which members of the public join team leaders on a camping expedition to search for Bigfoot evidence. They organize about two dozen expeditions per year and charge a fee of $300–$500 per trip. The organization also takes donations and sells merchandise on its website. Last, members of the group are able to parlay their appearances on Animal Planet's reality show *Finding Bigfoot* into paid speaking appearances at cryptozoological conferences.

Conferences with cryptozoology themes appear annually throughout the country in venues like casinos, Veterans of Foreign Wars and other meeting halls, campgrounds, and college campuses. Attendance ranges from a couple of dozen to over a thousand. Some conferences with a general supernatural theme also include speakers on topics like ghosts and UFOs, while others focus specifically on one cryptid. The Ohio Bigfoot Conference attracts hundreds of Bigfooters every year to discuss the latest findings in the field, and an annual Champ Camp attracts a handful of passionate lake monster researchers every summer to a campground on Lake Champlain. Conference appearance fees depend on how well known the guest speakers are and travel distance and accommodations. Some local speakers might be offered a small fee for travel expenses, while more well-known speakers might get between several hundred dollars and a couple of thousand dollars, as well as having their travel and accommodations paid for. All of this work helps cryptozoologists pay the bills, but it simultaneously undermines their credibility. By making it appear as though their claimed cryptid sightings are nothing more than a get-rich-quick scheme, these funding sources play into skeptics' suspicions that fraud and trickery are rampant among those who report supernatural phenomena.

Indeed, hoaxers seeking attention, cheap thrills, viral Internet fame, or having other motivating factors are a problem for cryptozoologists. Hoaxes are nothing new—recall the hucksters who cashed in on the Jersey Devil panic of 1909 with the poor kangaroo they painted green—and these pranks are even easier today with readily available apps that allow smartphone users to quickly insert a slightly blurry falsified Bigfoot into a photo. Of the many hoaxes out there, one of the best documented is known as the Georgia Hoax. In 2008, a used-car salesman named Rick Dyer and his associate, sheriff's deputy Matt Whitton, claimed they had encountered a Bigfoot corpse while walking through a forest in Georgia. They released a photo of a body stuffed inside an empty refrigerator at a press conference. The Bigfoot Field Researchers Organization quickly identified what it really was: a widely available Halloween costume that had been stuffed with animal entrails. Dyer, hoping he could fool the world twice, returned in 2014 with a new story. He claimed he was on a Bigfoot expedition near San Antonio and lured a Bigfoot (whom he later named Hank) with some pork ribs into his camp and shot the creature. After months of stringing people along with video messages and reports, he eventually hit the road to several states with a Time to Believe tour. Dyer charged people to enter a trailer to look at Hank's body preserved in a glass display case; by the time he was done, Dyer reportedly had pocketed $60,000 in profits from the stunt (Krulos 2015).[5]

---

5. For reasons unknown, perhaps simply becoming sick of the hoax, Dyer admitted in April 2015 that the story was false. Hank had been created by a costume and model maker in California out of latex and fake hair (Krulos 2015).

Another group that threatens cryptozoologists' tenuous claims to scientific legitimacy is skeptics. Within the mainstream scientific community, cryptozoology is often dismissed as pseudoscience because the evidence presented thus far has been fabricated, misidentified, or is inconclusive. This skepticism is well represented by Jim Harding, a herpetologist in Michigan State University's Zoology Department who told me during an interview, "My impression is that most animal biologists probably would take a skeptical view of cryptozoology, while at the same time maintaining an open mind about accepting new data that is gathered and reported in a responsible and professional manner." Although, Harding added, from what he had seen, "mostly on TV, . . . cryptozoologists often skip the steps that would legitimize their research in favor of snap judgments, instant publicity, and self-promotion" (Krulos 2015: 172). Skeptics like Harding argue that the methods and standards of evidence used by cryptozoologists do not meet the minimum requirements for sound scientific investigation and that therefore any claims made on the basis of such evidence are suspect.

Often skeptics exhibit a particular zeal for dissecting or debunking cryptozoological claims. They explain away the Patterson-Gimlin footage as a guy in an ape suit, the Mansi photo as a funny-looking piece of driftwood, Mokèlé-mbèmbé as nothing but local folklore, and the Mothman sightings as mass hallucination. In the case of the Chupacabra, skeptic and researcher Benjamin Radford followed the thread back to the original eyewitness, a woman named Madelyne Tolentino, in his book *Tracking the Chupacabra* (2011). Radford found the story of her Chupacabra sighting to be inconsistent and implausible. He discovered that shortly before her sighting she had seen the 1995 movie *Species*, which featured an alien creature similar in description to the Chupacabra. Once Tolentino started the Chupacabra craze, any shadow in the Puerto Rican night, dead livestock, or other mysterious happening was attributed to the Chupacabra. When the stories began to circulate in the southern United States, the creature's description morphed to a hideous, hairless, ill-tempered animal that walked on four legs. Skeptics and scientists quickly deemed the miserable-looking creatures as dogs, coyotes, or raccoons suffering from severe cases of mange (Radford 2011). By reframing cryptozoological claims as either outright fraud or inaccuracies caused by imprecise methods of data collection and analysis, skeptics are able to call into question every piece of purported evidence. Because these skeptics also often serve as gatekeepers to the mainstream scientific community, this leaves cryptozoologists perpetually on the outside looking in, seemingly condemned to the realm of pseudoscience.

THE ALLURE OF CRYPTOZOOLOGY

In the face of what seem to be insurmountable odds, one may wonder why cryptozoologists continue to pursue their research. On an individual level, part of what continues to motivate cryptozoologists is the potential of making a truly earth-shattering discovery. As cryptozoologist Loren Coleman (Figure 10.3) noted in an interview, committed cryptozoologists ignore setbacks like hoaxers and shrug off skeptics while maintaining an optimistic, open mind. They try to focus on the small percentage of cases that present compelling mysteries (Krulos 2015). Part of the thrill of cryptozoology is that it has odds comparable to winning the lottery. The chances of capturing definitive evidence is slight, but the possibility of definitively proving the existence of a creature like Bigfoot or the Loch Ness monster keeps cryptozoologists intrigued. Beyond the thrill of discovery, cryptozoologists also seek the respect and admiration of fellow researchers and fantasize about going down in the history books as the one who solved one of the world's greatest mysteries. Cryptozoologists maintain their enthusiasm by telling themselves that science has many secrets yet to unlock. Their unofficial mascot, the coelacanth, reminds them of this. Likewise, cryptozoologists appeal to the notion

Figure 10.3 *Loren Coleman, cryptozoologist and International Cryptozoology Museum founder, standing with a display that includes a Bigfoot statue and a model of an Orang Pendek, a cryptid primate rumored to live in Sumatra. Photograph courtesy of the International Cryptozoology Museum.*

that the sheer number of reported cryptid sightings lends credibility to the existence of such creatures—so many people have reported seeing cryptids that they cannot all be delusional, can they?

Beyond any benefits for the cryptozoologists themselves, one could argue that their efforts serve a social function as well: cryptozoologists allow the public to maintain a sense of excitement and enchantment about the undiscovered possibilities in a world in which it may often appear as though there is nothing left to discover. This re-enchantment includes the search for cryptids as well as interest in New Age spirituality and other beliefs and practices that reinject mystery into a world that is dominated by all-encompassing scientific and religious explanations. In describing re-enchantment, Christopher Partridge likens the mind-set of those who desire enchantment to the phrase "I Want to Believe" that appears on a poster in Agent Fox Mulder's office wall in *The X-Files*. As Partridge writes:

> Unsatisfied by disenchanted worldviews, unhappy with traditional, institutional religions, inspired by an increasingly re-enchanted popular culture, but not yet certain of new ideas that seem strange and irrational to their secularized minds, they move from the pre-liminal stage of detached curiosity to a liminal "I want to believe" stage in which new worldviews are entertained and old certainties seriously questioned. (2002: 249)

Ironically, for people who desire re-enchantment, the lack of definitive proof for or against the existence of cryptids is actually a positive thing. As long as no absolute consensus exists as to the status of Nessie, Bigfoot, and the other creatures described above, the public can maintain a sense that *maybe* there is more to the world than current science can tell us.

CONCLUSIONS

Cryptozoology stands at the intersection of folklore and fact. Thus, it serves multiple functions for various audiences. For those who simply "want to believe," the allure is in the mystery surrounding eyewitness reports and conflicting claims. For more serious cryptozoologists, the thrill is quite the opposite: they hope to make a breakthrough discovery by use of scientific methods of data collection. Cryptozoologists dream that, after enduring years of ridicule from mainstream science, they will have the last laugh when their dogged research uncovers definitive proof of the existence of cryptids. Last, those who have commercialized cryptids do not much care about proof *or* enchantment as long as they can continue to earn a living from the researchers and tourists alike who flock to their locales. Like any enigma, cryptids are open to multiple interpretations, none of which are demonstrably more valid than the others. As has been the case for hundreds of years, cryptids will likely continue to be monsters to some, myths to others, and simply misunderstood living creatures for those who choose to believe.

REFERENCES

Beck, Fred, with Ronald A. Beck. 1967. *I Fought the Apemen of Mt. St. Helens*. Self-published.
Brown, Jonathon. 2014. "Loch Ness Monster: Nessie's Back, Just in Time for Scotland's Big Year." *The Independent*, April 27. Available at http://www.independent.co.uk/news/uk/this-britain/loch-ness-monster-nessie-is-back-just-in-time-for-scotlands-big-year-9294548.html.
Coleman, Loren. 2002. *Tom Slick: True Life Encounters in Cryptozoology*. Fresno, CA: Craven Street Books.
———. 2003. *Bigfoot! The True Story of Apes in America*. New York: Paraview Press.
———. 2007. *Mysterious America: The Ultimate Guide to the Nation's Weirdest Wonders, Strangest Spots, and Creepiest Creatures*. New York: Pocket Books.
Coleman, Loren, and Jerome Clark. 1999. *Cryptozoology A–Z: The Encyclopedia of Lake Monsters, Sasquatch, Chupacabras, and Other Authentic Mysteries of Nature*. New York: Fireside.
Coleman, Loren, and Patrick Huyghe. 2003. *The Field Guide to Lake Monsters, Sea Serpents, and Other Mystery Denizens of the Deep*. New York: TarcherPerigee.
———. 2006. *The Field Guide to Bigfoot and Other Mystery Primates*. San Antonio, TX: Anomalist Books.
Dockett, Eric. 2017. "The Teddy Roosevelt Bigfoot Story." *Exemplore*, August 7. Available at https://exemplore.com/cryptids/Teddy-Roosevelt-Bigfoot.
Edwards, Guy. 2012. "Americans More Likely to Believe in Bigfoot than Canadians." *Bigfoot Lunch Club*, March 4. Available at http://www.bigfootlunchclub.com/2012/03/americans-more-likely-to-believe-in.html.
Godfrey, Linda S. 2012. *Real Wolfmen: True Encounters in Modern America*. New York: TarcherPerigree.
———. 2014. *American Monsters: A History of Monster Lore, Legends, and Sightings in America*. New York: TarcherPerigree
———. 2016. *Monsters among Us: An Exploration of Otherworldly Bigfoots, Wolfmen, Portals, Phantoms, and Odd Phenomena*. New York: TarcherPerigree
Grossman, Samantha. 2012. "Top 10 Not-So-Extinct Animals: Javan Elephants." *Time*, January 25. Available at http://content.time.com/time/specials/packages/article/0,28804,2105239_2105240_2105245,00.html.
Hill, Sharon A. 2010. "Being Scientific: Popularity, Purpose and Promotion of Amateur Research and Investigation Groups in the U.S." Master's thesis, State University of New York, Buffalo.
Keel, John A. (1975) 2002. *The Mothman Prophecies*. New York: Tor Books.
Krulos, Tea. 2015. *Monster Hunters: On the Trail with Ghost Hunters, Bigfooters, Ufologists, and Other Paranormal Investigators*. Chicago: Chicago Review Press.

Kruse, Robert J., II. 2015. "Point Pleasant, West Virginia: Making a Tourism Landscape in an Appalachian Town." *Southeastern Geographer* 55 (3): 313–337.

Lapseritis, Kewaunee. 2005. *The Psychic Sasquatch and Their UFO Connection*. Seattle, WA: Createspace.

Love, David. 2013. "Loch Ness Monster Museum Wars: Centre Owner Arrested after Admitting 'Taking Custody' of Rival Attraction's Sign." *Daily Record*, June 22. Available at http://www.dailyrecord.co.uk/news/scottish-news/loch-ness-monster-centre-owner-1977664.

Loxton, Daniel, and Donald Prothero. 2012. *Abominable Science! Origins of the Yeti, Nessie, and Other Famous Cryptids*. New York: Columbia University Press.

McCrann, Grace-Ellen. 2000. "Legend of the New Jersey Devil." Available at http://www.jerseyhistory.org/legend_jerseydevil.html.

Nelson, Bryan. 2009. "Lazarus Species: 13 'Extinct' Animals Found Alive." *Mother Nature Network*, November 5. Available at http://www.mnn.com/earth-matters/animals/photos/lazarus-species-13-extinct-animals-found-alive/rediscovered.

Partridge, Christopher. 2002. "The Disenchantment and Re-enchantment of the West: The Religio-Cultural Context of Contemporary Western Christianity." *Evangelical Quarterly* 74 (3): 235–256.

Pierson, Fallon. 2016. "Man Photographs Creature That Resembles Legendary 'Mothman' of West Virginia." *WCHS 8*, November 22. Available at http://wchstv.com/news/local/man-photographs-creature-that-resembles-legendary-mothman-of-point-pleasant.

Pohlen, Jerome. 2013. *Oddball Wisconsin: A Guide to 400 Really Strange Places*. 2nd ed. Chicago: Chicago Review Press.

Radford, Benjamin. 2011. *Tracking the Chupacabra: The Vampire Beast in Fact, Fiction, and Folklore*. Albuquerque: University of New Mexico Press.

———. 2015. "Loch Ness Monster: Facts about Nessie." *Live Science*, April 22. Available at http://www.livescience.com/26341-loch-ness-monster.html.

Radford, Benjamin, and Joe Nickell. 2006. *Lake Monster Mysteries: Investigating the World's Most Elusive Creatures*. Lexington: University Press of Kentucky.

Wamsley, Jeff. 2005. *Mothman: Behind the Red Eyes*. Point Pleasant, WV: Mothman Press.

Willis, James A., Andrew Henderson, and Loren Coleman. 2005. *Weird Ohio: Your Travel Guide to Ohio's Local Legends and Best Kept Secrets*. New York: Sterling.

11

ALIEN ABDUCTION NARRATIVES

A Proposed Model and Brief Case Study

Scott R. Scribner

Along with popular awareness of UFOs, reports of alleged alien abduction of humans achieved considerable social prominence during the late twentieth century. Alien abduction literatures offer many proposed explanations for these reports, mainly as physical, psychosocial, or religious events. In light of the methodological weaknesses of these explanations, I have proposed a nonlinear chronological Teller-Narrator model[1] for explaining the social salience of alien abduction narratives (Scribner 1999a). In this chapter I briefly review some of the major theories that propose to explain alien abductee reports, review my model for understanding alien abductee narratives (AANs), and conclude with an applied case study of one of the most widely popularized accounts of an alien abduction.

AANs are claims that strange beings took the Teller—typically from a bed or automobile at night—and subjected them to quasimedical examinations and other bizarre treatment. These accounts include expressions of fear as the victim is kidnapped and undergoes painful or humiliating procedures. AAN Tellers may go public by themselves or may contact and be interviewed by an AAN researcher. The resulting narrative consists of a report of a person who is seized, transported, and experimented on by strange creatures. On the

---

1. Rather than "Teller," I prefer "Storyteller." However, Diana Tumminia criticized my term in a discussion with me in 2005 because the word "story" might imply that a report is fictional at the outset. Because there are no purely objective accounts—even in science—I consider this bias unfortunate, but I use the terms "Telling" and "Teller" to avoid those assumptions.

basis of a controversial interpretation of data from a 1991 Roper Poll, some UFO abduction researchers claim that two million Americans may have been abducted by aliens (Hopkins, Jacobs, and Westrum 1992). According to the French scientist Jacques Vallee, "The folklore of every culture" contains "a rich reservoir of stories about humanoid beings that flew in the sky" (1969: 57). Vallee also contends that those beings "used devices that seemed in advance of the technology of the time" and "abducted humans" who "reported an alteration of the sense of time when they were in the beings' company" (vii; for reports of "missing time," see Scribner 1999b).

There is a qualitative difference between modern reports of UFO sightings and AANs. The former focus primarily on questions such as "*What* is happening? What is *causing* this?" while the latter bring to the fore questions of meaning and response ("What does this *mean*? What must be *done* about it?").[2] These different but interrelated perspectives highlight the distinction between (1) a *phenomenon* out there that both reflects and affects our continuously evolving views of the universe and (2) *human events* down here that simultaneously mirror and influence our way of life. Greg Wheeler (2000) identifies this distinction as the interaction between *Weltbild* (world picture) and *Weltanschauung* (worldview), which together constitute a dynamic cosmology—not unlike William Force's articulation of a "cryptoscience" in Chapter 1.

The prevalence of reported encounters with UFOs and aliens has not escaped the attention of scholars and academics. In the 1950s—a busy period for UFO sightings—Carl Jung wrote *Flying Saucers: A Modern Myth of Things Seen in the Skies* ([1958] 1969).[3] Apparent cultural parallels among reported experiences of alien abduction also inspired Thomas Bullard (1991) to investigate whether the narrative structure of AANs resembled traditional folklore. Contrary to expectations, Bullard found that modern AANs are not as culturally diverse as folklore, suggesting a common source or influence that is transcultural, such as neurophysiology. Vallee has written extensively about the cultic potential of AANs. In *Dimensions* (1988), Vallee points out

---

2. While early twentieth century UFO sightings stirred widespread interest, most responses originated from the military and private hobbyists. It took the increased prominence of AANs to reflect a level of fear comparable to that caused by Orson Welles's *War of the Worlds* (1938) radio program, broadcast on the eve of World War II.

3. Although Jung took the UFO phenomenon seriously, his use of the word *myth* was characteristically misunderstood by our utilitarian culture. To the modern Western mind, myths are tantamount to fiction and not, in the actual meaning of the word, a "sacred story." As a result, most people do not see myths in terms of the functions they fulfill as sources of shared human meaning that convey personal identity as well as membership in a group.

that the activities of UFO cults make it more difficult to study the "core phenomenon." He theorizes that some UFO narratives have been created by secret groups as social experiments or as cover stories for military activities. Vallee cautions us to take seriously the AAN's seductive power to influence mass psychology.

PERSPECTIVES ON ALIEN ABDUCTION

Significant differences exist among those who believe in alien contact, including the visitors' intentions. One faction fears invasion or human-alien conspiracies (e.g., Budd Hopkins, Jacques Vallee, and David Jacobs). Another appears to welcome alien "salvation" (e.g., Leo Sprinkle, Edith Fiore, Richard Boylan, and perhaps John Mack). A third group remains neutral about alien intentions (e.g., Raymond Fowler and Whitley Strieber). These differences may forecast a form of UFO denominationalism, and the religious implications have been discussed at length (see Lewis 1995).

Differences in attitudes and temperament may partially explain the variety of beliefs toward UFOs and alien abduction. Many UFO believers accept UFOs and aliens as physical realities (Friedman 1996). Other believers assert their reality, while conceptualizing the UFOs or aliens as nonphysical; some resort to spiritual explanations (R. Thompson 1993), while others prefer a more secular approach (Strieber 1987). Believers in nonphysical UFOs tend to be philosophical dualists, and some propose that UFOs (and alien abductions) constitute a bridge between matter and spirit (K. Thompson 1990).

UFO agnostics (skeptics) believe that UFO sightings and alien abductions are likely the result of misperception, confusion, delusion, or mental illness (Sagan 1995). These agnostics frequently endorse the possibility of alien life elsewhere in the universe but do not believe that UFOs visit Earth. Skeptics include those who offer rational explanations of AANs without prejudice but with the clear implication that UFOs and alien abductions are chimerical events (i.e., not real). Although they deny the reality of alien visitation itself, skeptics can still believe that the supernatural *stories* of such encounters have significant social and cultural importance (see Lewis 2000, 1995; Tumminia 2007).

UFO atheists (debunkers) assert that UFOs and alien beings do not come to Earth, and they may believe that UFO reports and AANs are pernicious or at least threaten the mental health of individuals who become involved (Klass 1989). Debunkers "know" that alien abductions are not real (if they were, they would be investigated as kidnappings by the Federal Bureau of Investigation, according to this group) and believe that the dissemination of UFO stories constitutes a dangerously irrational trend, or even outright deception or fraud. Debunkers tend to be philosophical materialists. Many debunkers also tend to discount any reports of supernatural or paranormal events and disdain religious claims.[4] Debunking has proved ineffective in discouraging the proliferation of AANs or even in slowing claims for the transforming effects of such experiences. The history of religious disputes—including twentieth-century attempts to eradicate belief in communist countries—suggests that confrontational approaches may tend to strengthen believers' resolve. Belief systems growing out of AANs also can produce powerful defensive protections—fundamentalist and even cultic—to resist criticism.

Despite their disputes, believers and debunkers alike may impose implicit materialist interpretations on the same phenomenological gestalt. Both sides attempt to hold their ground as champions of common sense, whether about flying saucers or swamp gas. However, each side focuses on some specialized forensic method or theoretical framework, which narrows their attention to not include the totality of the human experience. In other words, all sides can become hypnotized by their methods.

"WHAT IS HAPPENING?" EXPLANATIONS OF AANS

The most familiar theory of UFOs and AANs in popular culture—and the one that most closely fits the modern scientific worldview in its popular form—is the extraterrestrial hypothesis. This hypothesis proposes that throughout history visitors from other physical places in the universe have visited Earth via space ships, and may have even created humanity through genetic engineering. According to this theory, aliens abduct people for their own purposes, much like humans who capture terrestrial animals for study. The main problem with the extraterrestrial hypothesis is that it does violence to our current understanding of physics. The distances of Earth from other star systems is so great that the amount of technological effort and fuel required to travel that distance seems insurmountable to us and hardly justifiable for extraterrestrial zoology.

The terrestrial hypothesis, in contrast, proposes that UFOs originate somewhere on or inside the Earth. Their crafts may be piloted by strange (earthly) beings, or they may be UFO-shaped animals (Brookesmith and Truzzi 1992). The vehicles may fly from hidden bases, from under the oceans (Sanderson 1970), or even from inside a hollow Earth (Bernard 1969). In another variation of the terrestrial hypothesis, there are no alien beings but only top-secret vehicles flown in Earth's skies by government military forces.

---

4. Ironically, some conservative Christians also practice UFO debunking on the basis of a theological doctrine that supernatural events ended in New Testament times.

A conspiracy-driven version of this hypothesis suggests that these groups may be kidnapping human beings, who remember alien images because they were drugged or hypnotized.

Most scholars and academics articulate nonbelief theories: that UFOs and alleged alien abductions are natural phenomena, hallucinations, or a product of psychosocial variables. Their differences are housed within disciplinary camps that use different frameworks for interpretation. It is beyond this chapter to review all these nonbelief theories for UFOs and alien abductions, but I review a few to illustrate the diversity of approaches found in academia.

Alien abduction experiences have been attributed to natural electromagnetic phenomena, seismic movements within the Earth, and microwave or ionizing radiation (Budden 1995; Rutkowski 1988). In contrast to naturalistic approaches that explain UFOs and alien abductions as the result of external natural phenomena, neuropsychologists view human awareness as structures and processes within the brain. Neurophysiological explanations of AANs include the work of Michael Persinger (1992), who found that identifiable deformations of perception occurred in cases of deliberate disruption of cortical function, particularly in the temporal lobe.

Psychologists have offered their own explanations for UFOs and alleged alien abductions. The experimental psychologist Nicholas Spanos (1996) proposed that AANs are complex false memories arising from the interaction of human needs within our specific cultural period, in which technology dominates nearly all aspects of everyday life. A Harvard study (Clancy et al. 2002) attempted to explain the emotional distress of abductees and found that people who believed they had been abducted by aliens had the same physiological responses as persons who had experienced "real" trauma.[5] Alvin Lawson's (1989) birth trauma imagery studies also fall into this category: Lawson hypothesized that AANs originate in the experience of a person's birth or other trauma in early life.

Social psychologists interpret human behaviors in terms of—or as influenced or imposed by—social interactions. Leonard Newman and Roy Baumeister (1996), as well as Daniel O'Keefe (1982), identify narratives as personal constructions that bring coherence and meaning to experiences, which can be applied to make sense of the narratives people tell of alien abduction. Studies of rumor and urban legends (Allport and Postman 1947) emphasize the role of social interactions in creating and disseminating group narratives. The creation of unusual stories can originate from different motives (e.g., psy-

---

5. Because the Harvard study's governing assumption was that alien abductions are imaginary, its findings did not end the controversy.

chological disturbance, entertainment, boredom, anomie, power, or financial gain). Strange stories, such as an encounter with a UFO or an alien, can also result when people are affected by technological changes (Kipness 1997).

Sociologists consider AANs as a form of social contagion under some model of explanation such as the theory of memes, which posits a genetic model of social ideas that propagate, compete, and survive as genes do in the biological realm (Lynch 1996; Showalter 1997). Some sociologists see AANs as a subset of a peculiarly American construct, the kidnap narrative,[6] such as portrayed in the John Wayne movie *The Searchers* (1956). Anthropologists see AANs as imaginary social relationships, like those found in non-Western cultures with strong beliefs in ancestors and spirits (Caughey 1984). In American society as elsewhere, imaginary relationships are formed with celebrities, television and film actors, and fictional characters. Such relationships can have significant emotional consequences. Cultural anthropologists view AANs as primitive spiritual phenomena in the tradition of shamanic initiation rites (Eliade 1964; Harner 1980). This viewpoint sees AANs as modern shamanic journeys, arising from deep structures developed in human past but now exposed to technological change and urban conditions.

Religious anthropologists have studied the contactee movement and see AANs as a potential narrative basis for new religions (Lewis 1995). James Lewis's anthology *The Gods Have Landed* (1995) characterizes the UFO myth as millenarian, that is, concerned with the "end of time" both as historical movement and perceptual dynamic. Another explanation states that UFO stories constitute the basis of a new mythology that is developing in our highly technological age (Jung [1958] 1969). One of the most influential examples of the new-myth position is described in Keith Thompson's book *Angels and Aliens* (1990). Thompson proposes that aliens originate in an imaginal realm that mediates between the worlds of matter and spirit.

AAN cultural interpretation also takes the form of literary criticism. Combining social criticism and politics, Jodi Dean's book *Aliens in America* (1998) interprets AANs as the expression of dispossessed political groups, who use the narrative to dissent from modern bureaucratic institutions and an impersonal Big Science. In ethnic studies, the essay "Alien Abductions and the End of White People" (Newitz 1993) proposes that the "grey" alien imagery bespeaks white fears of losing their racial identity (their "whiteness") in a global culture. In the field of literary criticism, Stephanie Kelley (1999) studied the forms of rhetoric used in alien abduction stories. Using a narrative-mythic analysis that examines relationships between form and function

---

6. James Lewis told me this in 1997.

of the narratives, Kelley finds these narratives to be a highly significant living myth to those who told them.

The religio-spiritual hypothesis suggests that AANs are modern religious texts. AANs describe visits by heavenly beings that are similar to historical tales of entities from the cosmos that have interacted with humans. This hypothesis is based on similarities between AANs and traditional religious narratives, such as the Christian Gospels (Downing 1968). Even within evangelical Christianity, leading spokesman Billy Graham—in his book *Angels* (1995)—proposes that UFOs are angelic vehicles sent by God. Likewise, Hindu religious traditions contain many tales of beings from the heavens (R. Thompson 1993), and traditional Buddhism cautions about encounters with "skandha demons" from the heavens (Hua 1996).

Finally, among the most skeptical of all nonbelief theories are those claiming that UFOs and alien abductions are simply hoaxes or frauds. Examples include controversial cases such as Gulf Breeze and Travis Walton (described in more detail below using my Teller-Narrator model) (Gordon 1995; Klass 1989). Debunkers believe that these narrators are either hoaxers or dupes, spreading stories for financial gain and publicity or out of ignorance. Examples of such deceptions include the Philadelphia Experiment (Moore and Berlitz 1995) and reports of men in black (Barker 1956). In some metaphysical conspiracy theories, UFOs and alien abduction are plots carried out by cabals of the military, secret societies, fugitive Nazis with Atlantean technology, and so on (Kanon 1997).

"WHAT IS TO BE DONE?" AAN AS SOCIAL CONDITION OR PROBLEM

Along with many explanatory models for UFOs and AANs, medical, social, and spiritual approaches emphasize amelioration. Each model sees AANs as symptoms of social or health problems. In this sense, they illustrate the Weltanschauung-oriented approach (How should we live?). Psychiatry applies the medical model to psychological issues and emphasizes the chemical management of behavior. Psychiatrists attempt to rule out identifiable disruptions of consciousness due to subictal seizures, drug or alcohol use, sleep disorders, transient psychoticism, and other causes among people who claim to have witnessed a UFO or were abducted by aliens. Within a traditional psychiatric framework, AANs are considered hallucinations and delusions rooted in some form of psychopathology that may be manageable with medication. From this perspective, there may be life in outer space, but it is not visiting our patients.

Among psychoanalysts, AANs reflect intrapsychic conflicts rooted in the nervous system—a new kind of dream. These theories include object relations theories (e.g., infantile longing for a mother ship) and the problem of fear and paranoia as initial alienating conditions resulting from identity confusion, health problems, abuse, failure of adaptation, or a sense of threat. Tellers are hypersensitive watchers whose inner images derive from paranoid ideation (Slater 1983). Clinical psychologists consider AANs to be screen memories of actual abuse, such as childhood sexual abuse. Psychotherapists emphasize treatment of AAN-related distress, symptoms, and emotional problems.[7] In the view of many psychotherapists who work with abductees, AANs are expressions of trauma. Therefore, psychotherapists like the late John Mack, as he told me in 2002, conclude that it is better to empathize with Tellers than to argue about reality. In this approach, the reality status of aliens is set aside without judgment, but over the course of many therapeutic interactions, belief in their existence may become implicit. Researchers like Mack claim objectivity or neutrality, but their activities—such as attending American Indian rituals and New Age conferences—indicate movement toward the UFO believer camp.

The range of explanations for the AAN phenomenon is vast; I have covered only a sample, most of which are nondisconfirmable. All research starts by approaching phenomena from a context that includes predefined assumptions: physical, psychosocial, social, cultural, or religious. In almost fifty years of AAN research, these approaches have produced a blind alley instead of additional clarity. Yet even suspicions of hoax and deception do not cause interest in the phenomenon to wane. A scholarly approach must be based on what is known—human narratives, human values, and human behaviors—not mere speculation. Thus, I propose that we consider these narratives in terms of what is human within them rather than shift from one theoretical context to another without resolution. For these reasons, I suggest that the best approach is to focus on the narratives that people report of their alleged experiences with UFOs and alien abduction.

A TELLER-NARRATOR MODEL

Instead of presuming to objectively uncover what happened, I propose that we focus on the origins, development, versioning, and effects of the *narratives* and *images* produced about reports of UFOs or alien abduction. At a general level, AANs exhibit three common characteristics: *trance* (changes in awareness and behavior), *traumatic fears* (indications of strong emotions and psychological symptoms), and *therapeutic interventions* (often from family, friends, and professionals).

---

7. Or they do at least until their professional license is suspended, as happened to Richard Boylan in 1995 and Edith Fiore in 1997.

Trance: Are You Now—or Have You Ever Been—Asleep?

Altered states of consciousness—and the predisposition to have them—constitute the psychological dimension of AANs and underlie the variables that scientific psychology has attempted to measure. AANs contain many indications of alterations in consciousness, such as perceptual anomalies,[8] visions, sleep paralysis, and dreams. Accounting for a psychological phenomenon is made more complicated when hypnosis is used to acquire and explore these stories. Fear can appear within any disturbance of the "generalized reality orientation" (Shor 1959: 582). In trance, persons become more open to fears, whether the fear of hypnosis itself (even deep relaxation), disturbing emotions released in an undefended or dissociative state, or frightening dreams. Finally, preoccupation with pervasive media images can promote such altered states and therefore may act as a pervasive public source of hypnotic suggestion.

Traumatic Fears: Are You Now—or Have You Ever Been—Afraid?

The role of fear (or strong emotion) is the central factor in AANs (Fowler 1979; Hopkins 1981; Strieber 1987) and is often taken as signifier of alien presence and proof of reality status.[9] However, the presence of fear has not received sufficient attention. Fear must be the central focus of AAN study for three reasons. First, fear appears in all AANs, even those attributed to good alien beings. Second, fear constitutes a significant presence in AANs regardless of whether the events they describe are true or not. Third, fear is known to propagate through groups and cultures and through media channels (Sardello 1996).

Therapeutic Interventions: Are You Now—or Have You Ever Been—a Victim?

Identification of personal problems and victimization invokes the social dimension of AANs. Amelioration must face the presence of fears, anxiety,

---

8. Judging perceptions, impressions, or experiences as anomalous implies an existing framework against which they contrast. Otherwise, they would merely be normal or unperceived (which may be the same thing). Some signals or patterns we attend to deliberately (such as seeking a familiar face in a crowd). Anything we notice involuntarily or unexpectedly may be anomalous to some degree, especially if its meaning cannot be resolved soon enough to avert anxiety, fear, or panic.

9. Some UFO believers claim that debunkers' attitudes are attributable to their own fears (Hopkins 1981; Strieber 1987).

and alienation and include seeking the aid of friends, family, and medical or psychological professionals. Psychotherapy resources and support groups may be marshalled and made available. Some contacts are made with organized foundations set up by AAN researchers.[10]

In addition to these three common characteristics, AANs typically follow a process by which they transform from a description of a strange personal experience into a supernatural story that is consumed by the public. This pattern of narrative development is not unique to AANs and may be applied with minimal adjustment to different tales about anomalous encounters. I have found that the development of an AAN may entail up to six steps:

1. *Telling:* One or more people describe a strange experience, using emic explanations of the event and placing it within a local context.[11] For example, secular cultural judgments might attribute the disclosure to mental instability; whereas, in a more traditional religious setting, the disclosures could be appreciated as seership or spiritual election. The experience is described as having occurred in the past. This is a social necessity because an anomalous event reported as if in real time would be disconcerting to any witnesses who were not perceiving the same events.[12] The Teller is a person or group of people who through verbal report, writing, or other behaviors introduces a story into the world. Teller motivations can vary, but the story typically involves some category of anomaly—otherwise it would not be remarkable enough to be noticed.[13]
2. *Elaboration:* Private conversations ensue among contacts within an inner social circle, where the story develops further.[14] It becomes more elaborated and refined as the individual and the local social group seek understanding, consistency, and other forms of resolution. This development can produce early transcriptions, record-

---

10. These include Budd Hopkins's Intruder Foundation, Whitley Strieber's Communion Foundation, and John Mack's PEER group.
11. "Strangeness" is also a term of art in ufology; it denotes the degree of anomalous content in the story.
12. AANs that claim multiple eyewitnesses require additional analysis, as described in the brief case study.
13. This principle is the basis of carnival sideshows, which display outlandish—not mundane—attractions.
14. For example, in Budd Hopkins's (1996) Linda Cortile case, the inner circle was her family, but a Professionalization circle and Narrator already preexisted with her participation in a Hopkins support group and hypnosis by Hopkins.

ings, drawings, or other records that can become highly valued later as original sources. These initial records can also be modified over time. Contacts inside the local social circle of the Teller, such as family members, can further shape the story's development through the dynamics of their reception and response to the narrative.

3. *Professionalization:* Depending on the story's social context, strangeness, and impact on the Teller's well-being, professional contacts can occur outside the local social circle. There can be multiple contacts (e.g., police, medical, psychological, or journalistic). Specialized professionals called on for assistance supply additional contexts that can affect the story dramatically. In some instances, interviews, interrogations, or hypnosis may be employed to recover more memories that provide further transcripts as resources for the narrative construction. These artifacts may not be as valued by believers as the original sources, but they add credibility to the narrative as socially authorized judgments.

4. *Narration:* At a certain point, the story becomes significant enough to require a Narrator. The Narrator is a person, or group of people, with some combination of communication skills, social prestige, and media contacts who casts the story into the form that is presented to a wider but relatively localized audience. A Narrator organizes the evidence into a form of communication that becomes etic (public) and thus subject to out-group evaluations. A Narrator can have several motivations, including altruism, intellectual curiosity, psychological need, publicity, and economic gain. A Narrator can be the original Teller (e.g., Travis Walton, Whitley Strieber), a journalist (John Fuller), a private researcher (Raymond Fowler, Budd Hopkins), an academic (the historian David Jacobs), or a prestigious professional figure (the Harvard psychiatrist John Mack).

5. *Mediatization:* The AAN may be released to a local public in the form of a media product, initially in relatively small markets. For example, the story may appear in local newspapers or on television stations, radio, and specialized print or Internet publications. Regardless of the form, the narrative undergoes publication within fairly small, regional, or specialized networks of people. At some point, national and even global media can pick up the story. Mediatization marks a formal publication of the narrative, as packaged by the Narrator and disseminated by one or more media channels. Publication may also include key selected images that may play a critical role in the story's salience.

6. *Commodification:* Depending on the level of public interest stoked by news outlets and other basic media coverage, the entertainment sector begins to perceive the AAN as a viable commodity. For example, the AAN may be reformulated as a major book, television production, or motion picture. These interpretations of the event can differ quite dramatically from the original Telling or even its Mediatization, but commodities are designed to appeal to a broader and potentially global population's sense of what an AAN should be. Commodification marks the widespread presence of media images in print or on the Internet, television, and film.

On the basis of this model, the transmission of an AAN within society is roughly chronological, but its components can overlap. Once the narration has formed (i.e., after the Telling has occurred), it expands both backward and forward in time. The backward view has at least two aspects. At each phase in its development, people look *backward in time* for conditions, triggers, or motivations to help make sense of what happened. In addition, characteristics of earlier narratives can become conflated with the new one, leading to modifications and variations (for example, "this was Jesus" or "this is the same being that appeared to Dave"). This search for the evidence will inevitably fail to uncover the story's original truth because the narrative is ultimately a product of many interpretations of events. Nonetheless, people will search for clues that prove—in their minds, at least—what really occurred. This quest for evidence may be interminable, as opinions will differ as to what constitutes proof of an essentially supernatural tale.

AANs also expand *forward in time* in at least three ways. First, the form and content of one AAN will affect how future AANs are constructed. Stories about aliens abducting people from their beds at night have become so commonplace that this narrative structure is sure to affect people's perceptions of what may have simply been an instance of sleep paralysis. These preexisting narrative forms give support to future Tellers who develop their stories in ways that are congruent with public understanding of what an abduction experience should look, feel, and sound like. Second, the interpretation of a particular AAN can change as witnesses come forward. Delayed accounts of what occurred, whether first- or secondhand, will affect public perception of the original abduction narrative. Third, future AANs may affect the perceived credibility of past AANs even if the narratives are not related to exactly the same occurrence. For example, it can be argued that the Travis Walton case (described in more detail below) increased the believability of Betty and Barney Hill's 1961 UFO encounter narrative, because both occurred at night on dark country roads and featured a brightly lit craft that witnesses originally mistook for an airplane.

When the retrospective influences and prospective effects are added to the model outlined above, two further elements can be seen:

$$\Sigma x \leftarrow (T \rightarrow E \rightarrow P \rightarrow N \rightarrow M \rightarrow C) \rightarrow \Sigma n,$$

where Σx is the sum of retrospective experiences or events implicit in the story (x also denotes their ultimately unknown aspect). Like ordinary experiences or events, Σx is not subject to objective verification, although "event"—as contrasted with "experience"—claims can appear more amenable to forensic investigation. Searching for the causes of an experience is fruitless, but these are the focus of much UFO and AAN research, which may employ forensic techniques and hypnosis. The letters represent the steps in the development of an AAN: Telling, Elaboration, Professionalization, Narration, Mediatization, Commodification. Σn represents the sum of the potential for an unspecified and increasing number (n) of reported encounters of narrative elements by new Tellers and others in the model. These accounts may feed back into the evolving report of the Teller, affecting interpretations of the alleged event or experience and changing basic understandings of the original account. Past and future AANs are therefore embedded in a narrative matrix, such that each tale affects the others in some way.

It may be useful to think of the elements of this Teller-Narrator model as inhabiting periods within streams of time and not as discrete points in a strict chronological structure. Except for the implied xs and generated ns, some elements of this process of narrative development are optional or can be combined with others (for example, a Teller can also be a Narrator, as in the case of Travis Walton). Metaphorically, The Teller-Narrator model can be seen as kind of linguistic neuron within the cultural nervous system—with retrospective experiences and new Tellers' accounts as connections—that continuously propagates words and images in the world. These structures are to memes what DNA is to genes: an observable medium of an informational reality.

A CASE STUDY: THE TRAVIS WALTON ABDUCTION

I use the following case study to illustrate the usefulness of the Teller-Narrator model for understanding how an AAN emerges and evolves in a narrative matrix that includes preexisting abduction tales (both individual and mediatized), multiple (sometimes conflicting) witness accounts, news stories, and commercially produced versions of the original story that was told by

Figure 11.1 *Travis Walton and five coworkers with their awards for reporting the story of Walton's alien abduction. Photograph from Brenna et al. 1975.*

AWARD WINNERS: Travis Walton (foreground), who told of being abducted by UFO, shows off check for $2,500. Six others who saw incident share $2,500. Left to right are Allen Dalis, Kenneth Peterson, Mike Rogers, Dwayne Smith and John Goulette. Absent is Steve Pierce.

Travis Walton and his coworkers. The Walton case is controversial—some assert its validity, while others claim it is a hoax—and no effort is made here to determine its credibility as a real abduction experience.[15] It is important to understand that the construction of a Teller-Narrator model is independent from the evaluation of the scientific, or truth, value of a narrative. Precisely because of the controversy surrounding the narrative and its global spread by news media and other forms of publication, the Walton case serves as an excellent example of the Teller-Narrator model.

On the evening of November 5, 1975, Travis Walton—a twenty-two-year-old logging worker—was reportedly kidnapped by a flying saucer on a mountain road approximately twelve miles from Heber, Arizona. Six coworkers reported that a bright object had been hovering near the road after dark. They said that when Walton left his pickup truck and walked toward it, the object emitted a bluish-green ray that caused him to disappear. Walton reappeared five days later, when he telephoned his brother-in-law and was picked up twenty miles from the site of the alleged event. Later, Walton and his coworkers were paid expenses and an award of $5,000 (split among seven people, with Walton receiving the lion's share) for best UFO case of the year after they had supposedly passed polygraph tests administered by a newspaper and a UFO organization (see Figure 11.1).

---

15. Of the major public AANs since the 1960s, the Walton case has acquired the most suspicion of being a hoax (Lewis 2000: 211). However, because the Teller-Narrator model focuses on the development and propagation of narratives and images, the ontological status of an alleged event is not prejudicial to gauging its origins or effects.

The development of the Walton case can be mapped schematically by applying the Teller-Narrator model, given above, to the AAN, in which Σx can include any potentially influential media sources and commodifications of previous AAN origin stories, as well as retrospective and inferred reinterpretations of the abduction event itself. In 1975, the best-known AAN was the 1961 Betty and Barney Hill story, as recounted in *The Interrupted Journey* (Fuller 1966). It is hard for skeptics to overlook the broadcast of the NBC made-for-television version of the Hills' story, *The UFO Incident*, starring Estelle Parsons and James Earl Jones, on October 20, 1975—only two weeks before the alleged Walton abduction. It should also be noted that decades of science fiction books and films were available as stimuli. Walton reported memories that included the contents of hypnotic regression sessions intended to help him recall events that he allegedly experienced after being hit with the bluish light the craft emitted. Walton described awakening in pain in a hot and humid room. He said he saw robed doctors bending over him. When he realized that their faces did not look human, he jumped off the examination table, attacked them, and drove them away (an extremely atypical action in an AAN, wherein humans are typically easily immobilized by aliens). In the words of one reporter at the hypnosis session, "We taped everything and had the CBS crew film the kid's story given under hypnosis. It was a tale of little men with heads like fishbowls and skin like mushrooms" (Brenna et al. 1975).[16]

Absent any physical forensic evidence either at the scene of the alleged abduction (no scorched earth or trees, for example) or on Walton's body, believers look back to Walton's retrospective accounts that emerged during hypnosis as proof of his experience. Skeptics suggest that the entire story was a fabrication and point to the lack of physical evidence as well as inconsistencies in statements made by Travis's coworkers and brother to support his narrative of events. Skeptics also point out that Walton and other family members were described as having "a continual UFO history," including reports of ten to fifteen UFO sightings (Ground Saucer Watch 1975).[17]

Telling: The teller is Travis Walton himself. However, Walton did not make the initial incident report because he was reported missing for five days.

---

16. The description "heads like fishbowls and skin like mushrooms" closely describes the aliens in the 1953 film *Invaders from Mars*, which employed actual fishbowls and mushroom-colored suits. See the film stills at http://www.imdb.com/title/tt0045917/mediaviewer/rm2352798976.

17. In cooperation with J. Allen Hynek of the Center for UFO Studies, Ground Saucer Watch was the first UFO organization to appear on the scene of the Walton incident and interviewed his family before he returned from his disappearance. See Sheaffer 2016.

However, once he reappeared and began speaking about his experience, he became the primary Teller of his account and remains so to this day. In his books, Travis (1978, 1996) bases the credibility claims of his account on his identity as a "naïve country boy" (1996: 4) his status as a logger, and reliance on the six other "local boys" (4) who reported him missing and implicitly supported his later account. However, as the account gains wider social traction and commodification, Travis begins to emphasize his intellectual curiosity, his philosophical interests, and other qualities that might attract a wider audience.

Elaboration: The Walton case offers a highly unusual three-part elaboration. First, his inner social circle included the six members of his logging crew who—with Travis—witnessed the initial UFO sighting. The initial sighting was recorded in the police report as well as later descriptions in interviews and Travis Walton's 1978 and 1996 books on the abduction. Second, after Walton's alleged abduction, his coworkers reported their versions of events to the police and underwent interviews and polygraph tests that were requested because the police feared that Travis had come to harm at the hands of his crew. Third, once Travis reappeared after five days, his interrogation, interviews, and polygraphs occurred as interest increased dramatically.

Professionalization: The first professionals called on to evaluate the logging crew's reports, and then later Walton's claims, were law enforcement personnel who used their investigative context, techniques, and tools (including polygraph tests) to attempt to determine the true story. Once the story began to unfold and spread, however, many additional professionals arrived, including UFO believers and organizations, psychotherapists, journalists, academics, scientists, and a CBS news crew. Each new contact interpreted and shaped the narrative in ways consistent with their own presuppositions about (1) whether Travis and others were being truthful and (2) the meanings of the reports being made. All approached the account from the specialized contexts of each one's particular education, training, and worldview.

Narration: In 1978, Travis Walton first presented himself as his own Narrator in his book *The Walton Experience*, although it is unclear how much of it he actually wrote on his own. Later, the Narrator role was augmented when screenwriter Tracy Torme (who had previously worked on *Star Trek: Next Generation* and the AAN television series *Intruders*) converted Walton's book into a much more dramatic film script. Also taking on a Narrator role was Robert Lieberman, who directed the feature film *Fire in the Sky* (1993) of Walton's story. Consistent with the Teller-Narrator model, the feature film commodification established the narrative and imagery that most people know about this AAN. For example, the bright light that allegedly took Travis resembles a tractor beam, a staple of Star Trek imagery from its original series (1966–1969).

Mediatization: The 1978 mass-market paperback edition (181 pages) of *The Walton Experience* constitutes the first published autobiographical narrative of Walton's alleged abduction. By 1996, this book was significantly expanded (to 370 pages), revised, and retitled to leverage the film as *Fire in the Sky: The Walton Experience*, with the subtitle *The Best Documented Case of Alien Abduction Ever Recorded*. This 1996 subtitle looks back to the subtitle of Whitley Strieber's 1987 AAN bestseller *Communion* (subtitled *A True Story*), and points forward to Budd Hopkins's 1996 *Witnessed* (subtitled *The True Story of the Brooklyn Bridge UFO Abductions*).

Commodification: Both the 1978 and the 1996 book carried similar cover images of Walton helplessly blasted by a beam of light from the sky (although the 1978 image shows a flying saucer, while the 1996 image does not). Between the dates of these publications, the 1993 feature film *Fire in the Sky* became the second stage of the developing public narrative. Between these mileposts and since then, there were numerous television interviews, speaking tours, articles and interviews in support of or in opposition to the truth of the event. Travis Walton and other witnesses continued doing interviews and appearing on television for many years.

As with any AAN, images of the Walton story begin circulating with its first report in 1975 and continued as if ripples on a pond. The 1978 book and 1993 movie are likely the most significant influences for shaping the public narrative, but the *National Enquirer* story pictured in Figure 11.2 began framing the public story only six weeks after it occurred. For a more detailed analysis of the Mediatization and Commodification stages, it would be useful to build chronologies of media images both before and after the books and film. In addition, differences between the two editions of Walton's books could yield instances of changes and elaborations of the descriptions and imagery.

Walton's 1978 book constituted a relatively early popular AAN, occurring before the releases of the major AAN publication waves of the 1980s and early 1990s (Hopkins 1981; Jacobs 1992; Mack 1994; Strieber 1987). In terms of Σn analysis, further study could help determine whether there was an increase in abduction reports that resembled the published Walton account after it rose to popularity. Walton's AAN may have had a demonstrable effect on the form and content of many abduction reports that followed. Some examples include the development of sets of witnesses in the AAN

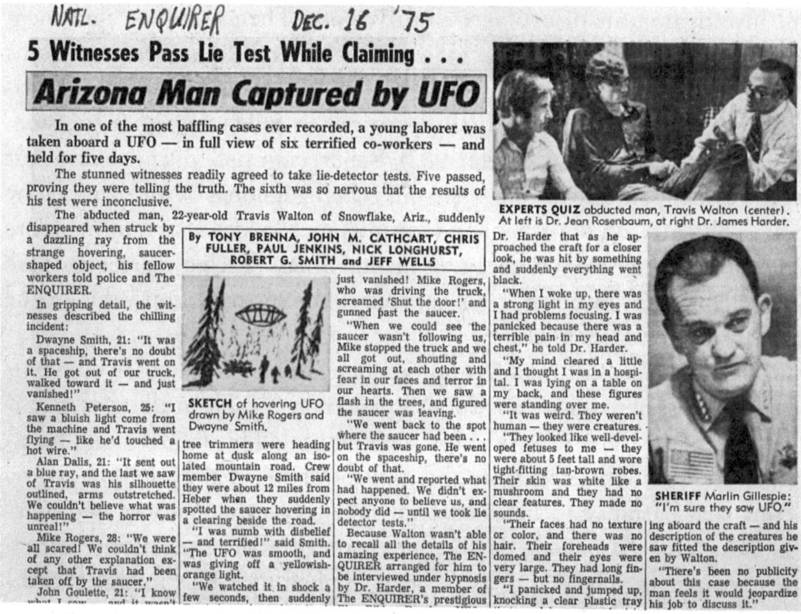

NATL. ENQUIRER DEC. 16 '75

5 Witnesses Pass Lie Test While Claiming . . .

Arizona Man Captured by UFO

In one of the most baffling cases ever recorded, a young laborer was taken aboard a UFO — in full view of six terrified co-workers — and held for five days.

The stunned witnesses readily agreed to take lie-detector tests. Five passed, proving they were telling the truth. The sixth was so nervous that the results of his test were inconclusive.

The abducted man, 22-year-old Travis Walton of Snowflake, Ariz., suddenly disappeared when struck by a dazzling ray from the strange hovering, saucer-shaped object, his fellow workers told police and The ENQUIRER.

By TONY BRENNA, JOHN M. CATHCART, CHRIS FULLER, PAUL JENKINS, NICK LONGHURST, ROBERT G. SMITH and JEFF WELLS

In gripping detail, the witnesses described the chilling incident:

Dwayne Smith, 21: "It was a spaceship, there's no doubt of that — and Travis went on it. He got out of our truck, walked toward it — and just vanished!"

Kenneth Peterson, 25: "I saw a bluish light come from the machine and Travis went flying — like he'd touched a hot wire."

Alan Dalis, 21: "It sent out a blue ray, and the last we saw of Travis was his silhouette outlined, arms outstretched. We couldn't believe what was happening — the horror was unreal!"

Mike Rogers, 28: "We were all scared! We couldn't think of any other explanation except that Travis had been taken off by the saucer."

John Goulette, 21: "I know

SKETCH of hovering UFO drawn by Mike Rogers and Dwayne Smith.

tree trimmers were heading home at dusk along an isolated mountain road. Crew member Dwayne Smith said they were about 12 miles from Heber when they suddenly spotted the saucer hovering in a clearing beside the road.

"I was numb with disbelief — and terrified!" said Smith. "The UFO was smooth, and was giving off a yellowish-orange light.

"We watched it in shock a few seconds, then suddenly

just vanished! Mike Rogers, who was driving the truck, screamed 'Shut the door!' and gunned past the saucer.

"When we could see the saucer wasn't following us, Mike stopped the truck and we all got out, shouting and screaming at each other with fear in our faces and terror in our hearts. Then we saw a flash in the trees, and figured the saucer was leaving.

"We went back to the spot where the saucer had been . . . but Travis was gone. He went on the spaceship, there's no doubt of that.

"We went and reported what had happened. We didn't expect anyone to believe us, and nobody did — until we took lie detector tests."

Because Walton wasn't able to recall all the details of his amazing experience, The ENQUIRER arranged for him to be interviewed under hypnosis by Dr. Harder, a member of The ENQUIRER's prestigious

EXPERTS QUIZ abducted man, Travis Walton (center). At left is Dr. Jean Rosenbaum, at right Dr. James Harder.

Dr. Harder that as he approached the craft for a closer look, he was hit by something and suddenly everything went black.

"When I woke up, there was a strong light in my eyes and I had problems focusing. I was panicked because there was a terrible pain in my head and chest," he told Dr. Harder.

"My mind cleared a little and I thought I was in a hospital. I was lying on a table on my back, and these figures were standing over me.

"It was weird. They weren't human — they were creatures.

"They looked like well-developed fetuses to me — they were about 5 feet tall and wore tight-fitting tan-brown robes. Their skin was white like a mushroom and they had no clear features. They made no sounds.

"Their faces had no texture or color, and there was no hair. Their foreheads were domed and their eyes were very large. They had long fingers — but no fingernails.

"I panicked and jumped up, knocking a clear plastic tray

SHERIFF Marlin Gillespie: "I'm sure they saw UFO."

ing aboard the craft — and his description of the creatures he saw fitted the description given by Walton.

"There's been no publicity about this case because the man feels it would jeopardize his job to discuss it."

Figure 11.2 *Clipping of the* National Enquirer *article covering Travis Walton's abduction story.*

waves mentioned previously, as well as Budd Hopkins's Linda Cortile case featured in the 1996 book *Witnessed: The True Story of the Brooklyn Bridge UFO Abduction* (where her kidnappers also use a "bluish ray").

The Travis Walton AAN illustrates the usefulness of the Teller-Narrator model and, in doing so, shows how the "true" stories of such encounters evolve over time. Tales such as those that appear in AANs undergo many transformations during their telling; they are reinterpreted by tellers, witnesses, believers, skeptics, representatives of professions (law enforcement, psychiatric, entertainment, and so on), and ultimately sold to a public yearning to learn more about these mysterious incidents (or be entertained by them). Through this retelling, the narrative interacts with other AANs, shaping their form and content even as they, in turn, affect retrospective interpretations of the original narrative.

CONCLUSIONS

Research on UFOs and AANs has always been controversial. There is a consensus that ufology—the study of unidentified flying objects and related phenomena—has failed as a science (Jacobs 2000; Sturrock 1999), implying that fifty years of study produced little of value. The field is so polemical that some investigators are discouraged or driven out. There is still no agreement on what constitutes a first-contact science (Wheeler 2000). Ufology remains on the margins, along with research on topics such as near-death experiences, out-of-body experiences, reincarnation, so-called past-life regression, and satanic ritual abuse (O'Keefe 1982). Believers in such phenomena assert that the evidence is already out there but is being ignored or undermined by skeptics. Skeptics, on the other hand, dismiss such evidence as nothing more than evidence of ignorance, deceit, or mental illness. Such disagreements are irreconcilable and do not help us appreciate the sociocultural value of the supernatural stories themselves.

The Teller-Narrator model proposed here allows us to understand this iterative process of narrative development and is applicable to all types of narratives—not just those related to the supernatural. This model could be effectively applied to the emergence and transformation of any public narrative, whether that narrative includes accounts of supernatural entities and practices (like ghosts, Sasquatch, witches, or voodoo practitioners) or more mundane phenomena. The eight-part schema applied to AANs in this chapter redirects attention to how narratives—supernatural or otherwise—emerge as social facts and highlights their important influences on culture regardless of whether the evidence contained within meets standards of scientific acceptability. The stories we tell about uncanny experiences keep belief in the supernatural alive and are therefore valid topics of scholarly examination in their own right.

REFERENCES

Allport, Gordon, and Leo Postman. 1947. *The Psychology of Rumor.* New York: Henry Holt.
Barker, Gray. 1956. *They Knew Too Much about Flying Saucers.* New York: University Books.
Bernard, Raymond. 1969. *The Hollow Earth: The Greatest Geographical Discovery in History Made by Admiral Richard E. Byrd in the Mysterious Land Beyond the Poles—the True Origin of the Flying Saucers.* Secaucus, NJ: Lyle Stuart.
Brenna, Tony, John M. Cathcart, Chris Fuller, Paul Jenkins, Nick Longhurst, Robert G. Smith, and Jeff Wells. 1975. "Arizona Man Captured by UFO." *National Enquirer,* December 16. Available at https://www.debunker.com/texts/walton.html.
Brookesmith, Peter, and Marcello Truzzi. 1992. *UFO Encounters: Sightings, Visitations, and Investigations.* Lincolnwood, IL: Publications International.
Budden, Albert. 1995. *UFOs—Psychic Close Encounters: The Electromagnetic Indictment.* London: Blandford.
Bullard, Thomas. 1991. "The Folkloric Dimension of the UFO Phenomenon." *Journal of UFO Research,* no. 3: 1–57.
Caughey, John. 1984. *Imaginary Social Worlds: A Cultural Approach.* Lincoln: University of Nebraska Press.

Clancy, Susan, Richard McNally, Daniel Schacter, and Mark Lenzenweger. 2002. "Memory Distortion in People Reporting Abduction by Aliens." *Journal of Abnormal Psychology* 111 (3): 455–461.
Dean, Jodi. 1998. *Aliens in America*. Ithaca, NY: Cornell University Press.
Downing, Barry. 1968. *The Bible and Flying Saucers*. New York: Harper and Row.
Eliade, Mircea. 1964. *Shamanism: Archaic Techniques of Ecstasy*. Translated by W. R. Trask. Princeton, NJ: Princeton University Press.
Fire in the Sky. 1993. Directed by Robert Lieberman. Hollywood, CA: Paramount Pictures.
Fowler, Raymond. 1979. *The Andreasson Affair: The Documented Investigation of a Woman's Abduction aboard a UFO*. Englewood Cliffs, NJ: Prentice-Hall.
Friedman, Stanton. 1996. *Top Secret/Majic*. New York: Marlowe.
Fuller, John. 1966. *The Interrupted Journey: Two Lost Hours "Aboard a Flying Saucer."* New York: Dial Press.
Gordon, Stuart. 1995. *The Book of Hoaxes: An A–Z of Famous Fakes, Frauds, and Cons*. London: Headline Book.
Graham, Billy. 1994. *Angels: God's Secret Agents*. Dallas, TX: Word.
Ground Saucer Watch. 1975. "Memo on the Walton Incident." December. Available at https://www.debunker.com/texts/walton.html.
Harner, Michael. 1980. *The Way of the Shaman*. New York: Harper and Row.
Hopkins, Budd. 1981. *Missing Time: A Documented Study of UFO Abductions*. New York: Richard Menck.
———. 1996. *Witnessed: The True Story of the Brooklyn Bridge UFO Abductions*. New York: Pocket Books.
Hopkins, Budd, David Jacobs, and Ron Westrum. 1992. *Unusual Personal Experiences: An Analysis of Data from Three National Surveys Conducted by the Roper Organization*. Las Vegas, NV: Bigelow.
Hua, Huang. 1996. *The Shurangama Sutra*. Vol. 8, *The Fifty Skandha-Demon States*. Burlingame, CA: Buddhist Text Translation Society.
Invaders from Mars. 1953. Directed by William Menzies. Los Angeles: Twentieth Century Fox.
Jacobs, David. 1992. *Secret Life: Firsthand, Documented Accounts of UFO Abductions*. New York: Simon and Schuster.
———, ed. 2000. *UFOs and Abductions: Challenging the Borders of Knowledge*. Lawrence: University Press of Kansas.
Jung, Carl. (1958) 1969. *Flying Saucers: A Modern Myth of Things Seen in the Skies*. Translated by R.F.C. Hull. New York: New American Library.
Kanon, Gregory. 1997. *The Great UFO Hoax: The Final Solution to the UFO Mystery*. Lakeville, MN: Galde Press.
Kelley, Stephanie. 1999. "The Rhetoric of Alien Abduction." Ph.D. diss., University of Kansas, Lawrence.
Kipness, David. 1997. "Ghosts, Taxonomies, and Social Psychology." *American Psychologist* 52 (3): 205–211.
Klass, Philip. 1989. *UFO Abductions: A Dangerous Game*. Buffalo, NY: Prometheus Books.
Lawson, Alvin. 1989. "The Birth Memory Hypothesis: A Testable Theory for UFO Abduction Reports." In *Cyber-biological Studies of the Imaginal Component in the UFO Contact Experience*, edited by Dennis Stillings, 125–142. St. Paul, MN: Archaeus Project.

Lewis, James, 1995. *The Gods Have Landed: New Religions from Outer Space.* Albany: State University of New York Press.
———. ed. 2000. *UFOs and Popular Culture: An Encyclopedia of Contemporary Myth.* Santa Barbara, CA: ABC-CLIO.
Lynch, Aaron. 1996. *Thought Contagion: How Belief Spreads through Society.* New York: Basic Books.
Mack, John. 1994. *Abduction: Human Encounters with Aliens.* New York: Scribner.
Moore, William, and Charles Berlitz. 1995. *The Philadelphia Experiment: Project Invisibility.* New York: Random House.
Newitz, Annalee. 1993. "Alien Abductions and the End of White People." *Bad Subjects,* no. 6. Available at https://bad.eserver.org/issues/1993/06/newitz.
Newman, Leonard, and Roy Baumeister. 1996. "Toward an Explanation of the UFO Abduction Phenomenon: Hypnotic Elaboration, Extraterrestrial Sadomasochism, and Spurious Memories." *Psychological Inquiry* 7 (2): 99–126.
O'Keefe, Daniel. 1982. *Stolen Lightning: The Social Theory of Magic.* New York: Random House.
Persinger, Michael. 1992. "Neurological Profiles of Adults Who Report 'Sudden Remembering' of Early Childhood Memories: Implications for Claims of Sex Abuse and Alien Visitation/Abduction Experiences." *Perceptual and Motor Skills* 75 (1): 259–266.
Rutkowski, Chris. 1988. "The Terrestrial Hypothesis: Geophysical Alternatives." In *Phenomenon: Forty Years of Flying Saucers,* edited by J. Spencer and H. Evans, 301–307. New York: Avon.
Sagan, Carl. 1995. *The Demon-Haunted World.* New York: Random House.
Sanderson, Ivan. 1970. *Invisible Residents: A Disquisition upon Certain Matters Maritime and the Possibility of Intelligent Life under the Waters of This Earth.* New York: Avon.
Sardello, Robert. 1996. *Freeing the Soul from Fear.* Great Barrington, MA: School of Spiritual Psychology.
Scribner, Scott. 1999a. "Alien Abduction Narratives." In *Encyclopedia of UFOs and Popular Culture,* edited by J. Lewis, 14–19. Santa Barbara, CA: ABC-CLIO.
———. 1999b. "Missing Time." In *Encyclopedia of UFOs and Popular Culture,* edited by J. Lewis, 204. Santa Barbara, CA: ABC-CLIO.
The Searchers. 1956. Directed by John Ford. Burbank, CA: Warner Brothers.
Sheaffer, Robert. 2016. "Skeptical Information on the Travis Walton 'UFO Abduction' Story." Available at https://www.debunker.com/texts/walton.html.
Shor, Ronald. 1959. "Hypnosis and the Concept of the Generalized Reality Orientation." *American Journal of Psychotherapy,* no. 13: 582–602.
Showalter, Elaine. 1997. *Hystories: Hysterical Epidemics and Modern Culture.* New York: Columbia University Press.
Slater, Elizabeth. 1983. *The Final Report on the Psychological Testing of UFO Abductees.* Washington, DC: Fund for UFO Research.
Spanos, Nicholas. 1996. *Multiple Identities and False Memories: A Sociocognitive Perspective.* Washington, DC: American Psychological Association.
Strieber, Whitley. 1987. *Communion.* New York: Beech Tree Books.
Sturrock, Peter. 1999. *The UFO Enigma: A New Review of the Physical Evidence.* New York: Warner Books.
Thompson, Keith. 1990. *Angels and Aliens: UFOs and the Mythic Imagination.* New York: Ballantine Books.

Thompson, Richard. 1993. *Alien Identities: Ancient Insights into Modern UFO Phenomena*. Alachua, FL: Govardian Hill.
Tumminia, Diana, ed. 2007. *Alien Worlds: Social and Religious Implications of UFO Phenomena*. Syracuse, NY: Syracuse University Press.
Vallee, Jacques. 1969. *Passport to Magonia: From Folklore to Flying Saucers*. Chicago: Henry Regnery.
———. 1988. *Dimensions: A Casebook of Alien Contact*. Chicago: Contemporary Books.
Walton, Travis. 1978. *The Walton Experience*. New York: Berkley.
———. 1996. *Fire in the Sky: The Walton Experience*. New York: Marlow.
Wheeler, Greg. 2000. "Cosmology." In *UFOs and Popular Culture: An Encyclopedia of Contemporary Myth*, edited by J. Lewis, 92–97. Santa Barbara, CA: ABC-CLIO.

CONTRIBUTORS

JANET BALDWIN lectures in anthropology and sociology. She is an independent researcher and ethnographer and has worked with mediums, trance mediums, and healers. She has published her findings in *The Ashgate Research Companion to Paranormal Cultures* (2013). Her most recent work involves extensive participation observation with shamans, exploring their spiritual practices using crystals, remedies, and forensic healing. She also works with astrologers, tarot readers, and other alternative practitioners to understand the evolving esoteric culture in Western Australia.

I'NASAH CROCKETT is a writer, cultural worker, public intellectual, and digital archivist. She received her B.A. from Sarah Lawrence in 2008, and her M.A. in Southern studies from the University of Mississippi in 2010. She is the lead curator for *Canebrake* (formerly *Antiblackness Is a Theory*), a space dedicated to the scholarship of the black radical tradition.

MARC EATON is an associate professor of sociology in the Department of Sociology and Anthropology at Ripon College. His research is driven by a dedication to ethnographic methods and a symbolic interactionist approach to understanding social life. He has applied these methodological and theoretical tools to the topics of online activism and, more recently, paranormal investigation. His main interest lies at the intersection of micro-level interpretive meaning-making processes and the macro-level power dynamics that shape these processes.

WILLIAM RYAN FORCE is an assistant professor of sociology at Western New England University and a student of social life. His research and teaching explore the accomplishment of identity at the intersection of culture, power, and language. His work covers contexts including punk and indie rock, crime TV, trick-or-treating, bar culture, and queer visibility.

RACHAEL IRONSIDE is a lecturer in the School of Creative and Cultural Business at Robert Gordon University, UK. She completed her Ph.D. at the University of York in 2016, where she studied social interaction and paranormal experiences. Her doctoral research was informed by video and ethnographic data collected during her participation in paranormal investigation groups over a five-year period. More specifically, her research focused on how collective experiences are understood and categorized as uncanny. Rachel's research interests fall into two areas: the study of social interaction and paranormal events and the role of ghost tourism in contemporary society. In keeping with her interests in ghost tourism she is currently involved in research projects that examine the role of dark histories and heritage on the Isle of Orkney and the value of ghost tourism to Scottish heritage sites.

TEA KRULOS is a freelance journalist and author from Milwaukee, Wisconsin. He is author of *Heroes in the Night: Inside the Real Life Superhero Movement* (2013), *Monster Hunters: On the Trail with Ghost Hunters, Bigfooters, Ufologists, and Other Paranormal Investigators* (2015), and *The End: A Journey through America's Apocalypse Culture* (forthcoming from Chicago Review Press). He also contributes essays on art, entertainment, social movements, and personality to *Milwaukee Record*, *Scandinavian Traveler*, *Shepherd Express*, and *VoiceMap*.

JOSEPH P. LAYCOCK is an assistant professor of religious studies at Texas State University. His books include *Vampires Today: The Truth about Modern Vampirism* (2009), *The Seer of Bayside: Veronica Lueken and the Struggle to Define Catholicism* (2014), and *Dangerous Games: What the Moral Panic over Role-Playing Games Says about Play, Religion, and Imagined Worlds* (2015).

STEPHEN L. MUZZATTI is an associate professor of sociology at Ryerson University in Toronto, Canada, specializing in the areas of inequality, crime, and culture. He has published work on consumerism and violence, state crime and crimes of globalization, the news media, working-class identities, advertising, risk-taking, and motorcycle culture. Stephen serves as a departmental representative to the Canadian Sociological Association and is a member of the editorial board of *Contemporary Justice Review*.

Scott R. Scribner studied physics and sociology at Rensselaer Polytechnic Institute, philosophy and cognition at the University of New Hampshire, and the relationships between religion and psychology at Fuller Theological Seminary's Graduate School of Psychology. His doctoral research examined interactions of fear with media images in alien abduction narratives.

Emma M. Smith is a criminology instructor at Humber College and a Ph.D. student in Ryerson University's Communication and Culture program. Her research interests include documentary representations of female murderers, reality television's (re)production of crime narratives, prison structures, the commodification of crime in popular culture and Canadian policing systems. Themes of gender, social inequality, and cultural identity infuse her research.

Jeannie Banks Thomas is a professor at Utah State University, where she is also head of the Department of English. She edited *Putting the Supernatural in Its Place: Folklore, the Hypermodern, and the Ethereal* (2015). Her feminist study of women's stories and laughter, *Featherless Chickens, Laughing Women, and Serious Stories* (1997), received the Elli Köngäs-Maranda Prize. Gender and the oral narratives (including legends) about material culture are the subjects of her book *Naked Barbies, Warrior Joes, and Other Forms of Visible Gender* (2003). She coauthored *Haunting Experiences: Ghosts in Contemporary Folklore* (2007), which won the Brian McConnell Book Award in legend studies. She is the former editor of the journal *Midwestern Folklore* and has been a member of the editorial boards of *Western Folklore* and *Folklore Historian*.

Dennis Waskul is professor of sociology and Distinguished Faculty Scholar at Minnesota State University, Mankato. He has authored or edited three books: *Ghostly Encounters* (2016), *The Senses in Self, Culture, and Society* (2011), and *Self-Games and Body Play* (2003). Dennis has edited or coedited three books: *Popular Culture as Everyday Life* (2016), *Body/Embodiment* (2006), and *net.seXXX* (2004). He has published over fifty empirical studies, book chapters, observational essays, and theoretical works; served as president of the Society for the Study of Symbolic Interaction; and served on the editorial board for journals including *Sexualities*, *Qualitative Sociology*, *Journal of Contemporary Ethnography*, and *Sociological Quarterly*. He is also a former associate editor of *Symbolic Interaction*.

INDEX

African Americans and voodoo, 152–169
American Society for Psychical Research, 79
America's Haunted Road Trip, 106
Ancient Ram Inn (Gloucestershire, England), 111
Angels (Graham), 216
Angels and Aliens (Thompson), 215
Alien abduction, 210–231; development of narratives of, 219–221; explanations for, 213–216; as hoax, 216; perspectives on, 212–213; Teller-Narrator model, 217–222
Aliens, explanations for, 213–216; extraterrestrial hypothesis, 213; terrestrial hypothesis, 213–214
Aliens in America (Dean), 215
Ape Canyon, 196
Apparitions, 66–68
Arcana, major and minor, 137–138
Association of Independent Readers and Rootworkers (AIRR), 119
Atlanta Vampire Alliance, 174
Auerbach, Nina, 183

Bader, Christopher, 2, 54, 140
Bauman, Zygmunt, 117
Berger, Peter, 19, 182, 184
Bigfoot, 195–198, 202
Bigfoot Field Researchers Organization, 197
Black, Danielle, 179

Black Hawk, 155
Black Mausoleum, 95
Book of Vagabonds (Luther), 120
Bullard, Thomas, 211

Cape Breton Island (Nova Scotia, Canada), 35–36, 40–43, 45–48
Cartomancers, 136–150
Chupacabras, 200, 201–202
Civil rights movement, 165–168
Cock Lane (London), 102
Coelacanth, 191, 192
Coleman, Loren, 191, 196, 203, 206
Consumerism, 99–106, 126–128, 201–202, 226–227
Cracker Jack Drug Store (New Orleans), 165
Cryptoscience, 21–32
Cryptozoology, 190–208; allure of, 206–207; Chupacabras, 200, 201–202; conferences on, 203–204; evil portents, 198–202; funding for, 203; and hoaxers, 195, 196–197, 201, 204; Jersey Devil, 201–202; lake monsters, 193–195; Lazarus species, 191–195; legitimacy of, 202–205; Mothman, 198–200, 201; in popular culture, 201–202; as re-enchantment, 207; sasquatch, 195–198, 202; skeptics of, 195, 205
Cultural authority, 6, 55–56
Cultural competence, 36–40

Dark tourism, 95–112; ghost hunting, 103–104; ghost tours, 102–103, 106; haunted attractions, 104–106; tourist motivations, 106–112
Dean, Jodi, 215
The Demon-Haunted World (Sagan), 21
Deren, Maya, 154–155
Dimensions (Vallee), 211–212
Dinsdale, Tim, 194
Divine Horsemen (Deren), 154
Donald Trump fortune-telling machine, 129–131
Dr. Phil, 178n6
Durkheim, Émile, 7, 20, 25
Dyer, Rick, 204

Economic inequality, 126
1886 Crescent Hotel and Spa (Eureka Springs, Arkansas), 104
Einstein, Albert, 23
Ellis, Bill, 96, 97
Epistemology, 83
Esmeralda fortune-telling machine, 129
Etteilla, 138
Evil portents, 198–202; Chupacabras, 200, 201–202; Jersey Devil, 201–202; Mothman, 198–200, 201

Faith, 76–77
Fangsmiths, 172–173
Ferrell, Rod, 177–178
Fire in the Sky (film), 225–226
Flying Saucers (Jung), 211
Forerunner legends, 42, 47–48
Fortune-telling, 116–134; development of, in America, 123–124; labor trends and, 125–126; machines for, 128–131; in popular culture, 119–120; professionalization of, 119; smartphone apps for, 132
Fortune Telling Hearing (1926), 122
Foucault, Michel, 184

Gébelin, Antoine Court de, 138
Georgia Hoax, 204
Ghosts, 27, 54–75; apparitions, 66–68; commercial, 58–59, 101–102; epistemological status of, 83–85; everyday, 55–56; forms of, 66–74; genres of, 55–61; ghost tourism, 102, 106–112; ghost walks and tours, 102–103; hunting, 76–93, 103–104; institutional, 59–61; and morality, 109; ontological status of, 81–83; phantasms, 68–69; phantoms, 73–74; poltergeists, 70–72, 95–96; professionalized, 56–58; specters, 72–73; wraiths, 69–70
Giants, 31
The Gods Have Landed (Lewis), 215
Golden Fleece Inn (York, England), 104
Goode, Erich, 127–128
Graham, Billy, 216
Grey Friars Kirk (Edinburgh, Scotland), 95–96

Haindl, Hermann, 145n
Haindl pack, 145–146
Hallucinations, 22, 24
Haunted accommodations, 104
Haunted attractions, 105
Haunted Museum, 105
Haunted places, 105–106
Hauntings: anniversary, 65; historical, 65–66; intelligent, 62–64; residual, 64–65; types of, 61–66
Hermetic Order of the Golden Dawn, 138–139
Hill, Betty and Barney, 221, 224
Hmong religious beliefs, 56
Hoodoo, 155, 164–165
Houdini, Harry, 122
Hufford, David, 6, 18–19, 24, 44, 55
Hunter, Jack, 24

I Fought the Apemen of Mt. St. Helens (Beck), 196
Intercultural communication, 37
International Cryptozoology Museum, 191
The Interrupted Journey (Fuller), 224
Interview with the Vampire (Rice), 184

Jameson, Fredric, 117
Javan elephant, 191
Jersey Devil, 201–202
Jim Crow, 165
Jung, Carl, 23, 211

Keel, John, 200, 203
Kelley, Stephanie, 215–216
The Key to the Tarot (Waite), 139, 142

Labor trends and fortune-telling, 125–126
Lake monsters, 193–195
Landrieu, Moon, 166

Late capitalism, 117
Laveau, Marie, 157–158
Laws of nature, 7–8
Lazarus species, 191–195
Leeds, Deborah, 201
Legends, 41–43, 95–96; forerunner, 42, 47–48
Legend tripping, 5, 35, 96–98, 106
Lewis, James, 215
Lincoln, Abraham, 122
Liquid modernity, 117
Loas, 155
Loch Ness Investigation Bureau, 194
Loch Ness monster, 193–195; financial value of, 195
Lord Howe Island stick insect (tree lobster), 191
Luther, Martin, 120

Mack, John, 217
Mackenzie, George (Bloody Mackenzie), 95–96
Magic, 9
Malinowski, Bronislaw, 127
Mardi Gras Indian, 155
Marie Laveau's House of Voodoo, 167
Megamouth shark, 192
Men in Black, 198
Minnesota State School for Dependent and Neglected Children, 59–60, 61
Modernity, 172
Monsters, 31; lake, 193–195
Moral panic, 177–179
Mothman, 198–200, 201
Mothman Festival, 201
Mothman Museum, 200, 201
The Mothman Prophecies (Keel), 203
Museum of the Paranormal, 105
Mysterious America (Coleman), 203

National Ghost Hunting Day, 104
New Orleans, 152–169
New Orleans Historic Voodoo Museum (NOHVM), 167

Occult Museum, 105
Ohio Bigfoot Conference, 204
Ontology, 81
Operation Deepscan, 194
Oppenheim, Janet, 121
Orishas, 155

Ostension, 47
Otherkin, 3–4
Ouija boards, 73
Our Vampires, Ourselves (Auerbach), 183
Ovilus, 83

Palmer House (Sauk Center, Minnesota), 58–59
Paranormal, 8–9
Paranormal investigation, 76–93, 103–104; provoking in, 87–88; in reality-based television, 79–80; reasons for, 85–88; scientific, 77–78, 81–82, 83–84, 85–87; and sensitives, 78–79, 82–83, 84–85, 87–91; subculture of, 79–81
Paranthropology, 24–25
Partridge, Christopher, 207
Patterson-Gimlin film, 197
Perlmutter, Dawn, 178
Peterhead Prison (Peterhead, Scotland), 98–99, 101
Phantasms, 68–69
Phantoms, 73–74
Pine Barrens (New Jersey), 201
Point Pleasant (West Virginia), 198–200, 201
Poltergeists, 70–72, 95–96
Possession, 155
Psychic abilities, 8, 59, 78, 79, 88–91, 119, 122, 173–174

Radford, Benjamin, 200, 205
Rational believers, 5, 29–30
Reality, 19; production of, 27–31; social, 25–26
Religion, 5, 6–7, 55–56, 108–109; faith in, 76; and fortune-telling, 120–121; New Age, 78, 124; voodoo as, 153–155, 167–168
Rice, Anne, 184
Rider Waite deck, 139–140, 146, 147, 149
Ritual, 141–143, 155, 160–162
Roadtrippers Ghost Guide, 106
Rockford, Lewis, 164–165
Roosevelt, Theodore, 196

Sagan, Carl, 21–22
Saint John's Eve festival, 158–159
Sasquatch, 195–198, 202
Science, 22–23, 77
Scientific method, 8–9

Scientism, 77
Shaw, George Bernard, 133
The Shining (King), 104
Sleep paralysis, 24, 44
Slick, Tom, 202–203
Social fact, 20
Society for Psychical Research, 79
Sociologies of everyday life, 25–27
Sociomental pareidolia, 28
Specters, 72–73
Spirit box, 83
Spiritualist movement, 5, 102
Spirituality, 76
Stanley Hotel (Estes Park, CO), 104
Supernatural: anthropological research on, 24–25; beliefs about, 1–3, 10–11, 54; defined, 6–9, 18–19; folkloric research on, 4–5, 24; methodology in researching, 35–51; in popular culture, 3; psychological research on, 4, 23–24; sociological research on, 5; and tours, 106

Tallant, Robert, 154, 163
Tarot, 136–150; as communal, 143–145; history of, 136–140; as introspection, 147–149; as ritual, 141–143; as self-empowerment, 145–147; tarot spreads, 141–142
Temple of the Vampire, 176
Thomas, George A., 165
Thomas, Keith, 1
Thompson, Keith, 215
Tourism, 98–112, 152–153; heritage, 153
Tracking the Chupacabra (Radford), 200, 205
Traveling Museum of the Paranormal and Occult, 105
Turner, Victor, 141

Ufology, 227–228
Unidentified flying objects (UFOs), 22, 210–217, 221–228

Vallee, Jacques, 211–212
Vampire and Energy Work Research Study, 174–175, 176
The Vampire Bible (Temple of the Vampire), 176
Vampires, 171–186; and donor's bill of rights, 174; and fear of coming out, 179; and helping professions, 179–180; historical characterizations of, 183; hybrid, 174; lifestyle versus real, 172–173; misunderstandings about, 175–183; moral panic over, 177–179; population of, 174–175; and psychiatric diagnosis, 175; psychic, 174; sanguinarian, 173–174; sexual, 174; vampirism as religion, 175–176
Vampire: The Masquerade (role-playing game), 177
Vodou, 154–155
Voodoo, 152–169; and the civil rights movement, 165–168; criminalization of, 164–165; and Jim Crow, 165; literature on, 159–164; mischaracterizations of, 153–154; and racism, 160–164; as religion, 153–155, 167–168
Voodoo in New Orleans (Tallant), 154, 163–164
Voodoo Spiritual Temple (New Orleans), 167

Waite, Arthur Edward, 139
Wallace, Anthony, 1
Walton, Travis, 222–227
The Walton Experience (Walton), 225–226
Wheeler, Greg, 211
Whitton, Matt, 204
The Wilderness Hunter (Roosevelt), 196
Williams, Richard N., 77
Wraiths, 69–70

Zerubavel, Eviatar, 27, 28, 29
Zoltar fortune-telling machine, 129
Zombies, 3